# DREAMING
## THE FUTURE

# DREAMING
## THE FUTURE
## The Ultimate Dream Guide

By Suz Andreasen

**ASSOCIATION FOR
RESEARCH AND
ENLIGHTENMENT**

A.R.E. Press • Virginia Beach • Virginia

A.R.E. Press
215 67th Street
Virginia Beach, VA 23451-2061

Andreasen, Suz, 1964-
    Dreaming the future : the ultimate dream guide / by Suz Andreasen.
        p.      cm.
Includes bibliographical references.
    ISBN 0-87604-436-4    (trade pbk.)
    1. Dream interpretation—Dictionaries.  2. Symbolism (Psychology)—Dictionaries.  3. Dreams.  I. Title.
    BF109 .A63    2004
    135'.3—dc21

                                        2001003620

# Contents

# Acknowledgments

I would like to thank my family and friends as well as my readers for all their support. Special thanks to the A.R.E. Press for seeing and knowing the message and the meaning behind this book. I also dedicate this book to dreamers everywhere who maintain the courage to voice and experience their dreams in material reality. Keep dreaming and the future will be yours.

# Introduction

*"For some must watch, while some must sleep.
So runs the world away."*—William Shakespeare

This book germinated from many years of work, not only in studying dream interpretation but also with chronicling my own dreams in personal journals for over twenty-two years. My curiosity began with my early readings about dream study and interpretation. Being the daughter of a psychiatrist, I was exposed to texts from Carl Jung and Sigmund Freud to J. Allan Hobson and Alfred Adler. Of course, this spawned into a curious fascination with any book relating to dreams, including dream dictionaries and dream guides. I searched for answers in dream dictionaries, only to come up empty-handed. I often found myself confused and frustrated. Why open up ten books to understand one dream? Many dream books kept me entertained intellectually but spiritually at bay. Other books seemed overly simplistic and inconclusive. How can a dream about a cat mean the same thing to every individual? Alternately, how can we explain the fact that so many of us observe similar and sometimes prophetic dreaming experiences?

My insatiable desire to probe the nature of sleep took me to new dimensions of thought. I wondered why so many dream researchers stay away from the spiritual act of dreaming. The obvious answer of being able to prove a theory scientifically holds strong. Yet, we cannot live our lives on what is seen before us. If we did, we would never have discovered the atom and would probably still believe that the earth is flat. In this paradigm of human limitation and potential, I remained hungry to know dreaming's purpose—not only in my own life but also on a universal plane. I wondered not only *why* we dream but also where our dreams might be leading us. Do we dream to discover ourselves or do our self-discoveries allow us to dream? Is it possible that the dreams we encounter in our sleep hold any relevance to what lies ahead of us? While the answers to these questions are surely found within the walls of personal wisdom, there are many things about the act, the evolution, and the purpose of dreaming that are palpable and accessible to each and every one of us.

I love to talk to people about their dreams, their hopes and their ideas. The dream examples you will read in this book come from individuals from many walks of life. Some are from profound historical thinkers in science and in art. Other dreams are from professionals and business people. Many are from people who have written to me through the Internet. I like to know what everyone is thinking about his or her dreams, be it the plumber fixing my sink or a priest I meet on the subway.

My goal is to demystify the dreaming experience and to take you through the fundamental aspects of interpretation looking at universal mythology, symbolism, prophecy, and association. This book will also teach you to understand the connection between your dreams and your life—past, present, and future.

*Think about it:* If you sit in your office and daydream about the future you would love to enjoy, the stocks you want to buy, the dream home you desire, you would probably consider this a valuable and realistic goal-making process. However, if you experience a nightly dream of your life's vision, you are very likely to dismiss it. Why? Because dreaming is a personal and intangible experience. Much like prayer, it offers us a window into our own souls.

Here is where my journey with you, the reader, begins. I want to bring you into a new world of personal awareness and, hopefully, make dreaming a more palatable and basic skill for all who read these pages. You will probably find it easy to relate to many of the dreams in this book because they are written by ordinary people from all over the world. You don't need a great deal of time or energy in order to interpret and connect with your dreams. All you need is a blank book and an open mind.

# 1

# Can We Dream the Future?

*"Take voyages. Attempt them. There's nothing else."*
—Tennessee Williams

Through our dreams, we discover new lands of miraculous sense and perception. Dreaming is the shape-shifting doorway to the human soul. Uncharted and without a map, we travel to new worlds. Most of us question the rationale and purpose of our nocturnal wanderings. The beautiful and strange mirage of dreaming often flies blindly in the face of reason. Nonetheless, we dream to discover how deeply we can penetrate the layers of self. Through this act of discovery, we walk through the portal of time and into the garden of tomorrow.

When we think of the future, we often picture the image of a blank slate, something unknown and open to us, holding infinite possibilities. We seek to embrace the world yet to be revealed to us. We dream of things we hope will come to pass for us, and we hope these dreams will come true. The concept of using our dreams as a testing ground for our most sincere personal planning process is one that many of us have questioned and explored. What if we could take our nocturnal visions, the dreams we encounter in our sleep, and experience those as a tool for planning our futures?

Holding this inspired thought in mind, consider the idea that your own potential is not something you only unveil through waking actions and strategic choices in your daily life. Have you ever pondered the grains of wisdom to be found in your nightly encounters with sleep? A friend of mine who is a lawyer says that he often daydreams but that he can't rationalize the comparison of his active aspirations and his nocturnal journeys. This makes logical sense and yet, it doesn't explain the creative and divine insight that many great thinkers have found during their nightly eight hours of uninterrupted sleep.

The structure of the benzene ring, for example, was first visualized by Austrian chemist Friedrich August Von Kekule in a dream. Kekule, who had already been seeking the answers to the components and structure of the benzene molecule, experienced a moment of insight in 1865. He dozed by the fire and had a dream in which he saw a snake chase and capture its own tail, thus forming a ring. Kekule awoke with the inspiration that the form of the benzene molecule is a ring. His idea proved to be correct: the basic structure of benzene is a ring formed of six carbon atoms linked together.

Within this famous illustration of dreaming and proposition, Kekule's dream reveals to us that our imaginations act as a propelling force that can spawn and design our many creative endeavors. Within each of us is the ability to envision our own destiny and to dream of a defined direction. When we ask ourselves basic questions like "How?" "Why?", "Where?" and 'What if . . . ?" we are actually formulating the building blocks of our unique and also inherent path. Nowhere is this insatiable hunger for truth more evident than during the mixed and wildly illusionary time we spend while sleeping. If we choose to embrace our nocturnal visions, we can benefit from a possible course we may never have charted in our waking lives.

The principles of relativity were discovered when Albert Einstein imagined what the world would look like if you could ride on a light beam. The last movement of *The Messiah* was delivered to Joseph Handel through the conduit of a dream. Jerry Lewis recently related a tale of his grandmother reminding him as an eight year old, to "live your dream. Don't listen to anyone else, just live it." As with all divine things in life, these words became a mantra for his success.

The blueprint for cartoon animation was first pondered in the mind of a seven-year-old Walt Disney as he lay in his bed on a farm near Marline, Missouri. Disney, in fact, drew some of his first sketches for neighbors and often spoke of a small mouse in his dreams that would later become the smiling face we know today as Mickey Mouse. Disney was a visionary who understood the wisdom in creating a reality from the magic of dreams, both sleeping and waking. Today, the Disney entertainment conglomerate is a billion-dollar industry. As the theme song from the film *Peter Pan* illustrates, "Any dream you dare to dream really will come true."

So, can anyone do it? Do we all foster the ability to see a given destiny, to create a conceptual walkway within the boundaries of sleep? Is it out of reach to believe that dreams can literally make you rich, both spiritually and materially? If you receive information in the your sleep about stocks, artistic and scientific discovery, or global events, should you take it literally or with an exploratory perspective? The answer surely rests in the journey of examining your own ideas and how they fall into place on the path of your own life. There are many tools and techniques you can use to chart and unveil the meanings in your dreams, which I cover in this book. Through exploring new boundaries of your own ideas, you will begin to learn how to gauge the difference between the various forms and types of dreams you experience and apply them to your active life. For now, just value that your dreams can and do exist within a plane of personal dynamic invention. Once you begin to work with your dreams you will find that no vision or inspiration, either of waking or sleeping, is beyond the reach of the human potential.

## WHAT WE SEE IN DREAMS

*"Sleep is a state in which every great part of life is passed."*—Samuel Johnson

Precognition and prophecy have both long played a role in people's fascination with the dreaming machine. From the beginning of recorded time, philosophers, scientists, and artists have theorized and discussed the potential and value of our dreams. Rooted in mythological traditions, we find a diverse array of stories and ideas about the nature of sleep and the purpose of dreaming. Many ancient cultures believed that dreams brought divination and prophetic nuggets of wisdom from otherworldly forces or from God. It's easy to understand why the vast and complex landscape of dreaming might have taken on a larger than life role to intuitive and spiritual cultures like the Aborigines or the Mesopotamians. Across the span of the world we know today, there were dozens of early societies that believed in the spiritual delivery and practical insight to be discovered in dreams. Proleptical examples of dream mythology can be found in texts from almost every ancient culture including Asian and Pacific regions, Africa, Europe, and Central America.

In Japanese mythology, for example, it is said that evil forces bring evil dreams. The good spirit of dreams, *Baku*, is a fierce creature with a lion's head, tiger's feet, and a horse's body. Baku is known as the "eater of dreams." When a person rises from a nightmare, he or she may cry, "Baku, eat my dreams," and Baku will turn the bad dream into good by eating up the evil forces.

This simple illustration reveals how one culture embraced the idea that dreams indicated individual control over the spiritual plane.

In India and Tibet, where Eastern traditions melded with Western thought, the concepts of reincarnation and the soul's value on earth played a role in ancient studies on the perspectives of sleep. Hindu writings from the Atharva Veda dating back to as early as 1500 B.C. reveal teachings that suggest dreams are part of a progressive problem-solving ability that we each carry within our own spirit and soul. This view on dreaming permeated and translated itself to the Asian regions where traditions of sages and Buddhist cultures flourished. The Chinese, who were the most literary in their attempts to understand the nature of dreaming, acknowledged in early texts that there were various levels of analytical thought and spiritual pursuit in the act and action of dreaming. In these conceptual traditions, they also respected dreaming as a soul's journey from the human body to another level of existence.

Dreams were also recognized by many early Pacific cultures as symbolic events. Aboriginal culture, the oldest living culture still in existence today, provides us with some valuable and vital clues to our mythological past. Many believe that aboriginal traditions lead the way to a more soul-specific view of the dream machine with their concept of Alcheringa or "Dreamtime," the soul of human evolution, which we will look at in chapter 6. Surely, Oceanic culture and its rich tradition of *mana*, or *the force*, carried the idea that the soul is part of a universal consciousness and that we, as humans, are here to follow a preordained and karmic course of events.

In the West, teachings from the Koran as well as from early Christian traditions brought new ideas about dreaming and its place among humanity. The Bible, both the New and Old Testament, is filled with wonderful illustrations of dreaming and prophecy. One of my favorite examples comes from Joseph, the husband of Mary, mother of Jesus. According to the New Testament, Joseph had a series of seven dreams where the angel of the Lord appeared before him. In his dream, Joseph is told of the coming of Christ when the angel said,

> *"Joseph son of David, do not be afraid to take Mary home as your wife, because what is conceived in her is from the Holy Spirit. She will give birth to a son and you are to give him the name Jesus, because he will save his people from their sins."*—Matthew 1:20-21

Another famous and well-known biblical dream is the dream of Pharaoh. This dream has been noted in many different variations and versions from its original report in Genesis to modern-day films such as *The Ten Commandments*. In his dream, Pharaoh was warned that seven years of hunger and famine would plague his kingdom of Egypt. Pharaoh took heed of this dream and was advised by Joseph, son of Jacob, to take action and save his nation from peril. Pharaoh acknowledged Joseph's words as a needed sign of change, accepting this combination of interpretation and diplomacy as a form of spiritual guidance.

While it would be hard to imagine such events taking place with today's heads of state or religious leaders, there is definitely a place where our present view of dreams and the ancient visions of others meet to form a cohesive structure of our individual inspirations and their relation to our lives. What we see in dreams often propels us to make choices even if we cannot actively see or acknowledge their value. Many people have told me that they don't dream at all and then asked me how they can "learn to dream." The truth is that we all dream. Some of us are better able to recall our visions and impressions, while others awaken with no recollection of any time spent in the dream machine.

Science has offered us a window into the biological and quantitative value of our nocturnal explorations, which we will look at in the next chapter. Within a given life span, for example, a person devotes about 50,000 hours to dreaming. That equates to six full years of our lives spent exploring the alternate universe of dreaming discovery. Knowing that we spend more time dreaming than we do getting a bachelor's degree, it becomes easy to say, "Perhaps I should give my dreams more consideration."

I like to think of dreaming as a place where we are free and unencumbered from our external selves. The soul takes flight and is able to wander where it chooses, see what it needs, and find value in what it must. There have been quite a few theories laid on the table about the nature of how the human soul might leave the body in pursuit of understanding and wisdom. I cannot say that my soul literally rises from my body at night or at any time of my waking life. I can, however, say that my soul and my physical body are one with each other and therefore part and parcel of every journey I take—awake or asleep. In this analogy, one begins to understand the concept of oneness with our sleeping sight.

Montague Ullman, an internationally known psychiatrist, noted for his work with dreams, illustrates this point in his analogy of the dreaming machine.

*"While awake, our view of ourselves is one in which we see and stress our autonomy, our individuality, our discreetness. We define our own boundaries and we try to work with them. What I'm suggesting, and which is not at all novel, is that our dreaming self is organized along a different principle."*

James Redfield, author of *The Celestine Prophecy,* puts it this way, "With our first move out of bed in the morning, we can remember the measures and thus move closer to the original consciousness as possible." Redfield, like many other writers and creative individuals, is pointing out that the value and promise of inner awareness is all laid out for us in the journey of sleep. It is integral with everything else that we do.

Once you allow yourself to understand that dreams are part of your individual fabric, a total part of your human experience, you then begin to acknowledge that the gifts which dreams may bring are worth exploration. Dreams are part mythology, part spirituality, and part brain function, combined to make a complete mental and psychological force of creative and, often, purposeful inspiration. In dreams, we have the ability to glimpse not only what is and what was but also what could be. These vibrant manifestations of the human spirit allow us to decode the basic text of our individual truth and, in doing so, take concerted steps in a given direction.

A good example of the potential that resides in our dreams can be found in looking at the basic skill of intuition and how that parlays into our choices. When you are driving your car and searching for parking space, your mind wanders. You think, "Where can I find a place to park my car?" If frustration takes over and you decide to give up and look in a new area, you have abandoned a given set of choices in favor of a new search. However, if you remain in a set area, you will eventually find ways to let your imagination and intuitive process take over. Your eyes follow the people leaving the stores and headlights turning on and off. Your ears pick up on sounds of engines beginning to churn. Your instincts tell you to turn left when you see everyone else turning right. Knowing when and where to look is what creates the manifestation of your actually finding a place to park your car. You find a parking space because you have combined the set of given circumstances with your own inherent skills in order to find your way toward what you needed.

While it may seem like a humorous approach to compare parking your car with charting your future intuitively, this model rings true when you *value the purpose of your own wisdom.* Dreams and their messages act in the same fashion as the intuitive impulses we feel in our daily lives. If we get a "feeling" about a person in our office or don't like the way someone sounds over the telephone, we usually adjust our behavior in order to handle the situation appropriately. In this paradigm of human action and reaction, we begin to unravel the dreaming mystery. Dreaming allows us to intuitively and spiritually evolve in the mere essence of its process and design. Indeed, it is often easier to gain access to our raw and unencumbered mental and emotional testing ground when we are asleep and free from our outer identities. Dreaming is prophecy, creation, and inspiration, combining the ingredients of the heart, the mind, and the human spirit.

## TITANIC DREAMS

*"Dream lofty dreams, and as you dream, so shall you become. Your vision is the promise of what you shall one day be."*—James Allen

The search for conclusive proof on prophetic dreams and their validity is one that has eluded many. Dreams that are defined by their ability to predict future events, either literally or symbolically, are frequently documented as psychic in nature. Illustrations and writings relating to futuristic dreaming can usually be found on the bookshelf under the heading of "occult" or "paranormal." While this literary marketing approach is interesting from a standpoint of popular myth, it devalues the inherent fact that precognitive and prophetic dreams can and do exist. They have been chronicled in an array of studies, some scientific and some by lay-people.

What fascinates me is that the study of dreams reveals that scientists and researchers, past and present, cannot disprove or discount the validity of precognitive dreams and their instruction. For most of us who want to understand our dreams, it remains unimportant if we call them "psychic," or we call them "cognitive," because these two areas of understanding are clearly interwoven. A dream is a way to gain access to the candid and often perceptive recesses of our minds and our souls. Much like the act of meditation, dreaming is something that requires us to relinquish rational traditions in favor of something greater than what we have been taught to understand. Carl Jung, the twentieth-century psychologist and dream researcher, put it best when he offered that "A dream, like every element in the psychic structure, is a product of the total psyche."

Though the history of dream study has mainly focused on the basic emotions, symbols, and images associated with sleep and its passage, there have been many famous examples of dreams that portend a future event either by association, or by story. Some well-known and precisely documented examples of dreaming and prophecy can be found in the sinking of the Titanic and the death of Abraham Lincoln.

The Titanic provides us with a distinct link to cumulous or collective dreaming experiences because there were over a dozen precognitive and prophetic dreaming events reported shortly before the disaster occurred, eight of which involved dreams. Many of these dreams were documented in books, articles, and the personal journals of relatives of survivors. As we all know, 1,522 lost their lives on a bitter April night in 1912 at the beginning of a new century of creative and industrial global change. These dreams clearly connect the unfettered dreaming minds of many to the sinking of the ship, either in form or in detail. The most riveting example of the four dreams cited below is from Mrs. Charles Potter, an English woman who awoke her husband in the middle of the night on Sunday, April 14, 1912.

### Mrs. Potter's Dream

*"I saw what seemed to be a high structure, something like an elevated railroad. There were people hanging on the outside of if as it they were holding their hands to the top of the rail of the guard fence. Many of them were*

*soaking wet and in nightclothes and they were gradually losing their hold and slipping down the inclined sides of this structure. I felt they were dropping to their certain death. They were all terrified and I felt terror so strongly that it weakened me, I'm so glad it was just a dream."*

## Mr. J. Connan Middleton's Dream

*"I dreamed that I saw the great liner floating on the sea keel upwards and her passengers and crew were swimming all around her. I saw myself floating in the air just about the floating ship."*

## Steven's Dream

*"I dreamed I saw mother in a crowded lifeboat, rocking in the ocean swell. The small white lifeboat was so crowded with people that it looked as if it might be swamped and sink any minute. The dream was something awful and frightening and all so real."*

## Mrs. Hughes's Dream

*"The most vivid dream I ever had was when I was fourteen. I was sleeping with my grandmother, who lived next door to us. I was on the main road in my town of Stoke-on-Trent, when suddenly I saw a very large ship a short distance away, as if in the middle of our park. I saw figures walking about on it and I just stood wondering what it was doing there and then suddenly it lowered at one end and I heard a terrific scream. I must have woke up screaming myself because Gran scolded me and told me to go back to sleep. After I fell back asleep, I saw the very same scene and when the people screamed, I must have again awoken, and Gran was very angry with me for waking her once more."*

Mrs. Charles Hughes, whose uncle, fourth senior engineer, Mr. Leonard Hodginkson, died on the Titanic, experienced this dream on the night of April 12, 1912, when she was fourteen. Mrs. Hughes told her mother and grandmother about this incident the next day. They would later learn that their family member had died in the disaster.

Within the paradigm of these dreams, we begin to catch a glimpse of how dreaming story lines and the human mind intertwine with one another in order to construct and reconstruct life events, past and future. While many writers have focused on the occurrence of "warning dreams" which these exemplify, it is vital as a dream worker to keep a balance and maintain your focus on probability instead of outcome. In our nocturnal journeys, it is easy to feel fear or concern when a dream or dream series seems to portend the death of a loved one or a natural disaster. I have encountered many seemingly precognitive dreams only to wake up and wonder about the probability and likelihood of these dreams really materializing.

A good example of the often senseless nature of futuristic dreaming is found in the journals of Charles Dickens. While one of Dickens's most famous works, *A Christmas Carol,* carries the main story line of spirits coming to life in the act of sleep, Dickens the man was a skeptic from the Age of Reason, devaluing dreams as anything more than a spicy meal from the previous evening. However, he did not fail to see the factual existence of these occurrences in observations penned within the pages of his personal journal.

### Dickens's Dream

*"I dreamed that I saw a lady in a red shawl with her back towards me . . . On turning round, I found that I didn't know her and she said, "I am Miss Napier." All the time that I was dressing the next morning, I thought—what a preposterous thing to have so very distinct a dream about nothing! And why Miss Napier? For I have never*

*heard of any Miss Napier. That same Friday night I read
and after the reading, came into my retiring room. Miss
Boyle and her brother presented a lady in a red shawl
who they presented as "Miss Napier"!*

Dickens's dream illustrates that dreaming the future need not
always portend a disastrous event. A dream may point to an
event in detail, but the event itself may hold no great significance. Often, our dreams can direct and guide us, but it is we
who give our dreams quantitative value. Over time, I have
learned that some dreams are merely illusions of my thoughts
and emotions that will most likely never transpire. Their purpose is either yet to be discovered, or merely anecdotal and symbolic. Within this context, it is easy to grasp that the choices we
make in our lives can and do dictate the shape of our own destiny. Self-determination is the connective tissue between our
dreaming aspirations and our waking fears. Some dreams act as
blueprints for events, and then, there are some dreams that
clearly illustrate the future.

Abraham Lincoln was a creative and deeply profound thinker
who suffered from depression in his lifetime. He kept a journal
for most of his adult life, writing poetry and other passages. He
often made note of his dreams and sentient thoughts. Lincoln
actively suspected that there were men who wanted to assassi-
nate him. He told his bodyguard,

*"Crook, do you know I believe there are men who want
to take my life? And I have no doubt they will do it . . .
I know no one could do it and escape alive. But if it is to
be done, it is impossible to prevent it."*
                    —Abraham Lincoln to bodyguard,
                    William Henry Crook, on April 14, 1865

In 1865, a week before his death, Abraham Lincoln had a
dream, which accurately foretold of his demise. Lincoln's dream

is richly metaphoric in theme and content and, yet, holds the main message of his death by assassination. Three days prior to his assassination Lincoln related this nocturnal vision to his wife and a few friends.

## Lincoln's Dream

*"About ten days ago, I retired very late. I had been up waiting for important dispatches from the front. I could not have been long in bed when I fell into a slumber, for I was weary. I soon began to dream. There seemed to be a death-like stillness about me. Then I heard subdued sobs, as if a number of people were weeping. I thought I left my bed and wandered downstairs. There the silence was broken by the same pitiful sobbing, but the mourners were invisible. I went from room to room; no living person was in sight, but the same mournful sounds of distress met me as I passed along. I saw light in all the rooms; every object was familiar to me; but where were all the people who were grieving as if their hearts would break? I was puzzled and alarmed. What could be the meaning of all this? Determined to find the cause of a state of things so mysterious and so shocking, I kept on until I arrived at the East Room, which I entered. There I met with a sickening surprise. Before me was a catafalque, on which rested a corpse wrapped in funeral vestments. Around it were stationed soldiers who were acting as guards; and there was a throng of people, gazing mournfully upon the corpse, whose face was covered, others weeping pitifully. 'Who is dead in the White House?' I demanded of one of the soldiers, 'The President,' was his answer; 'he was killed by an assassin.' Then came a loud burst of grief from the crowd, which woke me from my dream. I slept no more that night; and although it was only a dream, I have been strangely annoyed by it ever since."*

In life, Lincoln was a gifted and highly evolved intuitive individual. His humanitarian actions changed a nation. In death, his dream acts as a vision of his own ability to connect with destiny. The visual landscape of his dream is strong as the sounds of weeping overtake the dreamer. Yet, the message in his dream is one that every person can relate to. Lincoln's dream carries a clear message of love and loss, of hope and despair in a time of national crisis.

In reading Lincoln's dream, it is easy to form the idea that the events that would transpire approximately one week later were set in some type of karmic stone with cause and effect being inalterable. Here is where the parallax view of dreams and their meaning must be studied and understood before conclusions are drawn. The dream routine is part of an individual's make-up, like a dreaming DNA. Each of us carries our own unique reference file of experience, a brain/mind machine of our dreaming identities. A dream landscape can mean something entirely different depending on who experiences the dream. Dreaming provides us with a seamless environment, acting as an accessible doorway to our own hopes, fears, and desires. In taking the time to work with and understand our dreams, we gain knowledge, insight, and sometimes, *vision*. We create and define our dreams, and in turn, they create and define us.

## 2

# The History of
# Dream Interpretation

*" . . . dreams are that of which the subconscious is made,
for any conditions every becoming reality is first
dreamed."*—Edgar Cayce *reading 136-7*

The history of interpreting and understanding dreams took
shape on the global stage in the early nineteenth century with
the work of Sigmund Freud and the 1899 publication of his book
*The Interpretation of Dreams*. Freud took the study of dreaming away from folkloric traditions and into the realm of science.
Taking on the role of analyst and working with dreams as a tool
for diagnosing mental afflictions, Freud used psychoanalytical
thought as his model for research and discovery. His concepts
of wish fulfillment and manifest content lit a fire in the movement of modern psychological study. His heavy focus on symbolism and primal urges often led him to conclude that many
dreams were sexual in nature. Yet, his theories changed the
popular view of dreaming and dream interpretation to some-

thing to be taken seriously, an action and function to be respected and examined in relation to the various levels of cognitive thought.

Before Freud, however, there were many people exploring the nature of sleep and dreaming on another level altogether. In 1886, a group of scientific investigators in Great Britain probed the then radical concept of dreaming and prophecy by soliciting 5,360 average individuals for their futuristic dreams and follow-up testimonials. From this survey, catalogued by Frederic W.H. Myers and Frank Podmore, a vast library of dreams, published under the title *Phantasms of the Living,* was born. In this two volume book there is an entire section devoted to the publication of precognitive dreams and their value. While most of the 149 dreams listed dwell on death and foreboding omens, the hunger for dream understanding obviously lay present in the collective minds of the late nineteenth century.

During this same period of industrial history, a British aeronautical engineer named John William Dunne was exploring the dreaming dynamic through the use of his journals, which he kept throughout a thirty-year span. His curiosity began when he experienced a dream that foretold the eruption of Mount Pelée in Martinique. While his nocturnal prediction of the loss of 4,000 lives was inaccurate, (the death toll was actually 40,000) Dunne was convinced that dreaming was an act of mental time travel, allowing the dreamer to mentally probe the past and future much like we do in our waking minds. His book, *An Experiment with Time*, published in 1926 explores this quasi-scientific logic and ponders the notion that dreams provide us a glimpse into tomorrow.

The evolution of dream interpretation and the study of sleep from its inception to its present-day perspectives carries us into new dimensions of understanding. Research, science, and spiritual exploration have delivered some answers to the basic questions of sleep. Does everyone dream? How does the brain work when we sleep? How do we dream? Are dreams an emotional experience or are they abstract? Should we value your intuitive and creative left-brain activities or are dreams more of a right-brain experience?

Throughout this chapter, you will gain insight on how to begin to work with and dissect your own dreaming brain, by understanding the fundamental basics of dream study and what it can mean to your own development. This odyssey begins with the work of Edgar Cayce, who was a true pioneer in the understanding of prophecy, humanity, religion, and healing.

## EDGAR CAYCE: THE PHOTOGRAPHIC MIND

*"We are in a time so strange that living equals dreaming."*—Calderon

Great dreamers realize that the future is anyone's dream. No one understood this concept better than Edgar Cayce, the twentieth-century visionary, who explored his personal dreams and their meaning throughout the sixty-seven years of his life. Cayce believed that dreams offer us a window into the future. His psychic readings spoke extensively about dreams as a tool for transformation. He knew that our dreams act as compasses for our future choices. Indeed, the more we look at our dreams as a mirror for our waking lives, the greater our chance for wisdom and perspective.

Edgar Cayce was born in March of 1877 on a farm near Hopkinsville, Kentucky. His life story is a tale of true American adventure and pioneer spirit, as well as the story of a man who gave of himself honestly and devoutly to all he met. His childhood led him to believe in the teachings of Christianity, and he considered himself a Christian throughout the rest of his life. He worked for many years as a photographer, was a Sunday school teacher and a family man. Much like the printing process used in creating photographic works, Cayce's life was filled with positives and reverse positives, revealing a man who carried vision on multiple planes of thought and action. His calling as a visionary came at twenty-one when he found himself ill and unable to get help from the medical establishment. Cayce lost his voice and found no relief from the "snake oil" treatments, which were abundant in his day. Cayce turned inward and asked himself while sleeping how to diagnose his problem. He was given the answer to his call, "a congestion in the area of the voice box." Taking measures to cure himself, he regained his voice at once. After this, Cayce devoted his life to healing and the pursuit of metaphysical understanding.

To put Cayce's work and endeavors in perspective, the Cayce library today houses more than fourteen thousand psychic readings, which were given by Cayce from a sleeplike state over the span of forty years. These documents represent the largest catalogue of intuitive material from one specific individual. Cayce's work spawned a hospital and a healing foundation whose building still stands today in Virginia Beach. Published works about his gift are too many to list, but they exist in almost every translatable language. He is often referred to as "the sleeping prophet," because he entered a trancelike state in order to give psychic or clairvoyant readings on subjects from healing to prophecy to reincarnation.

In looking at Cayce's life, it is important to remember the value of his actions during the time in which he lived. He was working with concepts like prophecy, alternative healing, and also dream interpretation just after the turn of the century and during the great depression. This was an era when many people did not value alternative teachings, let alone have the time or money to explore self-healing and wellness. There were no health stores or fitness centers, no herbal mood elevators or yoga books. People lived to survive, and in need of help, they often sought out Cayce's insights.

In dreams, Cayce often experienced many elements of personal precognition and prophecy. He believed that the value of dreams was much like any human causational factor: If applied with positive and spiritual action, dreams could be used to change or even create the future. Cayce was a very complex man in some ways because he firmly believed in the laws of karma and in the concept of universal action and reaction. Yet, he consistently taught people that their destiny was in their own hands. Cayce had many students of intuitive study who over the years would send him their dreams for interpretation.

Cayce was one of the first individuals to advise people to keep a dream journal. He believed that the individual is usually his or her own best dream interpreter. While Freud was collecting data and analyzing other people's dreams, Cayce was encouraging people to master their own dream work, to chronicle their own journey. Cayce's readings commented that "any conditions ever becoming reality is first dreamed." (136-7) He firmly believed in the wisdom of dreaming, asking only that each individual take responsibility for his or her own destiny. A good example of the Cayce dream model can be found in this quote:

*(Q) How should dreams be interpreted?*

(A) Depending upon the physical condition of the [person] and that which produces or brings the dream to that body's forces. The better definition of how the interpretation may be best is this: Correlate those Truths that are enacted in each and every dream . . . and use such to the better developing [of yourself], remembering [that] develop means going toward the higher forces, or the Creator . . . [In] dreams, those forces of the subconscious, when taken or correlated into those forms that relate to the various phases of the individual, give to that individual the better understanding of self, when correctly interpreted, or when correctly answered. 3744-5

When a stockbroker came to Cayce for a reading in 1929, he asked about this dream:

> *"Got the impression regarding the market that we ought to sell everything, including the [high yield]. Dream concerning [my wife] . . . A bull seemed to follow [her] red dress. I tried to catch the bull. Some special reference to [certain stocks]. My impression was down, but I'm not sure."*

A month later, Cayce responded in readings 137-115 and 137-117 with the following thoughts:

> . . . many changes, as will be seen in a downward movement of a long duration . . . the body should dispose of all those [stocks] held—even those [of high yield] . . .
> . . . there must surely come a break where it would be panic in the money centers—not only of Wall Street's activity but a closing of the boards in many centers . . .

In the Cayce school of thought, this dreamer has the opportunity for change, should he follow a course of actions using his dream as a tool for perspective. The symbolism of the bull exemplifies a "bull market," and the dreamer, whose wife left him in the subsequent months, seems to be watching as his financial destiny chases his wife away. The crash of 1929 was to follow this dreaming event. If the dreamer arrives at a place of understanding and takes some action based on the dreaming experience, a process can begin which allows the dreamer to make soul specific choices, playing a role in self-determination and personal prophecy.

In a sense, Cayce was teaching people about intuitive sciences before they had a name. He created a niche and defined it. He was a visionary on multiple levels because he pioneered work in many areas that today seem commonplace. He was the father of the New Age and, much like the great writer H.G. Wells, someone born far too many years ahead of his time.

## Carl Jung: The Archetypal Master

*"Dreaming is the art of breaking the barriers of normal perception."*—Carlos Castaneda

The work and life of Carl Jung cannot be understated in relation to the history of dreaming and the study of the human mind. Jung, A Swiss-born psychologist and physician, was a brilliant man whose vast writings on dreams read like passages from a philosopher and spiritualist as well as a genius of modern thought. While a contemporary of Freud as was Cayce, Jung was the first person to openly address the concept that dreaming and the images of sleep stem from a common human source. His knowledge and understanding of religion, mythology, and symbolism allowed him to formulate the identity of archetypal themes among people from different walks of life and from different countries of origin. He deemed this metaphysical arena of truth in dreaming as "the collective unconscious."

Jung, the son of a protestant minister, felt that the metaphors of sleep were unified among mythological and religious traditions. Dreams were gateways to a mythic world of grand design, open to anyone who had the desire to enter. Dreams had a narrative, a voice, a story, and a plot. Water, for example, could universally reflect emotional and spiritual elements. Trees could be identified as a life-giving force, exemplified in texts from the Bible to the Koran. Jung believed that dreams were part of a process of self-awareness and awakening, allowing the dreamer to focus on the dream itself as opposed to an underlying source of the nocturnal event.

If you take the time to read some of Jung's collected works, you will begin to understand that his approach to dreaming and the human mind does not differentiate between the human "psyche" and "psychic structure." His writings are highly introspective as he explores the dynamics of the human spirit and the will to evolve. Jung did not believe in the notion of precognizant awareness. In most of his works, you will find that he openly states that he cannot prove or disprove the concept of prophecy in dreaming. To Jung, there was a definite distinction between dreams that *could be* and dreams that *will be*. In his article entitled "The General Aspects of Dream Psychology," he writes:

> *"The occurrence of prospective dreams cannot be denied. It would be wrong to call them prophetic because at bottom they are no more prophetic than a medical diagnosis or a weather forecast. They are merely an anticipatory combination of probabilities, which may coincide with the actual behavior of things but need not necessarily agree in every detail. Only in the latter case can we speak of prophecy."*

Acknowledging this, Jung also went a step further in probing the concept of the act and actions of dreams and their outcome. In the case study below, you will see how one futuristic dream openly played a role in Jung's personal and professional life. When a colleague came to him and recounted this dream, Jung intuitively recognized the dreaming message and noted that dream analysis deserves special attention, and that it can often be "a matter of life and death."

### Carl Jung: A Case Study

> *"I am climbing a high mountain, over steep snow-covered slopes. I climb higher and higher, and it is marvelous weather. The higher I climb the better I feel. I think, 'If only I could go on climbing like this forever!' When I reach the summit, my happiness and elation are so great that I feel I could mount right up into space. And I discover that I can actually do so: I mount upward on empty air and awake in sheer ecstasy."*

Jung, seeing the enigmatic message in his friend's dream, was concerned for his friend's safety. He urged the dreamer to climb with guides, saying *"My dear fellow, I know you can't give up mountaineering, but let me implore you not to go alone from now on. When you go, take two guides and promise on your word of honor to follow them absolutely."* Jung's friend did not listen, ignoring Jung's dream interpretations as an idiotic exercise. Jung never saw his friend again. Three months after having the dream, the man fell to his death. A guide standing below him literally saw him step out into the air while descending a rock face.

Jung deemed these dream happenings as *synchronicity*, or a causation-connecting event between individuals. Following this incident, in his article, "The Analysis of Dreams," Jung wrote, "No amount of skepticism and cynicism has yet enabled me to regard dreams as a negligible occurrence." In this divine thought of vulnerable human compassion, Carl Jung opened the doorway for a new generation of dreamers and their ideas.

## BRAIN WAVES

*"Dreams say what they mean, but they don't say it in daytime language."*—Gail Godwin

As the twentieth century steamed along with locomotive speed and the age of invention, so too did the model for dreaming and its study. In the era of space travel and new discovery, scientists hungered to know if psychic dreams or precognitive dreaming could be probed under a scientific model, with set criteria for research and understanding. They also wanted to know exactly how our brains functioned to create the language of our dreams.

The area of dream understanding was significantly aided by Eugene Aserinsky and Nathanial Kleitman in their 1953 discovery of *rapid eye movements* or (REM*)* that occur during sleep and which can be measured by EEG. Using laboratory techniques, it thus became possible to identify the various levels and stages of sleep. Dreaming could now be qualified and reported during the phases of REM sleep by measuring the brain activity or brain waves of thousands of subjects. This opened the door to a new outlook and approach to understanding our nocturnal mechanisms.

The physiology of REM sleep offered us two statistical truths. One is that everyone dreams. While REM activity occupies no more than 25 percent of the entire night in adults, virtually everyone has at least four dream periods per night at the rate of one every ninety minutes. The dream periods start out as short spans of ten minutes. They then stretch up to an hour or more as we end our sleep cycle. Typically, we remember our last dream in the morning because it is closer to the time we awaken or closer to the end of our last REM cycle.

The second mystery unraveled from early REM study is that many people dream in color, but they are usually unable to differentiate colors schemes in their dreams when they awaken. An excellent example of this comes from Helen Keller, who lost her sense of sight, hearing, and smell as an infant. She wrote in her autobiography:

*"Once in a dream, I held in my hand a pearl. I have no memory-vision of a real pearl. The one I saw in my dream must, therefore, have been a creation of my imagination. It was smooth, exquisitely molded crystal. As I gazed into its shimmering deeps, my soul was flooded with an ecstasy of tenderness. I was filled with wonder, as one who should for the first time look into the cool, sweet heart of a rose. My pearl was dew and fire, the velvety green of moss, the soft whiteness of lilies and the distilled hues and sweetness of a thousand roses. It seemed to me the soul of beauty was dissolved in its crystal bosom."*

The irony of Helen Keller being able to see and experience

color in her dreams—"the green of moss" and "the whiteness of lilies," stands as an example of the polarity found in dreams. This paradox links us to our own unearthed ability in the dreaming routine. Dreaming is not an activity that can be understood under one model of study. In looking at our dreams, we need to grasp the scope of all studies and then hold them alongside our individual capabilities—biologically, mentally, and spiritually.

Breaking new boundaries at the Maimonedes Medical Center in Brooklyn, New York, Montague Ullman and Stanley Krippner began working with dreams and their instructional purpose. Their mission was to see if dreams were indeed psychic and if they could carry a message through channels other than the human senses. As a physician, Ullman brought a distinctive look at the science of sleep as he endeavored to demystify the dreaming process, agreeing with Edgar Cayce that the dreamer was usually the best expert on his or her dream. In order to prove that dreaming was an experience that transcended the boundaries of a trained psychoanalyst or psychologist, Krippner and Ullman worked to study the nature of telepathic and prophetic dreaming to garner statistics on these nocturnal events. These studies asked: *Could dreams really connect us to one another?*

The results were impressive. From 1960 to 1972, twelve experiments were carried out. The format was simple: one participant, located in a separate building or room from the target subject (the dreamer), would concentrate on an image in order to attempt to "send" it to the dreamer and thus into the target participant's dream. Different images were used in the study ranging from abstract paintings to simple color-oriented mosaics and geometric designs. Dreams were timed and images were sent at the exact moment a given subject would be entering REM sleep. In initial trials, they were able to achieve a 50 percent ratio of acceptable examples of dreaming connection between the target individual and the "sender." They believed that in a dream state, a person could transcend their normal boundaries of thought in order to enter a more psychic and intuitive state. In one example, an individual was sent an image of Chagall's painting *Paris Through a Window*, which depicts a man viewing the Latin Quarter through his window. The city of Paris is clearly depicted along with the Eiffel Tower and many small buildings. The dreamer noted the following dream during the target period of REM sleep.

*"I was in the French Quarter and I was walking through different departments in a department store . . . It was an early village of some sort, it was some sort of blend of this romantic type of architecture—buildings, village, quaint."*

As the experiments progressed, Ullman and Krippner also attempted sleeping studies relating to prophetic or precognitive dreams but could not develop a model for understanding this complex and highly evolved aspect of sleep. From these trials, two books were published and more than fifty papers were written on the subject. Independent judges were used to score and rate the value of each dream and its ability to connect with a target image. The results? Out of twelve experiments, 83.5 percent of the dreams were accurately telepathic or, in other words, able to visualize the target images within the confines of the dreaming experience.

In looking at these various avenues of exploration and concentration, it becomes easy to see how science and the study of the brain began to play a role in our modern-day view of dreaming. But, how did the components of our brains play a specific role in the creation of our dreams? Are dreams really complete in form and creation or are they more like a stream of consciousness in action and structure?

The answers to some of these questions can be found in the work of Allan Hobson and Robert McCarley. In 1977, Drs. Hobson and McCarley presented a new a model of the dream process that challenged the many earlier psychoanalytical approaches to dream study. They suggested that dreaming is a physiological function and that dreams are determined by a "dream state generator" located in the brain stem. The brain stem system regularly activates the dream state, acting much like an "on/off" switch to mobilize the forebrain into dreaming action. Simply put, our brains are likened to a computer database. When we go to sleep each night, our brain stem searches our database to generate and create the dreaming genesis. All of our sensory functions, such as sight and sound and spatial orientation, are then instructed on what to do and how to do it, similar to computer file-sharing.

Hobson and McCarley deemed their model *Activation Synthesis*. In Hobson's world, dreaming is a behavioral state, much like waking. Now REM sleep and the emotions we experience in a given dream could be pinpointed to a neurobiological root. For example, in their examination of dream reports they found that 70 percent of the dream experiences related to the emotions of anxiety, elation, and anger. Following this statistic, the most common dreaming experience related to shame, guilt, and affection. Ironically, erotic dreams only ranked a low 5 percent on the dreaming scale, something that Freud would have been disappointed to hear.

Hobson also launched a full scale campaign to illuminate a new generation of dream thinkers about the truth in our dreaming potential when he fostered an art/science event at Harvard's Carpenter Center called *Dreamstage: a Multimedia Portrait of the Sleeping Brain*. The exhibit, which drew over 10,000 visitors, featured a person sleeping in a closed room behind a one-way mirror. The audience was able to view the dreamer in a sleep lab setting, hooked up to instruments monitoring his or her brain waves and body movements. These instruments would then convert a dreamer's REM pattern into laser light beams and sound, creating an electric light show of color and motion, all depicting what the dreamer was experiencing. Hobson's views represented the dawn of a new era of dream understanding and study. In his book, *The Dreaming Brain,* he writes:

> *"In assuming that our dreams may not only signal, but actually cause real-life events, the prophetic view has collapsed and the dreamer has assumed responsibility for the dream's actions. We humans seem to have as much difficulty delegating responsibility for important life events as we do accepting it. But there is a third way by which we may avoid the dilemma of unacceptable responsibility for unwilled acts. The scientific evidence now suggests that both life events (such as births, deaths, and accidents) and dream events (such as out-of-body and precognitive experiences) are all, in essence, unwilled natural phenomena: they occur according to their own laws, in which both determinism and chance are statutes, and the associations between them are as much casual as they are causal."*

Understanding the anatomy of the brain along with its motor functions offers us new insights into dreaming. Now, *Activation Synthesis* becomes a useful model for the dreaming machine. Of course, when it comes down to dreams, the real question relates not only to function but meaning as well. Do our dreams enlighten us? Will they make us smarter or challenge us more? Can they solve our problems, past, present, and future? The fact that we can produce such meaningful experiences from the act of dreaming proves that the brain is capable of a vast many things which we, as humans, cannot yet understand. Holding this concept in mind, we can then step into a new paradigm of dreaming and meaning. If we can "see" or picture a perspective path for the future in our active brain/mind, why can't we then be doing the same in sleep?

The coupling of the dreaming brain and the waking mind comes full circle in present-day logic and understanding. Many people today want to find their own answers, which is part of what reading this book will allow you to do. Interpreting your own dreams requires that you learn to probe the scope of your mind and to ask yourself about the nature of your own thought process. However, knowing that your dreams are part and parcel of your own gene pool—your psychophysical potential— you now stand ready to begin a new journey of exploring your dreams, understanding how their visions and ideas relate to your personal design of tomorrow.

# 3

# Tools for Mapping Your Dreams

*"Dreams are my truth. They guide me and link me to the divine."*—Judith Orloff

**M**ost of us carry the desire to have our dreams come true. We all have a wish, a star, or an idea that we hold in hope for the future. To dream is to live a vision, to embrace magic, to see the future and its possibilities. Dreaming is life. Great artists, thinkers, and visionaries throughout human history have triumphed by realizing their ideas and aspirations. Shakespeare dreamed his plays. Van Gogh painted his visions. Seeds planted from dreams grow beautiful trees. Everyone has a dream. Yet, how many of us act on our dreams and use them as tools for mapping our own unique and individual futures?

The journey of sleep takes us to a world where illusion and fantasy collide to create a cocktail of adventure. Tigers can speak and people have wings. Dreams often carry fancy and surreal symbols. Many dreams foretell future events or illustrate hidden emotions. Dreams are the stories of our lives. Though we ask questions and search for answers in the pockets of our daily lives, the results of our nightly wanderings often yield a profound insight. Upon awakening, we brush away the images and emotions, attributing them to nightly insanity. I frequently hear people say, "I had the craziest dream last night." In the eyes of the dreamer, one can see the contemplation of the event. He or she may be wondering, "Is this a sign of an impending encounter? What does this mean?" We all seek to understand our dreams, to conquer our internal journeys. Dreaming, much like life, is found in the details. To live the vision, we must value and understand our dreams.

I began a dream journal at a very young age. When I was twelve years old, I often dreamed of wandering around the streets of New York City. I look back on my writings and I can find descriptions of the tall buildings and the brilliant lights. I grew up in an Iowa town and had never seen the lights of Broadway. Somehow, in my sleep, these images made their way into my mind.

Years later, I moved to New York, where I still reside. Many of the images I described occurred fifteen, even twenty years later. Dreaming is about *path*. If we choose to follow the signs on the road of sleep, dreams can be a tool to enrich, even create our lives. I have always been served well by my dreams. My dreams have helped shape me, giving me guidance in my darkest hour.

Dream journeys are individual. They begin with self. Your dream journey begins through reflection and analysis. In order to retrieve your dreams and their meaning you need to begin by looking at the basics of dream forecasting. Remember that the future is all part of the fabric of your mind and spirit. Within each of us is a grand valley of insight. Soul and purpose are both found through the magical gateway of dreams. Nightly perceptions, no matter how unusual, or perhaps grand, reveal pockets of meaning. The task of the dream worker is to uncover these hidden nuggets. To understand and begin your journey of dreaming, you need to begin with some basic tools. Like any journey, you will need a compass. To gauge and follow your dreams, you begin with a dream journal.

My first dream journal was a hodgepodge of images and stream-of-consciousness thought. When we awaken, it can be difficult to record our dreaming sensations in a concise and understandable way. In order to map your dreams, you must first attend "night school." Educate yourself on your dreams and what they mean by keeping a dream journal. Your dream journal is the first step in dream understanding. You can write your dreams in a spiral binder or a bound blank book, whatever inspires you to put pen to paper. Endeavor to write as soon as you wake up, while the imprint of sleep is fresh. Keep this journal by your bedside, or on your night table. Your dream journal is vital because it acts as your nocturnal compass.

## NIGHT SCHOOL

*"Dreams are the touchstones of our characters."*—Henry David Thoreau

You may, at first, feel uncomfortable with the concept of getting up and writing. Many people do not have the time in their early morning hours to write. The pressures of getting to work on time or taking care of breakfast often take precedence over something like writing about a dream. Yet, this is the first step to dreaming your future. If you want to reap the rewards of your dreams, to create a better and more profound life path, you must write about your nightly insights, views, and emotions. If this seems complicated, try looking at it like this: *dreams are spiritual.* Much like prayer, they provide valuable aid in daily life. Would you take the time each day to pray or to meditate? Using a more concrete and simple analogy, do you take extra time in your life to e-mail a friend or read a book? All of these activities require time and effort, as well as creativity. Dream journeys demand the same rights of passage. In other words, effort can make all the difference.

The goal is to bring your dreams out of your closet and into your waking world. The Hopi Indian tribes of North America viewed dreams as the anchor of our inner worlds. Hopi society held dream guidance in high regard, cherishing the art of nocturnal voyage as a concrete tool for change. When you begin to value dreaming as a *tangible* and *purposeful* form of cognitive and spiritual thought, you realize its ultimate potential. Dreams play a role in illusion *and* reality. If you challenge yourself to take a few moments in the morning or early part of the day to jot down the details of your dreams, you have made the first step toward new self-awareness and personal transformation. You will be on your way.

## THE DREAM CHRONICLE

*"You are not wrong, who deem that my days have been a dream."*—Edgar Allen Poe

When you write about your dreams, it is important to follow some basic guidelines. The first thing to examine is your emotions. Take notice of residual sensations when you jot down your dreams. Follow your intuition. Begin by asking yourself what feelings linger from your nightly journey. What words or phrases best express your feelings in the dream? Did your dream tell a story? What happened in your dream? Know that your dreams act as a window into the purpose of tomorrow. By writing about your dreams in a way that reflects your individual personality and style, you create greater insight into your future. Often the nocturnal journey is highly personal. Write in a way that is informal and illustrative. Pay attention to details! Often the smallest image or feeling can relate an ocean of meaning. Fantastic voyages begin with humble origins. What counts is *approach*.

Dreaming lore is often complex and convoluted. While some dreams are simple in theme and subject, others are detailed in theme and ceremony. Dreams, like films, hold form and story. One example of a complex dream illustrates this point.

> *"My dream was one of the most vivid, colorful, and pleasant dreams a person could ask for. It was a beautiful, sunny day. Blue skies. I had a dream that I was flying in a mystical forest. I didn't have wings, and there were some other people with me. We also flew over a river. It was magnificent and I think about it all the time. Occasionally in the dream there would be young girls in the forest painting on huge canvases beautiful scenes of water lilies. I flew to a tall tree where a lot of my friends were coming down a hill. Birds were singing and I could smell the lilac trees below me. All of a sudden everything stopped! Then everything started going backwards. The birds were going backwards, the sun was moving out of the sky, the girls were walking backwards up the hill. I woke up rather amused but sad."*

This dream, which the writer titled "Mystical Forest" shows how detailed and elusive dreaming can be. It reminds me of a painting by Renee Magritte, entitled "Time Transfixed," because of its surreal qualities. When I first read the dream I was struck by the dreamer's ability to note the most minute images and symbols. Her dream resolves with the expression of her feelings. It reveals that the dreaming mind is creative and sensitive. In dreams, we write our own script. When you endeavor to chronicle your dreams, you create a motion picture of your life and your future. Remember that writing about your dreams is an act of inspired form, a spiritual journey. If you make the effort, you will reap great rewards.

You are probably wondering about the meaning of the " Mys-

tical Forest." We will cover the various insights of dream interpretation as we travel through the pages of this book. In the
meantime, you may want to test your interpretive skills and ask
yourself how you perceive this dream. You can grab a scrap of
paper or anything handy and jot down your ideas.
1. What is the prevailing feeling in this dream?
2. Which symbols or metaphors tell the story?
3. How does the dream story connect to your life?
Remember that your answers are completely interpretive.
There are no right or wrong ideas in the beginning steps of
dream work. The task of understanding and analyzing dreams
is to relate to other dreamers and walk with them through their
subconscious garden. Their dreams, much like your dreams, are
all part of the path of higher thinking and being. Like the air we
breathe, dreaming is a thing we all experience, a space we all
*share.*

## SYMBOLOGY

*"The word did not appear in truth, but in symbols and
images."*—Jesus

Dream symbols are vast and metaphoric. The importance of
dream symbology cannot be underestimated. When we dream
about the people we know and the events in our lives, we peel
away the layers of our inner beings. The act of dreaming illumi-
nates things in a mythical fashion. Later in the book, I will touch
on the important mythological and symbolic components of
dreams. For now, follow the guideline of writing about your
individual dream mythology. Make note of the most important
symbols, characters, colors, numbers, or objects. Begin your
dream journey by establishing which elements stick in your
mind. Ask yourself if a particular object or color figures more
prominently than other features of the dream. For example, if
you dream about a person you know wearing a diamond ring,

make note of its importance. What stands out more, the ring or the person? Perhaps a certain sound can be heard. You may feel overpowered by the size of a mountain or feel the spiritual pull of a religious symbol. All of these things tell a story and relate to your world. They reveal who you are today and who you will become tomorrow.

Dream symbols can act as emblematic guides for the actions in each dream. They reflect emotions, premonitions, and higher truths. Some dreams are simple and short in theme, yet still reveal a high level of direction. In one woman's dream, a fork in the road plays a single, yet dominant role.

**Jen's Dream**

*"My sister has a recurrent dream. She is driving down a winding road and she finds herself at an intersection. She is afraid because she is lost and does not know which way to go. By the end of her dream, she decides on a road and feels good because she has finally chosen the right path. When she wakes up she feels confused. What role does this play in her life?"*

In order for the dreamer to answer this question, she must first look at the symbol of the intersection. This is a very simple yet, richly metaphoric dream. The concept of a "crossroads" in life is not unique. We all reach times in our lives when important decisions must be made. How do we make our choices? Do we choose rationale or faith? The knowledge that our choices are correct because they are individual is vital. If we know that the act of choice is the thing that sends us in the right direction, we gain wisdom and experience. This particular dream can be summed up in the sentence, *"She decides on a road and feels good because she has finally chosen the right path."* The dreamer is using her dreaming experiences to improve her decision-making process. She gains empowerment and strength. She prospers in her decisions. Here lies the essential component to dreaming the future. The goal is to endeavor to read the signs of each dream in order to make improved choices for love, career, and life.

Look at it this way—symbols are no more than pointed representations of our mental and emotional minds. Symbolism is part of the global human language. Symbolic representations often yield profound universal truth in theme and in message. Take, for example, the symbol of the cross. In the world arena, it takes on the role of deliverance, healing, and salvation. Many people see it as a metaphor for their own spiritual path. You don't have to be a Christian to embrace its message, but you do need to be in touch with the concepts of human compassion and soulful awakening in order to connect with any type of archetypal message.

Does a dream with a major symbol such as a cross, a Star of David, or the ankh portend a calling or future enlightenment? *Perhaps.* However, more importantly, it is vital to look at the connection between the images and representations of sleep and their wireless to your own individual path. I always remind myself that no matter what the dream is telling me in symbol, I chart my own destiny. If I use the gifts of sleep to envision and create a better tomorrow for myself and for others, I am surely on my way to greater revelations in life and in spirit.

## Baby Steps

*"The dream was always running ahead of me. To catch up, to live for a moment in unison with it, that was the miracle."*—Anais Nin

When we begin to track our dreams, we often jump ahead of ourselves. Many people feel certain that their dreams may indicate a specific event to come. The truth is that many dream mysteries come to light over time. I have experienced numerous dreams that have revealed their meaning weeks, months, or even years later. Often, it is a question of comparison and association. Interpretation is about personal reflection. Seeking the answers in dreams is about learning from your inner emotions, spirit, and being. Intuition often has a hand in this mix of nocturnal logic. Significant answers come from asking the right questions. Dreaming is about the journey *and* the destination.

Dreams can often clarify. Association is very important. I once dreamed that I was passionately embracing a man who works in my office building. When I sat and wrote about the dream, I realized that this dream revealed specific needs I was feeling in my life. My relationship was not going well and I was yearning for romance and special attention. Though it is certainly possible that this man could have played a potential role in my future, it was important for me to look at the signs on my life's highway. Looking for the answers in sleep has much to do with charting a course and following it. It is a continual, never-ending story.

Wherever you are on your dream journey, it is important to remember the small steps. Be a dream detective. Uncover clues and eliminate meanings based on *your* compass. Ask yourself about the significant activities in your dreams. What are they telling you? When is the same feeling present in your waking life? Do you sense that a specific dream is leading you toward something or someone? Manifest your dream visions by knowing that they connect you to your place in the world. The messages in dreams are the connective tissue between you and your destiny.

*"My cousin just recently got married. In my dream I am wearing a wedding band, and I am under the impression that it is hers. I am also with her husband. He and I are running from people who seem harmful. We are in a car that will not move. Finally, the car starts and we get away, but when I look down at the ring, the stone is missing and the only thing left is the band. Then, I wake*

*up. Does this mean I am going to get married? Please help. "*

The dreamer wonders if she will marry since she dreamed of a wedding. However, the cousin's recent union tells the story. This is a fascinating dream because of the metaphor of marriage and the missing stone in the ring. I wish that the dreamer had written what type of stone was in the ring because stones often carry a valued and powerful symbolism. The essential element in this dream is the ring. Although weddings are very symbolic, this one is not greatly illustrated. To interpret the dream and its connection to her world, you must look at the picture and the symbols. Perhaps the dreamer is jealous of her cousin. The feelings are those of loss and discovery combined. She runs from unknown forces only to stop and wonder at the ring resting on her hand. Something is absent in her life. The missing stone says that she is seeking. Yet, a sense of self holds firm because the band, the circle of life, remains on her hand. Once the dreamer understands the void she feels in her world, the dream will aid her on her path to self-empowerment.

This dream illustrates that little details can make all the difference in better understanding your dreams. In the pursuit of dreams, we face many elements known and unknown. When you do your dream work, take the time to develop a sense of your dreaming mind. Trust your inner compass. Allow your dreams and your interpretations to guide you. Know your intuitive signals. Your dream memoirs are a mirror of you.

# 4

# The Roadmap of Dreams

*"Dreaming has meaning like everything else we do."*
—Carl Jung

Sleep is merely a gateway into the roadmap of dreams. Dreaming the future is what we all do when we close our eyes each night. The nightly journey takes us to places unconquered, unfound. We see what we cannot see in our waking minds. The inner self emotes and speaks. Through the magic of sleep, we find a path to new vistas of spirit and self. Dreaming the future is possible, if we understand that we are the living embodiment of the act of the dream. We are the life of the dream.

The panorama of the dreaming world is meaningless until you interact with it. Look at your dreams as you would archival footage from a video library. Your dreams tell the story of who you are, past, present, and future. Your dreams offer you a chance to evolve and change. You do the choosing on which direction to take. For example, each day, most of us drive, commute, or walk to work. If we choose an alternate route on our way to work, we will encounter a different series of views, experiences, and events. Much like an atlas, the dreaming map offers you a choice for your journey. Action must be guided by intuition and experience. The dream journal will aid you in your quest for understanding and context. By keeping a record of your dreams, you will begin to gain wisdom on how to create a more permanent vision of your life. Depending on the choices you make and the insights you gain from nightly vision, you will create a new and different set of circumstances for tomorrow.

I have experienced dreams of anger directed at those who have hurt me in the past. This is common in dreams of healing and recovery. A good example of charting the future from dreaming is the choices I made from taking note of those dreams. I held the residual emotions of morning and asked myself, *"Why was I angry?"* and *"What do I have to gain from continuing with hidden rage in my waking life?"* By looking at my emotions and the unique features of each dream, I rescued myself from resentment and gained tenfold in the act of forgiveness. Great rewards come from the smallest efforts. In dreaming, these efforts begin with the interpretations of our stories.

Begin by completing the following exercises and see how you fare. Remember that dreaming is individual. Don't get hung up on what you think may be the "right" answers. Just follow your instincts and complete the following sentences:

## THE DREAMING IDENTITY QUIZ

1.  My greatest stumbling block with dreaming is

2. The most clear dream memory I have is

_____

3. The more I dream, the more I think

_____

4. If my dreams come true, I am afraid that

_____

5. If I let myself feel my dreams, I usually

_____

6. I want to understand my dreams better so that

_____

Once you have taken the quiz, set it aside and move forward with other things. Later, you will look back at your ideas of dreaming in order to examine your progress. Remember that your dreaming identity carries a growth process, and it is up to you to journey toward greater understanding in the world of sleep and beyond.

## INTERPRETING DREAMS

*"The images before our eyes when we awaken are identical to the objects perceived in dreams."*
—Johannes Muller

Many dreams reflect a sense of the past. History and its place in our lives offers perspective. We are the result of our choices. The following is a dream submitted to me by one of my readers. A woman wrote to me confused and upset about a recent dream.

*"Okay, so a couple of nights ago, in a dream I had, I saw myself walking through what seemed to be an arts and crafts store, looking for finger paints. They were every-where, but I was specifically looking for the small ones. All I could find were the big, fat ones, and for some*

*reason, I couldn't give up looking for them! It was so confusing. I don't understand the significance of the finger paints. Help!"*

I replied: "I really enjoyed reading this dream because it reflects the colors and innocence of youth. Many of us, here in America, used colorful finger paints as children. To many, they represent freedom and creativity. The fact that you wanted the small paints reveals your search for your childhood. Do you feel that you have lost your innocence? Are you seeking out greater creativity in your waking life? Yours is a dream of rebirth. Once you go and buy some new paints or other creative tools, you will find a new sense of hope and spirit for future choices in life and love."

She wrote back: *"Amazing. Simply amazing! You hit it right on the money. I lost my virginity shortly following my father's death. I have been dating older men for years. My innocence is gone. Thank you."*

Because of this woman's dream and her better understanding of it, she now has the tools she needs to create change in her world. She can work toward renewal, or she can forget about the dream and move on. Either way, the act of taking note of her nightly voyage has already given her a wider and better view of her past. She now sees her innocence lost and her desire for advancement. As you can see, dreaming offers us choice. In taking a moment to understand the metaphors and signals of sleep, we move toward greater opportunity and stronger potential.

The art of interpretation is one worth the pursuit. Anyone can interpret a dream. In fact, the best interpreter of the dream is often the dreamer. My years of dream work have aided me in times of hardship as well as happiness. They have taught me that the mysteries of sleep are much like the mysteries of waking life. As you work toward better interpretation of your dreams, hold this thought: *Once you realize that your emotions, instincts, and hopes are all part of your twenty-four-hour clock, you cease to look at dreaming as something otherworldly.* You then begin to see that there is no distinction between the dreams you dream in your office and the dreams you dream in slumber. Think about it. How many times has your mind drifted off into a world where you are a famous rock star or a well-traveled entrepreneur? I have always found the term "day-dreaming" amusing because, in my mind, to dream is to create, to design your unique path, in waking or in sleep.

Dreaming, no matter when we do it, is the method as well as the *result.* The French mathematician and philosopher, René Descartes often questioned dreaming logic in his philosophical propositions. On the night of November 10, 1619, Descartes had a series of significant and powerful dreams relating to his quest for the truth in his thinking process and his life's goals. These dreams are documented in his writings and personal journals. He interpreted these dreams as a divine sign, an answer to his call of occupational pursuit. The journey of sleep spawned his later work with mathematical methods and analytical geometry. His dreams helped him unify the pursuit of science and humanity.

Through using the tools of sensation and emotion, the flow of dream interpretation begins to form. These components, along with symbolism and mythology, act as guides. Though the symbols and images of sleep hold the key, the personal odyssey is what creates the construction. The dreamer is the dream. Therefore, the interpretation is also part and parcel of the dreamer's life. When you look around you, do you find yourself experiencing emotions during the interludes of daily life? For example, I often find myself on a mental journey when I catch a glimpse of my image in a mirror or a store window. This is a good analogy for the discovery of sleep. Dreams are a net by which you can catch your spirit. When you write about your dreams, you take the time to *know* your dreams. Through action and interpretation, you are then taking the time to know yourself.

## EMOTIONAL RESCUE

*"Learn from your dreams what you lack."*—W.H. Auden

Understanding your dreams links you to your life. In many tribal cultures, there is a belief that the human soul leaves the physical body during sleep, in order to connect with a higher plane of thought. The Kahunas of Polynesia, the Inuit tribes, and the Zulu societies all believe in the soulful transmissions and transcendental vehicles of sleep.

These shamanistic myths resonate in their relation to personal perspective and experience. Dreams connect to human emotions in many ways. Dreams can heal, dreams can conquer, and dreams can open our eyes. The goal is discovery. When you dream do you feel sad or angry? Are you joyous in your dreams? These questions and their answers unlock the mysteries of tomorrow. Continue to keep in mind that as you journal your dreams, the story unfolds. Having a frightening dream one night does not necessarily portend a scary encounter the next day.

Earlier, I mentioned some of my dreams of anger. I have also experienced many dreams of joy, fear, and sadness. All emotions play an integral role in the dreaming process. Begin your dream odyssey by knowing how you feel about each dream. Nothing is more profound than the feelings you have when you awaken. Always journey into the eye of awareness. How did it feel? What did you sense? Where is this dream leading you? Dreams are emotions and responses. Look at the heart of the dream, for it is *your* heart.

Universal themes resonate in the minds of most dreamers. Many people dream of flying and climbing, of falling, or being chased. Others dream of their teeth falling out or public nudity.

In fact, throughout my work with dream interpretation, I have received hundreds of dreams on the subject of teeth falling out. Another common theme is that of trying to speak with no voice.

*"I have had this recurrent dream for years. It starts with my finding that I have a loose front tooth and then all my teeth start falling out. Though I try not to move the teeth in my mouth, I know they will fall out. What's your analysis?"*

*"In my dream, I am trying to scream, but nothing comes out. I talk in my sleep and have screamed before. What does this mean?"*

Both of these dreams show vulnerability and stress in the dreamer's waking life. I have experienced each of these dreams and when I wake up, I just shake them off like a bad cold. I understand that some dreams are a sign that I have been working too hard or that I am feeling the pressures of a given burden.

Look at your dreams as you would a good novel. Some parts can be riveting and others, part of the narration. One chapter may be a link to another part of the larger story that the author has created for the reader. With dreams, however, *you* are the author. You create the book and tell the tale. In knowing this, you begin to engage the ability to distinguish between dreams of stress and dreams of valuable emotional importance. Below is an excellent example of a dreamer who has found happiness and enlightenment in his dream.

*"I was standing in my yard in the evening. In front of me was the biggest tree I had ever seen. It had thick and twisted roots everywhere like a bunch of ropes intertwined. It stretched upwards to the sky and I could hardly see the stars because the leaves of the tree almost blocked the sky. It was probably big enough to*

*be visible from space! I started to climb it, but never finished. Judging by how I felt throughout, it was probably one of the happiest dreams I have ever had. "*

I love this dream because it is a beautiful illustration of success and attainment. Though symbolic, it is mainly an adventure of sentient enlightenment. Joy is abundant. Trees are the image of life force. In Christian tradition, paradise is centered by the Tree of Life, the perfect representation of harmony and spiritual growth. The dreamer climbs this monster tree toward the sky and the result is a feeling of tremendous happiness. This dream shows us the potential for joy and bliss in dreams. Depending on how the dreamer chooses to use this joyous nocturnal event, he can begin to set new goals for himself. The dream gives him a gift of achievement. His dream is patting him on the back and saying, "Continue to live with zest!" Much like the happiness of waking, the happiness of sleep acts as the connective tissue between suggestion and action. When I feel joy in my life, it urges me toward greater desire for purpose and change. This dream illustrates that powerful dream emotions open the door to the walkway of life's goals.

The emotional legacy of dreaming is varied. Many dreams reveal elements of searching. Through interpreting the sensations and subtle meanings in your dreams, you will discover new ways to overcome obstacles. Our nightly wanderings can take us to places we cannot face in our waking hours. This holds particularly true with relationships and affairs of the heart. Love is a force of grand and mythical scale. Dreams are no exception when it comes to the bridges and horizons of human relationships.

*"The other night I dreamed I was swimming in a pool. My girlfriend, who has moved away, was on the other side. I swam towards her, but the pool kept getting wider and wider. The more I swam, the wider it got. I*

*called her name, but she kept walking away from me. I
woke up yearning for her presence. I felt lost. What does
this mean?"*

The fact that the dreamer's girlfriend moved away tells the
story. He feels unsure of the relationship's direction. As he
swims, he searches. The widening gulf of water reveals feelings
of fear and loss. Perhaps he feels that his girlfriend is leaving
him behind. Crossing the lake is a metaphor for his struggle to
"hang on" in the relationship. The distance he is crossing is in
reality, his reaction to the void of love lost or denied.

As you work more with your dreaming experiences, remember that your emotions play a pivotal role. Symbols and metaphors, much like the colors on a canvas, create greater definition
in your dream paintings. They are the highlights, the innuen-
does and the arrangements of your dream song. The feelings
you experience, the perceptions you encounter are the brushes
that paint the strokes of your dreams. Value your intuitive incli-
nations as the foundation of your story. When you combine your
emotional sensations with your daily experiences, you begin to
master the art of dream interpretation.

## THE DREAM CONNECTION: AN EXERCISE

Write down a dream (hopefully in your new dream journal)
that you have recently experienced. Your dream map will have
three columns. In this exercise, you will interpret your dream,
looking at who or what the dream is about, why it occurred and
how it relates to your life. In the example below from some of
the dreams you have been reading, you will see how you can
begin to dissect and understand your dreams.

| WHO/WHAT | WHY | HOW |
|----------|-----|-----|
| My girlfriend | We are separated | I need to find closure |
| My mother | I miss her guidance | I need to communicate |
| My job | Too much stress | I need a passion or career |

While these examples may not be exactly the same as your dream, they are nonetheless useful in any dreaming story. Even the most basic dream is usually constructed of these three elements. Understanding the components of your dreams and how they motivate you will take you into a new way of looking at your future. How can I make choices that will enrich my life? How can I stop procrastinating on self-improvement? Dreams are your fuel for a more purposeful tomorrow. Use them as you walk forward on the highway of life.

## METAPHORICALLY SPEAKING

*"Then let us fly upon the wings of sleep."*—August Strindberg

Metaphors and symbols are avenues for the expression of our souls. When I think of metaphors and symbols, the film *The Wizard of Oz* invariably comes to mind. I have always loved this movie because it gives the gift of dreams and hope combined in a symbolic tapestry of innocence and magic. In fact, the entire film is that of Dorothy's dream. She journeys to find the answers to deeper questions regarding life and happiness, only to discover the truth in her own backyard. The road of dreams is paved with this type of magic. Understanding the symbols in your dreams begins with unveiling the façade. No matter how unusual or distant a symbol may seem, your task, much like Dorothy's, is to pull the curtain and find the reality.

Consider this: Symbols are nothing more than words and pictures. The hieroglyphics of the mind are another form of communication. I once dreamed of a huge white rhino. The dream was very simple. I was standing in a field when this large creature crossed my path, slowly moving on to other pastures. I spent days searching through my dream dictionaries and buying new books on dreams, only to come up empty-handed. I found no book to explain why I encountered this large and beautiful beast in my sleep. I was very frustrated because I wanted an answer as to why I had experienced this dream. My emotions told me that this was an important dream. Yet, I could not find the symbolic reasoning. Finally, I asked a friend of mine who is from Zimbabwe about the white rhino. He commented on their possible extinction and then he mentioned how graceful they are. Finally, he said, "They are unique, you know—special."

Bingo! I had finally found the resolution to the symbolism. The dream revealed a search for uniqueness and the quest for imagination in my life. At the time, I was working in a retail job, and though I was not unhappy, I was certainly seeking a greater purpose in my soul. My dream unveiled a need for a creative journey and the identification of my own special qualities.

I tell you this to illustrate how important it is to do your own homework. No book gave me that answer. I found it by doing my own dream detection and following my intuition. I pursued the path of my emotions in search of the deeper meaning in my dream. Through the act of mapping my individual dream journey, I began to change my life's circumstances.

Metaphors bring a cascade of acquired thought and representation. A bird flies from a hand; the ocean has a voice. Not all surreal metaphors convey happiness and bliss. Some images can be painful or convoluted in form. Dreams communicate with us in a variety of phantasmagoric messages. As dream detectives, we journey to decipher the images and apply their science to our lives. As you work with the symbols and metaphors in your dreams, remember to look at the connection between the images and your life. Ask yourself where the dream is leading you. Does the dream ask a question of you?

> *"My husband and I are separated. We are filing for divorce. He left me. I dreamed that my ten-year-old daughter came back from visiting her father. She handed me this bouquet of flowers with a carnation and a rose, each having their own water flask tied to the front of the bouquet. The water in the flasks was boiling and the feeling I got was that my future ex-husband's professed undying love is lethal."*

This is a powerful and richly metaphoric dream of love lost and anger spawned. The rose is a symbol of love and passion. Roses reveal the essence and beauty of romance. Yet, in this dream the roses reflect the illusion of love and the ties to her ex-husband through the daughter's innocence. The daughter, the giver of the bouquet, is not aware of the pain in adult passion and the complexities of the relationship. The boiling water represents anger and undercurrents of toxic love.

Since the dreamer awoke feeling that her husband's love was lethal, her emotions are surely the most significant part of this nightly voyage. Here is another excellent clue to how dreams connect us to our life's choices. If the dreamer regards the dream as a sign to let go of hostility, she begins a journey toward further healing. Divorce can be brutal. Since the roses carry the boiling water, they will surely die. This dream questions the future. It is the dreamer's task to examine choice. She can carry her anger or she can release it and embrace forgiveness.

> *"I am chasing a woman to whom I am very attracted. We are both walking on different pendulum-type objects. There are thousands of them, all swinging back and forth. I try to step from one swinging pendulum onto*

*another, hoping to get closer to her. Each effort fails, and the distance increases as each pendulum I jump onto swings me even further away from her. The lighting is poor, she is very far away, and I can only make out her silhouette. I never reach her. What does this mean?"*

This dream reveals feelings of frustration and desire. The dreamer pursues the woman of his dreams. The harder he tries to grasp her, the wider the gulf becomes. The pendulums are very interesting because they are metaphoric in subject. They symbolize the concept of time. Time is running out as he chases after her. When you look at this dream from the perspective of time and action, the question of solution comes into play. Here is where the art of interpretation and dreaming action become paramount. If he decides to ask her on a date, how will his world change? Even if he faces rejection, he will be confronting his fears and questions.

Only the dreamer can answer these larger questions for him- or herself. Your task as a dream detective is to perpetually consider what each dream image means to *you*. Through reflection, your dreams will bring you to a place of awareness. Your dreams will connect you to your magnetic mind. As you work with the predictive myths of your nightly path, remember that your feelings and personal associations are of value. By integrating the dynamics of your dream metaphors and associations, you will gain new perspective. Perspective is the doorway to the unfolding story of your life.

## ASSOCIATION

*"The dream is the truth."*—Zora Neale Hurston

One of the most valuable truths in dreaming is that you never know what you will find around the next corner. Try as we may to understand the peaks and valleys of nocturnal flight, it seems that as humans, we inevitably end up scratching our heads. The mind's associations can be mystifying or elusive. Frequently our association to things or people relates to familiarity or memory. For example, I keep a photograph of my mother and myself on my desk. In the photo, I am six years old. My mother and I had spent the day picking sunflowers in a nearby field. The photo is warm, green, and honest in its image of my mom and me. I keep it on my desk because I associate it with sunshine and happiness. When my days are long and I am tired, I look at my photo and it invariably lifts my spirits.

Defining the unique and often arbitrary meanings of dream associations proves itself a difficult task. Our sleep connections lead us to new horizons of introspection and grandeur, but not without careful dream examination. What counts is how each dreamer arranges his or her connection to the features of the dream story.

I often dream of the ocean. To me, water is healing. Symbolically, water is viewed as a life-giving force. However, water in dreams means something entirely different to an individual who has fear of it. This illustrates the paradox of dream association. Dream association is often about problem solving. As you walk further on the path of dreaming, you will begin to see that some associations mean nothing, while others act as a connect-the-dots for your dream quest. Dreaming is action and relationship. Much like a great artist or filmmaker, your role as the dreamer is to combine all of the sensory elements of your dream—audio, visual, emotional, and spiritual. Ask yourself how you view the dream. How does the dream relate to your waking life? Each dream scene leads you to the next vista. In the stolen moments of your dreams are the answers to your waking questions. Your dreams are your vehicle. They drive you to fill needs, solve problems, and overcome struggles. Deciphering the elusive association between you and your dream is a right of passage.

A page from my own museum of dreams illustrates this point. I dreamed of a man I know loosely through my health club. I see him infrequently. His name is John. Our conversations usually focus on work and his pursuit of an acting career.

### Suz's Dream

*"Last night I dreamed that I was standing in the entrance to my health club speaking with John. We stood face to face and looked at one another. I smiled and he said, 'Would you like to go out with me? I want to take you to church and to California.' I was surprised as I have never had any romantic feelings for him and a church is the last place I would think to go on a 'date.' Nonetheless, I told him I would. He asked me to wait in the lobby of the club. I sat for a long time and grew impatient. When I went to look for him, I found him with a small, blonde, very young looking woman in a nurse's uniform. I felt awkward. The girl left. He then, took my hand and said, 'I can't wait until we get to California.'"*

I interpreted this dream to mean that John would like to know me better on a business level. I also sensed that he might view me in a "pure" way as he asks me to attend church with him. I associate church with purity. I spent a few years working on the West Coast, and I equate California with work and the entertainment industry. These relationships led me to my dream conclusions. In my dream, California represents John's acting career. In my dream journal, I note these ideas and possibilities, and then, I move on. In dream interpretation, it is always important to follow the flow of your associations and connections. Don't dwell on one topic. Write about each dream, jot down a few ideas on what you think it might mean, and then allow yourself to integrate the dream into your daily life. Journey into the heart of the larger picture.

The link between your world and your dreams is what creates your individual dream history. As you chronicle your dreams, you will begin to see patterns emerge. While some dreams hold greater truths for your future, others are leading you to realization or perhaps introspection. What counts is each dream and what its contents mean to *you*. Think of your dreams as works in a museum. The walls of the museum are your dream journal, your collective memories. You are the curator. You choose which dreams hold a prominent position on the walls of your museum. Your dream museum is the ever-unfolding story of your world.

## SEX AND IDENTITY

*"Learning to understand our dreams is learning to understand our heart's language."*—Ann Faraday

Most of us find sexual or romantic dreams indelible. We awake to curiosity about the dream and its connection to the lover or the feeling. Sex is about expression. As I mentioned earlier, many people dream of sexual feelings for people they do not know or know in a formal way. Often the subject and plot of these dreams point back to desire and individual persona. To dream of connection with others forces us to face ourselves. In addition, the act of sex is one of intimacy. Vulnerability often plays a role because the act of love and passion requires us to take risks and remove façades.

When we dream about a person in our waking life, we find ourselves asking if they hold a part of our future. This holds particularly true in dreams of a romantic or sexual nature. Most of us have dreamed about someone we know in a sexual way. Dreaming takes us to places we dare not go. Many people find themselves in bed with a co-worker or passionately kissing a neighbor. This does not necessarily portend a budding affair or office romance. Understanding the meaning in each dream is much like deciphering a book of personal codes. Each dreamer must learn to track his or her individual passage. If we seek out the deeper meanings in our nightly journeys, we become experienced travelers. To dream is to travel on a journey of greater wisdom.

Sexuality holds a special place in dreaming study because of the works of Sigmund Freud. Freud believed that many of our dreams relate to unconscious or subconscious desires on a primal or sexual level. While this holds true for some dreams, other dreams reflect our individual views of gender and identity. The dream below is a perfect illustration of this merger.

### Janet's Dream

*"I have had the same dream since I was very young. The dream takes place in a cloud of deep purple smoke. During the dream, I am watching a couple who is sitting in a yoga-like position with their legs intertwined. The couple is naked but not engaged in any sort of sex act. As I watch the couple, I am overwhelmed by the emotion in their eyes. As I watch them, their facial features and body shapes start to change but their expression is steadfast. They start "morphing" into different people of all different sizes, shapes, and colors. Sometimes, the man is a woman and the woman is a man. I watch the couple change from an older woman and younger man to a gay couple, a very old couple, an interracial couple, and an Asian couple. The same expression, however, lingers in the eyes and smiles of all the changing faces. Toward the end of the dream, I see a Native American couple with the same eyes holding the same expression. Tears start running down the cheeks of the very young woman and her belly swells rapidly as if she were pregnant. She opens her mouth to scream and grabs the man's arm. The man disappears. The woman is lying down and she is no longer pregnant. She is staring into the dark where her lover has disappeared, sobbing violently and uncontrollably. Her eyes open wide in surprise and then I realize she is me! Please help me figure out this haunting dream."*

Dreams of metamorphosis often indicate the dreamer's desire for a direct connection between different aspects of life. Many people dream of the transformation from man to woman or loser to winner, for example. These themes connect us to our past and to our future. They represent the desire for change. Janet's dream is fascinating because it encompasses every aspect of primordial human odyssey—race, sex, birth, and emotion. This dream is the ultimate illustration of change. It is an excellent example of our perceptions of sexuality, identity, and humanity.

### Lori's Dream

*"In my dream I am shopping for lingerie. I cannot make up my mind about what I should purchase. All of the items seem too erotic for me to buy. When I finally decide what to choose, I wake up! What does this mean?"*

Lori is connecting to her sense of image and femininity. The metaphor of lingerie and shopping tells the tale of her search for greater connection to persona. Her sexuality is in play. The dream explores its place in her waking world.

### Mike's Dream

*"In my dream I kissed my best friend's wife. We sat on a park bench in front of a beautiful garden. We passionately kissed. I cannot remember anything else because my mind went numb. I am not attracted to this woman at all! What does it mean?"*

Mike's dream provides the perfect illustration of dreaming magic. We often dream of those we know in a sexual way, even if we have no conscious interest in them. It is *possible* that Mike has hidden desires for his best friend's wife. Alternatively, and more likely, his dream could relate to his best friend. Perhaps the sexual interlude reveals his desire for a closer relationship with his friend. I wrote back to Mike and asked him if he had been out of touch with his friend. I also asked him if he had recently felt out of touch with his place in his world. Is his identity in question at work or in his personal relationships?

He replied: *"I have not spoken to my friend in over a month. We had a fight over money. I also have changed jobs. Thank you. I plan on giving my friend a call."*

Mike has allowed his dream to serve him well. His attraction in the dream to his best friend's wife proved to be nothing more than a myriad of identity concerns. Now he can make choices to better his life and his relationships. Dreams like Mike's are common. While some dreams lead us to new avenues of personal exploration, others lead to love affairs. Your dream compass is the mechanism of guidance. If you encounter an erotic dream about someone and you feel attracted to him or her, you may be moving toward a relationship with that person. The answers are all within you. Your dreams are your story.

Remember that creating your dream museum and chronicling your dreams take time. Over years of dream journaling, I have learned to distinguish between dreams that portend a budding romance and dreams that tell me I should look at issues in my day-to-day life. Dreams, much like sexuality, are personal, intimate, and sensory. Your dreams will carry you through the interjections of life and love if you follow their messages. More importantly, they offer you a path to the wisdom of your personal motivation and desire. Your dream desires can reveal your deepest yearnings. Much like any instinctual pursuit, process counts. Manifest destiny is not the act in the dream, but the act you take after the dream.

## DEATH, SPIRITUALITY, AND AFTERLIFE

*"Was it a vision, or a waking dream?"*—John Keats

Dreams have soul. Dreams provide faith. As you work with your dreams, understand that the mirages of sleep contain a link between you and your spirit. What you see, hear, feel, and sense in dreams connects you to your greater life path. I have often found that dream messages are just as important as their vision. The essential question is how our dreams can aid us in our spiritual odyssey. How can we improve the structure of our lives according to the *soul* of dreaming journeys?

Though many people dreamed of the sinking of the Titanic before the event, very few dreams actually forecast the arrival of death. Dreams of prophecy do occur, and we will examine this phenomenon in the next chapter. For now, your goal is to journey into the heart of the divine. Every dream is a journey of the spirit. Dreams relating to death, spirituality, and afterlife often contain many universal symbols and images. Crosses and other religious symbols may be present in spiritual dreams. Friends and loved ones who have passed on appear as if they live once more. Many of these dreams relate to the process of healing. Bereavement and death are an eternal question for humankind, as no one truly knows what lies beyond the doorway of life.

### Carole's Dream

*"I dreamed that I found out that I was dying and I wanted to be put to sleep! The only people that were in the dream were my parents. Then at the last minute I changed my mind and decided to live!"*

Carole's dream is one of rebirth and renewal. Her experiences on the wings of nightly grace take her to the land of personal opportunity. The dreamer is given insight into the very nature of her existence. Death, for her, is a *choice*. Carole has since found a new relationship and bought her first home. Her dream has taken her to a new place of prosperity.

**Tia's Dream**

*"I was sitting with my parents in a mesa-like home and there was a huge mound in front of us with caves. There were cats running around the mound having fun. My cat just died in real life. Then, we noticed two owls in separate little caves and one of them took off and flew toward a tree. His belly was very white. Then, the phone rang and I woke up."*

This dream is fascinating because in Navaho and Lakota tradition, the owl symbolizes death or the departure to "another world." The dreamer has no knowledge of this fact. Tia's dream takes us into the dimension of the dreamer's connection to universal thought and soul. How and why did the owl fly into her nocturnal world? This dream, much like my dream of the white rhino, reveals the magic of archetypal messages.

Since the dreamer mentions that her cat has died and that the owl flies toward the sky, this dream represents the ascension of her cat's soul. The owl also represents knowledge. Athena, the goddess of wisdom, had an owl on her shoulder, enabling her to speak the universal truth. Tia has gained perspective on death through the experience of her dream. The symbol of the owl has aided her in seeing a higher truth in the passing of her cat. She can now begin to rebuild. The dream connects her to her views of life and afterlife.

Dreaming is the oil in the salad of life. Without it, there would be nothing but vinegar. Our souls are like unmolded pieces of clay. With each day and each step of life, we form our concepts and ideas through human expression and experience. Sometimes, the simple act of dreaming supplies spirit and hope for tomorrow. Many of us wonder about the journey and evolution of our own soul. This is where problem solving in our dreams begins to take on a greater dimension. How can your dreams help you to understand the quandaries of your life? How do your dreams carry you into new dimensions of better decision-making and process? Below is an excellent example of one dreamer's odyssey with faith and her changing views on spirituality.

> *"My dream started out with a woman taking me up in the air. She brought me to a tree. The tree was so tall that you could see everything below. Suddenly, she let me go and I just kept falling. As I was getting closer to the ground, I started to fall at a slower speed. There, I could see an open pit that looked like a grave plot. Around this was a bunch of women in white, just waiting for me. I came to the ground and I thought I saw my mother but I was not sure. No one would talk to me and all I could do was cry and ask to go back home. In an instant, the women in white began to go away. I just cried and said 'I want to go home. I am not ready to die!'"*

I love this dream because it exemplifies the saga of spirit. This dream symbolizes a higher purpose for humanity and the universe. The dreamer rises to the top of the earth, led by a woman. Next, she falls endlessly and experiences the sensation of fear as she approaches the ground and the grave. White is the color of purity and reincarnation. There are many images of birth and death represented in this dream. The dreamer's mother appears, as the angelic woman fades. This dream is indicative of curiosity about the meaning of death. The dream reflects wonder over death's relationship to the spiritual world.

While some dreams are a direct wireless to our souls in theme and in content, others are the bridges between heaven and earth. In times of catastrophe or tragic loss, dreams can bring tremendous healing and transformation. Internal wounds often remain in the heart and mind of the individual. Internal scars are much like external scars. Dreaming gives the following dreamer a chance at forgiveness.

*"My mom committed suicide one month before my fifteenth birthday. I have the following recurring dream. I am at an airport, taking my older sister to her flight. I see her off on her vacation. The airport has its boarding and exits outside. I am standing at a big window waving goodbye to my sister when I look over and see my mom getting off a plane. She looks great, healthy, and smiling as if nothing has happened. That is when I wake up! I am now thirty years old and on occasion, I still have this dream. What do you think it means? I usually wake up with a sense of excitement as if maybe she will be back someday."*

This is a very important dream because it represents the soul's evolution. This dream delves into the deepest aspects of the concepts of suicide and the afterlife. In most religions and spiritual systems, suicide reflects a lost soul. In some Christian traditions, it indicates eternal damnation. This concept brings great suffering for the families and friends of suicide victims, as all souls should ultimately rest in peace. In the dream, Stephanie's mom is arriving from an unknown place. She is smiling and waving at her and her sister. Her soul appears to have found salvation! In a sense, this reflects that the dreamer has found a place for her loss. Depending on the dreamer's choices, she can now gain some form of closure and forgiveness. If her belief system allows, she can nurture her world and heal this wound through spiritual insight and love. She has a chance for disassociation from the terrible stigma of suicide.

As you journey into your dreams, focus on your individual beliefs. What does your belief system tell you about your dreams? How do dreams of spirit relate to your world? Do you feel your dreams are guiding you on a specific path for the future? Dreaming itself can enrich your soul and bring new transcendence in faith. When you review your dreams and work with them, understand that each dream carries a specific place in the timeline of your life. Don't feel pressure to experience complete epiphany in your dreams. The dreaming journey, much like the life journey, requires time and patience.

By now you have probably begun writing about your dreams and are filling your journal with ideas. As you write about your dreams, move toward creating a universe unique and true to *you*. Dreaming is *personal*. Receive your dreams. Ask your dreams to answer you! The nightly voice is often introspective and profound. Trust the dreaming kaleidoscope. Sit back and watch the pieces of your nightly world fall in to place. Work on integrating your dreams into your life. Know that each day reveals a new opportunity to combine the perspective of sleep and the action of waking. Your future lies in the mutual agreement of these two grand forces. Remember that dreams are here to guide you, aid you, and reveal your journey.

## DREAM MAPPING: AN EXERCISE

In order to begin to connect your dreaming patterns to your dreaming purpose, you will need to challenge yourself and your interpretive skills. Now that you have all of the tools you need for dream analysis, you can begin to learn from and benefit from your dreams. Choose a dream from your dream journal, perhaps one that you wrote a week or more ago. Reading an older dream often yields new insight because you have had time to gain perspective and distance from it. Choose a dream that you find striking—not only visually, but also emotionally. Read through your dream. Complete these phrases:

◆

1. In my dream, I missed the chance to

_____

2. The image or symbol that struck me most deeply was

_____

3. To me, this image or symbol represents

_____

4. In the dream, I felt

_____

5. I associate this feeling with

_____

6. The dream asked me why

_____

7. The dream is telling a story about

_____

8. The dream also relates to

_____

9. I think the dream is telling me to

_____

10. I can begin to change my life by using the dream as

_____

It is important to recognize all of the dynamics of sleep and how they can then slingshot back to your daily life. Not all dreams carry an active message, but they usually carry some form of direct meaning. Allow your interpretive skills to take over and see where your dreams are leading you. Take stock of how you can build on your present-day view of life in order to use the wisdom of dreams for a new and more promising tomorrow.

**5**

# Sleeping Sight

*"I have dreamed in my life, dreams that have stayed with me ever after and changed my ideas. They have gone through me like wine through water and altered the color of my mind."*—Emily Brontë

**P**redictive dreams are part of the nocturnal imprint. I have experienced many dreams that have landscaped future events. Over time, I have learned the importance of valuing the relevance and significance of each dream and its relation to my own life. Sleeping sight, much like the vision of waking, is often inspired. Dreams are creative and emotional. Dreams can guide, dreams can forecast, and dreams can heal. In time, you will find that you can mold your waking life to accompany the perspectives of sleep. Think of yourself as the accidental tourist. You are wandering in a land, unfamiliar and foreign. Nonetheless, you prevail by using your dreams as your spiritual source of exploration.

Dreams of prophecy and vision exist within each one of us.

Earlier, I mentioned Abraham Lincoln's portentous dream. His dream is an excellent example of a prophetic dream because it outlines in accurate detail events yet to occur. Though Lincoln had no way of knowing it, he was looking through the mirror of his world, into the incremental details of his future. Lincoln was surely a creative and soulful individual. Because of his efforts to explore the crevices of his mind and his spirit, he charted a new course for dreaming and meaning.

As you begin to decipher the patterns and unique qualities of your dreams, know that precognition is not illusive. In search of the bigger picture, you will learn to discern the difference between the various aspects of predictive dreams. Some dreams may be leading you to an event in vague and enigmatic design. Other dreams will be clear and visualistic in their construct. Understanding the nature of precognition requires effort and exploration. Take your time in chronicling your dreams. Don't expect to be dreaming your future every night! Use your dreams as a resource. Interpret them as an attempt to read an unknown text. Remember that the future is an unrolled carpet, a lost desert highway. Dreaming is forward motion. It is your job to steer your world in the direction you desire.

As a dream worker, follow the path of predictive dreaming by knowing that you are part of the process. You are the visionary. Dreams are the matrix for mind and soul. Understand that dream forecasting is an integral part of your psychic and intuitive self. "Night vision" is candid and real. Since dreams provide important information about your inner life, it is your task to determine the purpose and place for your insights. Ask yourself questions about each dream. Does a particular dream relate to a larger story? Do you sense that events in your dream will transpire? Examine the various distinctive sensations in each nightly voyage. Understand that dreams, much like a series of puzzle pieces, group together to form a larger image of life, spirit, and tomorrow.

## DREAM FORECASTING

*"We are the music-makers, and we are the dreamers of dreams . . ."*—Arthur William Edgar O'Shaughnessy

When I began to harvest the garden of dreaming, I often found myself questioning the value of each dream and wondering where it fit into the greater view of my life's path. I read many books in order to find my way in the futuristic hallway of night vision. I found myself wondering how much our dreams relate to the ever-present aspect of free will. Personal choice is always paramount in human spirit and life plan. Since this is true, what is the difference between dreams of prophecy and dreams that merely offer us a glimpse of what *could be?*

By now, you have started a dream journal and are intuitively following a charted course. As you get your sea legs, you will discover the vast and complex dynamics of sleeping sight. The basic concepts of dreams and their relationship to your future will begin to take shape as you build on your dream experiences. Remember that dreaming is part of your thought process and part of your life.

Learn to *integrate* and *celebrate* your dreams. Dreams are the link between you and your cognitive soul. The mechanisms of sleep offer you a place to hang your hat and to make instinctive choices for your life's plan. Dreams are the clouds in your sky and the fish in your ocean. Spend some time getting to know your dreams. When you find a comfortable perspective on your dreams, you begin creating the vision of your life. Remember that you are the beginning, middle, and end of the infinite story. As the dream below illustrates, you are the linear prophecy of your dreams.

### Cyndi's Dream

*"In my dream, I was with my best friend's boyfriend. We were on our way to a park where we live. We met up and*

*sat underneath the night sky to see the fireworks. It was so beautiful! Three weeks later, my dream came true. Everything was just as I had dreamed it. Recently, I have been dreaming other things that led me closer to him. My dreams clue me in on how he and I can get closer to each other. I even dreamed that he wanted to take me on a trip of some kind. If one dream came true, could these others come true as well?"*

Precognitive dreaming is still very much a mystery as no definitive scientific research has been found on what makes us "see" the future. However, it is obvious that Cyndi's dream brought her insight about impending events between her and the man of her desire. Her dream occurred exactly as she had seen it in her nocturnal flight. Does this mean that all of her dreams will come true?

As you explore your dreams, seek out the liaison between sleeping karma and waking action. Cyndi's dream illustrates the importance of perspective and path. Dreaming, like life, has its struggles. Though Cyndi has experienced the déjà vu of dreaming, she still has a role in the greater plan. Her dreams may be leading her to this man, but her actions are what count. Does one dreaming manifestation lead to another? Ultimately, the choice is hers. The wireless is leading her to her best friend's boyfriend. However, her cognitive mind and her value system will create the impetus for her future decisions.

If you sense that your dream is showing you a glimpse into the future, take note of the sensations you experience. Express your thoughts, emotions, and ideas in your dream journal. *Respond* to your dreams. Make them part of your daily life. It is important to remember that many seemingly insignificant dreams may hold valuable pieces of information. Precognitive dreams are profound. They rest in a strong visual and emotional cradle. Dreams that portend future events may reveal their purpose weeks, months, or even years later. Think of your dreams as you would pieces of an archeological dig. You are creating a dream infrastructure from your findings. Many people write about their dreams and feel that they hold no special significance, only to open up a dream journal years later and discover the profound wisdom of the past.

Sometimes we cannot see the reason or meaning behind the dream experience. Try as we may, our minds cannot always connect to the result of each dream. Here is a page from my dream journal, which illustrates the complex wonder of futuristic dreaming. I wrote this when I was eighteen. I had a crush on a boy who had just graduated and moved away. I did not know him well.

### Suz's Dream

*"I dreamed that I was with Brian. We met on a huge snow-covered hill. He looked so lovely. We began talking. He told me that he was going to be a writer. I told him that I was going to be one, too. He was surprised. We talked about it and he told me that he had written a 'one-way novel called Vienna.' I wondered what a 'one-way novel' was. Then we started sledding and we rolled in the snow together. I woke up."*

The value of my dream, much like an antique, appreciated over a span of time. One obvious aspect of the dream, which I now live, is my career as a writer. However, an interesting event transpired four years after I had this dream when I was a college student. I spent one summer in Europe with a Eurail pass and I wound up in Vienna. One day, as I was walking down a small street in the beautiful city, I spotted Brian. I could not believe my eyes. We talked and went out for drinks. I helped him find a place to stay. Even more interesting is the fact that I did not discover the prophetic nature of this dream until many years later when I began to work more extensively with my dreams. My waking mind of young adulthood could never have conceived that I would visit Vienna, nor that Brian would be a part of my journey. However, my dream revealed through indirect detail, that we would cross paths in future days.

Fragments from the dream crucible bring information. Each dream has its own unique and potentially useful qualities. Time and reflection will bring you the dream purpose and meaning. Some dreams bring direct perception of future events by nature of their stories and their metaphors. Dreams can predict the future or merely be reflective of possibility. As you work more extensively with the secrets of sleep, know that your work is never complete. There is always another door to open on the timeline of dreams.

### Claudia's Dream

*"Here's a very strange experience I had twenty years ago, when I was fifteen years old. I dreamed that my cat Ollie walked up to me and said 'goodbye.' The next morning, after I woke up, my mom came into my bedroom and broke the news to me that Ollie had been hit by a car and killed during the night! How can that be logically explained? Coincidence?"*

Claudia's dream had an emotional impact on her life. The synchronicity of the dreaming metaphor and her cat's death left her pondering the aspect of coincidence. Many of us wonder whether our dreams are picking up clues from our reality or vice versa. Though no one knows the answer, time tells the larger story. Since Claudia dreamed of her cat saying "goodbye" before the event of death, she has split a small atom of the pre-cognitive dreaming design. This dream illustrates that while we may dream of an event in form, the actions often deviate from the dream story. This fact makes your work as a dream detective more significant and vital. You may wonder how to differentiate between dreams of emotion and dreams of precognition. Do you follow the *sensation* of sleep or the literal line of dream *action*?

Many great thinkers have pondered human ability to control and diagnose sleeping sight. The renaissance painter Leonardo Da Vinci often questioned vision, creativity, and prophecy. He asked, "Why does the eye see a thing more clearly in dreams than the mind while awake?" This is an excellent question. For example, if Claudia had the ability to "see" her cat saying goodbye in waking life, she could then create a new set of dynamics in anticipation of loss. However, her dreams brought her the information that her cat was passing on. Her dreams opened the door for a new avenue of thought. The signals on her dreaming highway have brought her inner senses to life.

You may be questioning your ability to dream the future. Remember that you do not have to be a prophet to experience prophetic dreaming. People from every walk of life have experienced the phenomenon of night vision. Precognitive dreams usually involve friends and family, or people with whom we share a close emotional connection. However, some precognitive dreams involve global events, strangers, or public figures. The diversity of precognition cannot be underestimated.

**Carl's Dream**

*"In June of 1995, I dreamed of a large and vibrant mural. It was a painting in three panels. In the three panels, I could see a movie or an event taking place. I had the distinct impression that there were three parts to the story and that it was my job to understand these three pieces of the mural. When I looked more closely at the painting, I could see war torn streets and people looking for food. There was a strange map on the first panel that read 'Kornica.' I remember thinking how beautiful this place must have been at one time. A small boy ran across the first panel into the second panel. I heard the noise of bombs and I woke up. I was very sad because I remember wanting to know about the other two parts of the story."*

Later, Carl learned that his dream illustrated in distinct detail, the events that had yet to unfold in Kosovo. The dream occurred during an important year in the Serbian conflict. The city of Korenica was one of the places where mass destruction had taken place. Carl had never been anywhere outside of his native country of Great Britain. Yet, his dreaming mind took flight and found information about the impending war in Serbia. To this day, he wonders what the other two parts of the mural represent.

If dreaming the future were as simple to understand as the alphabet, we would all surely be using our dreams as a greater tool. As you explore your dreams and begin to look at how they relate to your life, endeavor to understand the ebb and flow of your nightly journey. You will find that while some periods yield vivid and significant dreams, other timeframes will bring none. Dreams, like the singular beauty of a snowflake are unique and complex. You may, at first encounter difficulty in seeing the difference between dreams of future events and dreams that reflect emotion, association, or identity. Use your intuition. Allow your instinctual process to guide you as you write about and live your dreams.

As you can see from some of the dreaming insights in this chapter, the act of discovery is yours for the taking. Not only do you possess the ability to make your dreams come true, but you also hold the secret to your dreaming dialogue within the pages of your dream journal. Simply put, your dreams are your life. Like Da Vinci's and Disney's, your life is the visionary projection of your dreaming story. The dreams you dream today are the wisdom and definition of tomorrow.

## DREAMS THAT GUIDE

*"The dream reveals the reality which conception lags behind."*—Franz Kafka

One of the things I love most about dreaming is the sensation we all share when the topic comes up in conversation. Faces light up when people talk of their dreams. Everyone has a dream he or she wonders about. I follow my dreams and in doing so, I endeavor to focus on the message. In my years of working with and paying attention to dream messages, I have grown to view my dreams as a comfort, a guide. Dreams are the arms of soul that embrace me each night to fill my world for the morning.

You've probably heard someone say, "I had a dream last night that I won the lotto! I hope it comes true!" We all want our wishes to materialize. Often, we dismiss our nightly journeys as flights of fancy. Yet, dreaming, much like waking offers opportunity. As you walk on the path of dreams, remember that your dreams are mental execution of undone work. Your task is to *question* your dreams. Maybe you won't win the lotto, but if you demand more from the dreaming experience, you will gain more in return. On the broadband of dream waves, learn to understand the connection between dream thought and dream potential. While precognitive dreams can forecast future events, other dreams act as beacons on the ocean. These dreams shepherd us in our ideas, our visions, and our decisions.

You may be wondering how to distinguish between dreams of certainty and dreams that point in a given direction. How do you make your choices? Should you follow the feeling of the dream or the overall picture? Should you do what your dream is telling you to do? Below is an excellent example of a guiding dream and the dreamer's subsequent actions.

### Sarah's Dream

*"I had to write a proposal at work to land a new account. I was very nervous and unsure of myself. I had never written a formal proposal for a deal of this magnitude. In my dream, the woman to whom I had to give the proposal came to me and said 'If you want to win, focus on marketing. Marketing is the key.' I woke up with a very positive feeling but I was still unsure. I had never*

*studied marketing. I went out, bought a book on the subject, and wrote my proposal based on marketing techniques. Two months later, the proposal was approved and I was promoted."*

The dreamer awoke and realized the potential value found in her dream. Had she not acted on the intuitive impulse to further explore the dream message, she probably would not have accomplished her goal in business. This dream illustrates that while dreams offer us choice, we are the active ingredient in the chemistry of vision. When Sarah chose to take notice of this dream, no matter how elusive the possibility seemed, she embraced change. She created a new set of dynamics for career advancement because she paid attention to the messages of sleep.

*"I was in love with a man to whom I felt a very passionate connection. His name was Noah. He was ten years younger than I was and though I felt that our relationship would not work out, I pursued it in spite of myself. Looking back, I wonder why I put myself through such a relationship. He broke my heart in more ways than I can count. I had this dream after we spent our first night together. In the dream, Noah was in my living room and he walked over and sat down on my coffee table. As he did, I saw that he was about to sit on my glasses. I yelled out, 'My glasses!' but it was too late. When he stood up, there lay my glasses, completely flattened. I picked them up, and as I did this, I noticed that they looked different. They had been transformed into these new glasses with heart shaped lenses. The glass was shattered, but the heart-shaped frames amazed me. I remember standing there, holding them and the looking at them in disbelief. Noah and I just stood there smiling in awe of these glasses. I woke up."*

Dreams of future events often take on different shapes and

forms. In this dream, the dreamer seems to know that the man she loves will break her heart. He shatters her sight, her illusions of love. Yet, she chooses to love anyway. This dream touches on the element of heart and direction. It illustrates that we cannot always walk in the direction that our dreams point us. In affairs of the heart, this holds particularly true. To love is to live a dream, no matter what the outcome. This dreamer is wiser for the journey although her love was ill-fated.

I have experienced many dreams that expressed a future heart of disappointment. Did these dreams keep me from loving? No. Yet, as I wrote of each dream, I learned more about *how* I love and how to improve my life as I went forward in my subsequent relationships. Dreams are like personal therapy. They heal and explain some of our deepest emotions.

Does every aspect of each dream have a value for the future? No one will ever know the answer with any certainty. Often dream fragments hold pieces of a bigger picture. Your dreams may carry significant meanings relating to your life. Dreams are private and, yet, still entirely cognitive. They can be rational and even illuminating. Dreams connect us to each other. Dreams lead, accompany, and even advise. I often have people approach me and tell me about their dreams. A few weeks ago, a man who was repairing my sink told me of a recent sleeping event that changed his life and his relationships.

### Jose's Dream

*"I dreamed that I was blind. Everything was black and I could not see. I felt lost and unsure of myself. I knew I was blind and though I was not panicked, I knew I had to do something to find my way out of the blackness. I felt two hands cover my eyes and then I heard a voice. It was my brother. He said, 'If you want to see, you have to open your eyes. I can help you see.' He took his hands off my eyes and I could see again! I felt amazing. I woke up feeling that I had to make changes in my life."*

When I asked Jose what changes he felt he needed to make, he told me that for a long time, he had been in an empty relationship. He had lost a great deal of money in speculative business ventures. His brother had been trying to help him, but he felt he had let him down. From his dream, he expressed a new sense of hope and promise for future choices. I enjoyed listening to him talk of his sleeping vision because the image of sight plays a key role in the imagery of his story. He has been blinded by his choices. The closed eyes of sleep have opened his eyes for a new perspective on waking movement.

As you read this book, you have probably found some dreams that seem much like your own. You may have encountered similar nocturnal journeys that you feel are leading you to new perspective. As you begin to question and interact with your dreams, work toward embracing the theme, message, and emotion of each voyage. Many dreams ask us to examine their messages. What counts is how we *react*. The dream source springs from your deepest emotive being. As you journey on the dreaming ocean, always remember to receive your dreams. *Respond* to your dreams. Create your future. Design and build your world.

## DREAM TASK: FIND YOUR INTUITIVE LINK

Many people are blocked by their dreaming emotions and unable to identify their intuitive sensations. You awake from a frightening dream or a romantic dream and you think, "Will this happen? I felt so strongly." In your growth as a dream worker, you will start to have the ability to discern the difference between dreams that contain fear, hope, and expectation, versus dreams that offer insight, vision, and prospective truth. In the following exercise, you will be asked to pinpoint the fragments of your dreams and ask yourself how they relate to your future. You may need to read through several dreams from your journal in order to complete this exercise. *Take your time.* Free associate with your dreams. It is vital for you to begin to see your dream journey as a movement of experiences, which are leading you to a summation of instinctual ideas and choices.

1. My dreams have materialized in the form of

_____

2. My emotions say _____ but my

sense is that I am being directed toward _____

3. The strongest impression I have felt was

_____

4. I am applying what I have learned in my dreams to change

_____

5. Intuitively, I know that my dreams are about

_____

After you complete this task, begin to use a new mental model for your dreaming mind. It's not enough to have vision; you also need to know how to use it. Light a candle before sleep and reaffirm your own belief system, spiritually, mentally, and emotionally. Ask your waking mind to bring your sleeping brain wisdom to guide you through your life. *Trust yourself.* Remember that dreaming and the insights of our nocturnal journeys are a lifelong pursuit. Once you begin to make concrete steps toward opening yourself to your intuitive gold mine, you will then be able to pursue a manifest destiny of your own choosing.

## Dreams Of Healing

*"Dreams are rough copies of the waking soul."*
—Pedro Calderon de la Barca

In times of crisis and stress, our dreams shed light on greater struggles. They offer us hope in the darkness and they bring us a world of renewal. One of the best things about healing dreams is that they gift us with a message as well as with the sensation of repair. Dreams tell us that "everything will be OK." Dreams provide us with a warm hug or an emotional injection of faith.

Mary Allen, author of *The Rooms of Heaven,* found healing in her dreams following the suicide of her fiancé. Her book chronicles her journey through devastation and repair from tragic loss. As she puts it, "I think of my dreams as messages that come to me from some larger spiritual presence who knows everything about me and wants me to learn and grow and heal."

Certainly there is a greater plan of nourishment and renewal in the very act of sleep. How dreams connect to the spirit is within the ideology and spiritual eye of the dreamer. In many cultures, dreams are regarded as the sleeping prophecy of our waking existence. For example, the Quechua tribes of the Peruvian Andes believe that dreams are the human window to world creation and soul. Aboriginal cultures foster the idea that dreams provide for and guide the human spirit. These anthropological legacies are a part of the greater universal theme of forgiveness, compassion, and healing.

### Patty's Dream

*"My friend died in a car accident on New Year's Eve. The other night I had a dream that we were dancing, and he told me that if I got a dime and put it in a locket I would remember him forever."*

This dream is a lovely sentiment for a friend departed. On a spiritual level, the friend is healing the dreamer through the avenue of sleep. He instructs Patty to keep his memory alive. The numbers one and ten also play an interesting role in this dream. One is the number of wholeness and completion. Ten is also a derivative of one. Lockets reveal the beautiful sentiments of reflection and keepsake. Patty's dream embraces her. She gains tenfold in this wonderful dream of healing and remembrance.

During times of loss, you may find yourself questioning your dreams and wondering if they hold a window into greater strength and resolve. We all look to the skies and question our purpose. Dreams act as the invisible bridge between the known and the unknown. Your dreams measure and detect your spiritual universe. Can you move beyond your pain and fear? Are you ready to face new horizons of happiness and peace? Often religious or spiritual messages appear in order to reconnect us to our personal sense of faith and divine light.

### Barbara's Dream

*"I had a beautiful dream in the beginning of my breakup with my husband. I awoke feeling like God had sent me a message of healing. I was standing by the edge of the ocean and I looked down to see if there were any sharks. There was a slow moving ballet of beautiful fish. They were positively entrancing! All of a sudden, I felt movement beneath me. My first impulse was fear. What if I should fall? Then, I realized that I was standing on a giant slow-moving fish and I felt completely safe and willing to trust wherever the fish was going. I hang on to that dream when I am fraught with pain about the loss of the relationship."*

As Barbara's dream illustrates, dreams often act as keepsakes for a place in time. Dreaming is the act of renewal or the rebirth of self. Your dreams are the transitional hallway into your future. Barbara's dream served her well. In times of doubt, she reflects on this nocturnal moment and knows in her soul that her choices were the best ones for her during a difficult time in her personal life. Her dream turned loss into gain with its message of trust. Dreams of healing anchor us to hope and, in their motion, bring us a new vision of waking.

I believe that we are blessed by our dreams. Most of us have gone through periods of change and loss, only to find that rescue is found in our inner strength and our sense of faith. Some dreams reflect the healing of self and the rebirth of life. I have rediscovered my soul's mission in the amazing light of my dreams. One dream which comes to mind when I write about healing happened during a very difficult period of my life. I was going through a medical nightmare. I had undergone several frightening cancer biopsies over a period of two years. Though the results were always negative, I continued to find myself in the doctor's office for more tests. The emotional legacy of constant fear was staggering. I finally found myself facing a final surgery with a specialist. I felt terrified and alone. The dream that I had the night before my last surgery tells a mythological story of my own healing future.

**Suz's Dream**

*"I dreamed that I was running away from something across a large green field. I came to the bottom of a hill and found a small creek. Facing the creek on the other side was another hill. When I tried to jump the creek, I failed. I was confused and afraid. Then, I looked across and saw a wolf standing on the opposite hill. I looked into his eyes and at first, I was afraid. Then, I felt my fears subside and he said, "If you need help, all you have to do is ask." I was stunned. Suddenly a small wooden door appeared in the face of the hill. The wolf walked inside the door and closed it. I quickly jumped the creek and knocked on the door three times. 'Will you help me?' I asked. The wolf opened the door and came*

*out with a baby wolf at his side. He took my hand and he
led me to the top of the hill. We sat in a circle around a
small campfire and the wolf said, 'This is my son. His
name is Achi.' I woke up."*

The next morning I had my surgery. I not only came out of
anesthesia quickly, but I also finally found out why I had been
having so many health issues. The doctor that performed the
procedure properly diagnosed my health issue and since I have
regained strength and wellness. A week after my surgery, I
called my cousin in New Mexico to tell her about my dream.
She is a member of the Lakota tribe and I knew she would ap-
preciate the wolf imagery. The wolf is sacred to the Native
American people as he represents guidance and the force of
healing. When I told her the dream, she said, "Achi means *little
moon* in Lakota." I was surprised and mystified by my own
dreaming brain. Though I have visited New Mexico, I have no
knowledge of this Native American language. At that moment,
I understood how deeply this dream was prophesying my well-
being and my healing future. I was able to face the years of
living in fear and begin to rebuild my life from the ashes of
disrepair.

What I cherish dearly about the wonder of dreams is that
each of us holds the ability to discover the bounty of power
within the simple act of turning out the lights and snuggling
into bed. Personal issues and the worries of each day fade away
in the comfort of rest and repair. As you glance through your
dream journal and read your dreams, you will find ways to
mend your life and create change through your sleeping visions.
You don't necessarily need to pay a therapist or get a deep tissue massage to regenerate your power or heal your soul. Often,
all you need to do is go to sleep and open your soul to life's
possibilities. In your dreams, you will find that you can *rescue
yourself.*

# 6

# Dream Archaeology

*"As I live, my dreams become the substances of my life."* – S.T. Coleridge

**D**reams, like the flow of rivers, are vast and ever changing. The course of their presence is determined by the direction of our minds, our spirits, and our choices. Depending on which side of the river we choose to stand, we alter our destiny. Free will and choice are part of the plan. If we choose to navigate, we move with the tide of our dreaming spirits, we become the explorers of our unique and undiscovered dreaming country.

Dream archaeology is a way of looking at our night visions with an eye toward finding wisdom and greater understanding. We are digging for lost clues to the past as well as the future. Sometimes in searching through our dreams, we find prophecy and insight. At other times we find feeling and metaphor. A good analogy for this process is the concept of an electronic card catalogue. When you are looking for information, you might search at the library or on the Internet. You seek out answers focused on themes and topics. The same can be said for dream archaeology, or the study of your dreaming narration.

Dreaming reveals aspects of personal history; lingering in nuance, clues for future potential reside. A dream about your mother might relate to your current job situation. A dream from ten years ago may be telling you how you need to change your life today. I always like to remind myself that dreams are my own way of elevating my thinking process, freeing my mind from daily cares. In the sublime land of dreams, time remains in stasis and I am able to see and feel things that rest beyond the reach of my waking mind. For example, in the following dream a woman searches for an emotional connection to her former spouse.

**Lucy's Dream**

*"I dreamed that I was with my ex-husband in Paris. He handed me an empty picture frame and we walked across a black-and-white marble floor together. A voice over a loudspeaker called the Orient Express. I remember thinking we would then go to Turkey. As we held hands I felt something new for him. The odd part is that we always wanted to go to France but never had the chance."*

This dream is interesting from an archaeological standpoint because the writer ended up reconciling with her husband three years after the dream occurred. They did go to France, where they purchased several antique frames. Six years after the trip to Paris, she went into business and opened an art store. Her specialty became framing and reproduction of antique framing styles. The dreamer has yet to visit Turkey or to understand the significance of the marble floor. If she hadn't taken note of that dream, none of the following things may have occurred. More importantly, the dream opened a door to her spirit and emotional environment, materializing in form and content over a long span of time.

As you delve deeper into your own dreaming stories and works, it is essential to regard your dreams as a part of your own timeline. Always keep your own frame of reference in perspective. *When* did I feel this way? *Why* did I do that? When you uncover possible target areas of value, it then becomes important to ask the deeper questions. How have my dreaming symbols played a role in the person I am today? Where does my identity fit into my dreams? How does the motion of each dream connect to subsequent dreams?

While it is true that we all want simple and quick answers, it is important to continually keep in mind that writing down our dreams is ultimately our best tool in the analysis of our nightly dialogue with life. Now that you have begun the journey of chronicling and studying your dreams, it is time to examine them for their wisdom, to survey the dig for clues to your future. Begin by tracking your earliest dream memories. You can try looking at the conceptual ideas of your past by examining dreams about childhood or dreams that carry a message from the vault of your individual history. You might also examine how your early dreams have evolved into the dreams you are currently experiencing. Your intuitive choices will define your outlook and take on a greater role in your life.

## DREAM DIG: AN ARCHAEOLOGICAL MISSION

Choose a dream from your dream journal that has perplexed you either symbolically or emotionally. Try to focus on a dream that has intuitive strength or one that you sense has a greater undiscovered purpose. After reading through your dream a few times, use the following chart to excavate the artifacts of your nocturnal patterns.

In your dream journal, divide a page into two columns. At the top of each column write "Then" and "Now." Within each column, answer the following questions:

Where are you directing your energy, past and future?
What are your dominant feelings?
What were the major events?
Who are the key players in your story?
How are your intuitive senses being used?
Why do you feel this way?

Initially, you might find it difficult to relate the acts of a dream to the acts in your waking reality. Don't be alarmed. Simply let your mind free associate and follow the images of your dream along with the images of your active mind. Eventually you will come up with some concerted answers and you will connect the dots between then and now. These answers will aid you in your journey of dreaming awareness. You are now ready to face your dialogue with time and the flow of creative spirit that connects your past to your present.

## DREAMTIME

*"In dreams we catch glimpses of a life larger than our own."*—Helen Keller

The connection between time and the act of dreaming is as old as humanity. In Australia, where *Dreamtime* is more than a concept of passing our nightly hours, the power and movement of the dream join forces. The Aborigines believe that Dreamtime represents a place beyond the physical dimension where the energy of ancestral spirits and divine creation become one. Dreamtime is *soul time.* This god/man connection to life eclipses our waking concept of time and asks us to be enlightened by the metaphor of the dream. In our dreams, we can go beyond selfhood and connect to a state of timelessness, rehearsing for tomorrow's promise.

When you begin to look at dreaming from this standpoint, you cease to separate the act of dreaming from the spiritual plane. Dreams become *transcendental* in nature and *transforming* in effect. Dreamtime can connect a material or natural element such as a window or a tree to the metamorphic spirit of an individual. In essence, "the dreaming" as it is called, is a state of enlightenment, a continual push toward spiritual realization and intuitive vision.

How can a dream shape you? How can a dream from long ago define how you feel today? How can it create a better "you" for tomorrow? Once you embrace, work with, and understand your dreaming archaeology, you begin to grasp the eternal value of the dreaming machine. In the practice of defining and orienting yourself to your dreams, you will find higher awareness and, sometimes, richer perspectives on your past. A good example can be found in the following dream where myth and love connect to form a message of identity and change.

### Sarah's Dream

*"I have had this dream from the time I was a small child. I am about the size of an ant and wandering around in the grass in my back yard. I'm just looking around when suddenly I walk around this really big blade of grass and there sits a gigantic wedding cake. Just as soon as I see it, I am normal sized again and I am alone in my back yard. Suddenly, a booming voice comes out of nowhere and says, "You have ten minutes to pick up all the sticks in the backyard or your parents will be executed." With all my strength and speed, I start to pick up the sticks and just as I am going to pick up the last stick, I glance at the time clock and see that I have about a minute left. I think I am safe. As my fingers are about to touch the last stick, the buzzer goes off and the announcer says, "Time is up. Your parents are now executed . . . executed . . . executed." I usually wake up and feel*

*terrified, alone, and afraid to go back to sleep. I started*
*having this dream when I was about seven and I still*
*have it to this day. I am now twenty-four though in my*
*dream I am always still seven. What do you think?"*

The changes that occurred in Sarah's life when she was seven
years old define and shape the person she is today. The dream
accesses her intuitive and mythological doorway to the truth.
Time has frozen in her dream and she remains a seven-year-old
child. Her dream explores the realms of unity and division. The
wedding cake is a symbol of nourishment. Her size changes
much like Alice in Wonderland and she feels dwarfed by the
subject of marriage in some way. When she returns to normal
size, a voice tells her that she has to pick up sticks, or her parents will cease to live. She believes that time is ticking away.

In essence, Sarah's dream is about picking up the pieces of
her parent's marriage. Time plays a key role in her dreaming
story. Her dream reveals her inner fears and doubts about the
subject of commitment and the mythology of marriage. If she
can take hold of her past and examine her inner feelings on the
topic of love and the passage of time, a greater understanding
of her own identity will then emerge.

Time also plays a role in the dreaming scene when we look at
how it affects our ideas of tomorrow. Dreamtime can be a window into our deepest fears or our grandest hopes. Often dreams
offer us a new way of handling events that are traumatic or difficult to face. The definitions of how we perceive a given situation and how our dreams resolve the dilemma can take us into a
new scope of looking at the world.

### Max's Dream

*"For the past three weeks I have been experiencing the*
*same dream. I'm having a liver transplant and have*
*been on the list for two years now. The hospital just*
*called me. All my dreams are about my having the*

*transplant done, but I don't remember coming out of the
hospital or waking up in the hospital after the transplant. I can't make heads or tails out of it. Am I going
home after the transplant, or am I going six feet under?"*

For three weeks, Max experienced this troubling dream scene
only to feel frustrated by his lack of ability to foresee the outcome of his surgery. He wants to know if he will live through
the surgery and his dreaming mind won't allow him to let go of
this frightening thought. His intuitive track is being blocked by
his fears. Since he has spent many years waiting for a second
chance, the dream takes him to the gateway of his future but
leaves him short of the resolution.

I wrote back to Max and suggested he think of his dream in
terms of his fears. Does a lack of vision in the dream make him
feel he will die? Does he have to "see" his body come out of
surgery in order to know he can live? Isn't living in fear a death
in itself? When he replied, this is what he said, *"Thank you so
much. I had the surgery two weeks ago. I am so relieved and
you were right. My dream was telling me that I needed to let go
of the past and embrace the life I had, whatever happened. Since
that time, all I dream about is running through my backyard in
the green grass. I feel free again."*

Many dreams ask us to make choices in our lives years before we see the material results of their directive force. The
value in this type of dream can be found days, weeks, months,
and even years after. It's important to recognize that time inter-
acts with our ability to be proactive in life. We will discuss this
in the next section on dream incubation, or the maturation of
your dreams. Keep in mind that while you may sense that a
dream has a meaning that is relevant today, the essence of your
own spirit influences how your life evolves and grows. Following this understanding of the human timeline, we can then understand the importance of writing about our dreams and noting

how we feel about them. In the process of reviewing old dreams, we are then able to conduct a higher level of learning about and understanding our personal path.

### Rabbi Rabinowitz's Dream

*"I have always kept a journal. I recently was reading through my old journals and I found this dream. The amazing part is that today, thirty years after the dream, I realize its meaning. I believe the dream was calling me to my destiny. In the dream, I am walking. I see a cavelike room with a light shining down from a round hole in the ceiling. I stop and look into the cave from a circular opening—large enough to step into if I bend my head. The cave is dark except for this light that shines on a large cedar tree trunk. I do not see the top or any branches. I see the dark, moist, textured bark and note its beauty. I see the tree roots, many, exposed, intertwined, piled on top of each other, long and short, some are knurled but all go down into the soil. Next to the tree is a small temple and a door. I am at the entrance and I have to make a decision whether to enter the cave or walk on. I feel in awe but overwhelmed and walk on. The dream ends, I awake knowing that I will return to the cave and explore it; the decision has already been made regardless of what I did in my dream."*

In the Rabbi's dream, he is literally being called to temple. The symbolism is wonderful with his view into a cave and his wide-eyed desire to explore and learn more. The cedar tree is an ancient mythological representation of life and understanding. In this dream, the young man peers into the light of his soul in order to discover a spiritual truth. While he had no way of knowing this as a child, the Rabbi found that his dream brought him comfort and wisdom later on. In reading through his old dreams, he saw that some choices were put in place in the moment of his dream's inception. In a sense he gave birth to his life path that night. Much like early paintings from a master artist, he can now take stock of how far he has come and take comfort in his early visions.

Through our dreams, we often find new ways of looking at the world. Yet, the question usually lingers. If my dream is to come to pass, when will it do so? How long before my dreams come true? As mortals, we have no way of knowing any concrete answers to these questions. Yet, dreams are the lifeblood of creative choice, soulful action, and thinking movement. Dreams incubate and form over time. The results of their visions depend on whether we grow as humans, how we live our lives, and if we choose to follow the infinite illumination of the dream itself.

## DREAM INCUBATION

*"Sleep seems to hammer out the logical conclusions of my vague days."*—D.H. Lawrence

The passage of time acts as an hourglass or a meter for our daily goals and hopes in life. As we drive in our cars or sit at our desks, we often find our minds pondering how long it will take to accomplish a given task. What time will it be when I get home? When will my bills arrive? How long before I meet my soul mate? Dreams allow time to suspend itself in order for a deeper process of reasoning and incentive to take place. When a dream acts as a signal, much like a stop light at an intersection, it gives us a window to grasp a given truth. These dreams function as a turning point in our nocturnal reality, opening doors to the infinite unknown.

In order for a symbolic event in a dream to be realized, the idea must at some point take hold in your waking mind. If the dream is to occur, then the intuitive process needs to share a link to the purpose of your dream. Dream incubation provides that link. Dream incubation is the period of time between the dream itself and the material manifestation of the night vision. While many dreams never come to pass, others may happen in form but not in content. Some dreams will yield a bit of information that is of value and others none at all. Much like a fall harvest, there are some good crops and some bad.

Why are memories of people, objects, and events in some dreams so vivid and striking? Often, dreams can repeat themselves in theme and in message. They act like an alarm clock, going off every twenty-four hours or so to remind us that it is time to face our inner life. When we finally see their meaning, we are then able to move on with our lives. Some dreams can reveal a given sensation of destiny, and yet, we are unsure of how to handle the force of their message when our lives overlap with their presence.

## Richard's Dream

*"I keep having the same dream over and over again. It's been going on for at least the last seven to ten years. I am thirty-three. I'm always walking through a high school. It's not my own. This dream always starts between classes. I'm walking to my next class, and I am talking to my friends. Behind me, I can sense a woman, and I look behind and see who it is, and the only thing that I can remember about her is the fact that she has long, black, straight hair. I can never recall her face. I know that she is my girlfriend, my soul mate if you will, but I cannot remember anything about her, except for her hair. Amazingly enough I do remember sometimes that she smiles at me and it is a warm smile. Recently I began dating a woman and I fell in love with her. I realized she was the woman from my dream. How strange is that? I am thinking of asking her to marry me, but I feel weird basing my feelings on a dream. What do you think?*

Richard poses an excellent question. While his dream was surely leading him to the woman of his future, he is wise to question the root of his decision-making process and his instinctual choices. Dreams can transform us, guide us, and link us to tomorrow. However, the nature of our individual character is what makes our life plan. If Richard is wise, he will take his time and allow his instincts and his value system to work together in unison in order to make solid and positive decisions in his new romance.

One way to gain a greater foothold on the nature of dream incubation is to address the patterns of your sleeping ideas, after the dream occurs, or after you read through it in your dream journal.

1.   Track predictions and feelings along with the accuracy of your dreams.
2.   Follow repeated symbols.
3.   Chronicle personal associations.
4.   Ask yourself how probable your dream may be.
5.   Trust your instincts.

A good example of dream incubation and the role it plays in predetermination can be found in the next dream where time and vision collide to form choices that fail to meet expectations.

**Mandy's Dream**
*"A year ago, when I was still working at my old job, I had a dream. I was a cosmetics salesperson then. In the dream, I looked up and there was a big clock ticking away. You could hear the sound of it so loudly. As I looked out over the floor there were many people shopping. Out of nowhere, a lady approaches me and hands me a traffic report. It was a piece of paper with lots of lines and information and it said 'Traffic' at the top. I*

*asked her why she was giving me this and she replied,
'You will do this one day.' At the time, I did not understand the dream. But six months later, I interviewed for
a job at an advertising firm as a traffic manager. I
thought this dream was telling me my destiny. But now
I am in this job and I am more miserable than I have ever
been in my life. Why did I dream this?"*

Mandy cannot see the connection between her future and her past. Dreaming, much like life, is about the journey and not the result. While Mandy's dream led her to move up on her career ladder, she found that the job was not to her liking. Does this mean that the dream had no value? The answer is that the dream was leading her to make new choices. Her destiny, in work, in life, and in love, is in her hands. If she can find a way to value her current situation as a growth experience, she will make progress on her journey of self-empowerment.

Many dreams offer simple visions of places and people. They can lead us to find answers or to push ourselves to new discoveries. It doesn't matter how long it takes for the dream to represent itself in material form, but it does count that we take note of it. The incubation process is what allows us an opportunity to ruminate over our intuitive notions and to evolve into our future plans.

### Dominique's Dream

*"When I was a little girl and once a couple of years ago,
I had this dream. I am sailing in a small boat alone. I
come to an island that I know is Siam. I step onto land
and look around and I wonder why I am there and it's
really weird. The odd part is that I just got called on
assignment to Thailand. I am television reporter. I
wonder if I should try and take a boat ride. I can't wait
to go!"*

## Mark's Dream

*"I collect coins. In my dream I found a bunch of coins that I have been searching for at this coin shop I don't usually go to. I drove to Florida and also found some coins there. The dream stuck in my mind for about a month and then I finally decided I needed to go and see. I went there yesterday and they had three of the four coins I needed. The thing is that the owner told me he had just gotten them in that day. If I had gone to the coin store after my dream, he wouldn't have had them. How did I know to wait? When should I go to Florida?"*

Dominique finds that she is ready to embark on a new journey of soul-searching because her dream has told her that this trip to Asia may be a significant journey in her life. She is excited and hopeful because of her dream. Mark's dream also allows him a new hope for discovery in his pursuits as a coin collector. Why did he wait for a month to visit the store he had seen in his dream? Does he need to visit Florida or is it better that he wait and let life's natural evolution play itself out?

The answers are surely found in the intuitive spirit of each one of us. Mark's disbelief in the dream allowed him the perfect timing in order to visit his local coin shop and snatch up the coins he was searching for. If he runs off to Florida simply because the dream tells him to, he may not find what he is looking for. I have experienced many significant dreams that have never materialized. Some dreams mature and evolve in parts and over years. Remember my dream about Vienna? Aspects of that dream have come to pass and others are yet to be materialized. The blueprint and the design are there. In my own life, I follow my heart and my soul as I walk through choices and decisions. Here is where the doorway to your own dreaming future grows strong.

As you work with your dream journal try to ask yourself which dreams may hold information that seems causational.

Which dreams brought you wonder and awe? Which dreams offer clues to your own mysteries? Do certain dreams represent forthcoming landscapes? Which parts contain fact as opposed to fiction? How do these dreams parallel your waking reality?

## DREAM DIAGNOSTIC: AN EXERCISE

Choose a dream from your dream journal or one that you have recently experienced. Focus your energies on working with a dream that contains a directional basis or a dream that has a defined story line. As you work with this dream, concentrate your efforts on determining the core source of the dream. Allow your intuitive brain to work in unison with the symbols as you complete the following phrases.

1. In my dream, I wanted to

_____

2. In my dream, I felt

_____

3. The strongest character in my dream was

_____

4. The greatest message in the dream was that I should

_____

5. My dream connects to my past because

_____

6. My dream relates to my future because

_____

7. The dream could possibly foretell

_____

8. My greatest desire right now is to

_____

9. Because of my dream, I plan on

---

10. I now see that I can

---

After you do this exercise, you will see that the smallest changes in your thinking can have a profound effect on your life. Like ripples in a pond, our dreams reverberate throughout many different aspects of our lives. Your journey continues as you work with, probe, and investigate the underlying movement and conduits in your vast dreaming sea. This insight into your own mythology continues with the understanding of the dream series.

## THE DREAM SERIES

*"Traveler repose and dream among my leaves."*
—William Blake

Frank Lloyd Wright once commented that "the idea is salvation by imagination." When one or more dream characters maintain a dominant role in a series of dreams, they become players in an ongoing story. Like acts in a play or pieces of a puzzle, they form together and create a cohesive structure in the arena of our dreaming minds. These dreams act as a series of purposeful directives, a human map to our own inner dream sequence.

The dream series offers salvation through imagination because it gives us the ability to view a series of messages over time; usually from a figure we trust or identify with. Your mother might be a frequent visitor or a long-lost object may repeatedly act as a metaphor to bring information. Some people dream of celebrities or famous historical figures as messengers from beyond. It's all about association—who we see as our leaders or deliverers and how we connect these symbolic personifications to a repeated dreaming motif.

## Adam's Dream Series

*"I was in a garden of sunflowers and smelled jasmine nearby. It was a dream of expectation and the sunflowers were magnificent. I found myself in a grouping of very tall trees. I decided to sit amongst them and think for awhile. The sun came through with bursts of warming golden light. I heard the sound of waves in the distance. My mother, who is in many of my dreams, came to me and handed me a towel. I said, 'Mom, I don't need this.' Then I woke up."*

*"I dreamed I was in the same garden, beautiful and light, but this time it was raining. I sat beneath the trees and tried to shield myself from the rain. I kept thinking of my mom and the towel. Then, my mother came into the clearing and handed me a book. This time I took it. I woke up thinking that the dream is telling me that I have not outgrown her help. Then again, she's my mom, so maybe that's not right. I am trying to decide what college to attend, so maybe the book relates to that. What do you think?"*

While Adam's dreams are simple and direct, they clearly relate a dreaming allegory that deeply connects Adam to his mother. His mother acts as a guide, a teacher, and a messenger. His dream coupling is asking him to face issues with his identity and his future growth with college and other aspects of independence. Adam's dream series is a great example of how dreaming can lead us to new realizations when we are attuned to the metaphors of sleep. He is open to the fact that his mom plays a significant role in his dreaming world. This gives him a keen insight on new ways to take in the information from his dreams and embrace their greater purpose in his life.

As you work with dreams in a series, be in touch with your own dream mythology, as well as your associations and guides for each dream. Keep your eye on the key players and then work with the dreams much like you would pursue reading a crime novel or writing a personal memoir. Who plays a featured role? What is the message of the story? How do these anecdotes connect to your life? As you explore these archetypal themes, these mirrors of your mind, pay attention to the spiritual role of the dream series. Watch for changes in emotion and action with the knowledge that you are the hero of your own dreaming story.

## Melanie's Dream Series

*"A dream I had when I was very young stuck with me for the longest time. I dreamed that I met a man at a gas station, and he asked me to marry him. He had long hair and seemed very sweet. I had the dream when I was around the age of ten. When I was twenty-two, I met my future husband, who worked at an Amoco station, and at the time he had long hair. I didn't put the two together until after we were married."*

*"The dream about my daughter came when I was still dating my husband-to-be. I dreamed about being pregnant, and in the dream, I knew it was a girl, and so did my husband. I dreamed about being in the hospital, and it was too early, and I was worried. But the next thing I knew, I was holding my baby girl in my arms. I didn't remember any labor pains or anything. She had a head full of dark hair, and she was beautiful. I shared this dream with my husband. I rarely told my dreams to anyone. Well, I now have a three-month-old baby girl."*

*"I also had a dream while I was pregnant about my future which has not happened yet, but I feel will*

*happen one day. I dreamed that my husband and I were on our own land, riding horses. Our little girl was about six and riding a horse of her own, and my husband had our two-to-three-year old son on the saddle with him. I felt like this was a premonition of our future and that in a couple years we will have a little boy."*

Melanie, who currently works as a veterinary technician, says that she has "always felt that dreams mean something. Whether it's a weird little dream that has nothing to do with anything or a complex dream that seems to map out an actual event." In her dreams, her husband and mother both play significant roles in her dreaming stories and personal prophecies. She is able to focus on and relate to the metaphors of sleep with greater ease because her family is important to her. Melanie's dreams reveal that we can have many different dreaming groups with a variety of dreaming messengers. Her dreams have continuity and progression. They are a group of vignettes, taking her from one step in life to another, acting as both cause and effect.

In this symbolic anomaly, we begin to see how vital our dream messengers can be. Dreaming is life. We cannot base each decision on only one set of criteria. It is always vital to weigh and measure every aspect of a situation. If we remain open to different vistas and new ways of learning, we grow and gain wisdom as people. Just as life offers us new and eye opening experiences in each day, so do our dreams tell a tale of higher individual truth.

Dreams that are hallmarked by celebrities or characters from fiction are often found in the dream series. The mythological root of these featured players is easy to understand. People who have carried symbolic meaning in our lives, whether they are from books, movies, or the newspapers, can have a profound place in our dreaming consciousness. It doesn't matter if we know them personally or how they gained their place in our hearts. What counts is their core representation and value in our dreaming soul. The following dream series reveals this truth.

## Wynona's Dream Series
### 12/8/1980

*"I was at Bill's house earlier tonight because I had a fight with my Mother and I fell asleep on his couch. I dreamed that George Harrison died. My friend awakened me, and he asked me what I was dreaming about because I had been talking in my sleep. I told him that I had a really strange dream that George Harrison had died. Bill sat down on the couch next to me, looking white as a ghost, and said that he had just heard that John Lennon had been shot. I came home a few hours ago and made up with my Mom. I still don't understand why I would dream about George Harrison, when John Lennon was killed. I am very upset."*

### 12/5/1987

*"I was looking through a box of old photos at my grandparents' farm. I remember feeling like I needed the answers about their recent death. I looked under the bed and found an old shoebox. In it were a few pictures of John Lennon. He was smiling and he was playing golf in the desert and I remember thinking—' why would he do that? You can't hit balls in the desert.' I woke up wondering the meaning of this dream."*

### 10/16/1994

*"I had a dream last night that John Lennon came to me and told me that he had wasted his life writing songs and winning prizes. He told me not to make the same mistakes. He said, 'Focus on people. Pay attention to people.' It was so weird. I was aware in the dream that he was no longer living. But I felt his spirit was telling me something. Then I woke up."*

**10/22/2000**

*"Another dream with John Lennon. I was in an old hotel, or inn. It was very much like the ones I used to see when I lived in the UK: old wood, green lawn, lace curtains. There were a bunch of women sitting around talking about how great it was to be a Mom. I couldn't relate because I cannot have children. I walked to the second floor of the inn and I found a large banquet hall. All four Beatles were sitting around a table and talking. I felt like I was intruding so I just looked around. The windows were old and some had stained glass like a church. John came over to me and started to embrace me, to dance with me. It was a waltz and not at all sexual, but I felt completely healed from the experience. The feelings were the same ones you get sitting in the sunshine after the rain. I remember I woke with an incredible sense of happiness."*

Wynona, who works in publishing, carries a personal connection to John Lennon as a mythological figure, though she cannot specifically pinpoint why. To many people, he represented a peacemaker, a political activist, and an artist. To Wynona, he carries those meanings along with acting as an emblem for the truth in times of duress and confusion. As she goes through her life, this dream series character aids her in facing aspects of her own evolution—death, independence, and her inability to have children.

These dreams, which span a twenty-year period, illustrate the profound importance of identifying and working with players in a dreaming series. It doesn't matter if you are dreaming about Einstein, Mickey Mouse, or a character from Greek mythology. What counts is your approach to your own symbolism and your association with these figures. At first you may feel silly taking note of these dreams or working with dreams in a series. Don't pressure yourself to have all the answers. Dreaming is a lifelong process. Dreams mature as we mature. Dreams languish in indecision as we languish in choice. Only by identifying with and trusting in our nightly pursuits can we peer into the greater power of our ultimate potential. Dreams in a series act as a gentle reminder that our connection to others becomes our talisman to spiritual truth.

## Dreaming The Past

*"The dreamer and the dream are the same. Personified in a dream are those that move the world."*
                                                    *—Joseph Campbell*

In the land of dreams, anything is possible. I have come to know this truth through my years of working with, listening to, and writing about dreams. Many dreams parlay our deepest soul work into waking reality. They offer us a glimpse of the impossible and even the divine. Other dreams act as a seamless portal into the walkway of time. No matter how crazy or surreal they may seem, in dreams we can see, feel, hear, and even connect to a sense of spirit, a holy ghost if you will, of our own concrete perception.

Like elusive images from a squeaky, old movie projector, karma also has a role in the dreaming machine. We awake to ask, "Was I really there?" and "Was I dreaming or did that happen?" The experience of this perceptive dreaming *déjà vu* cannot be overlooked. The visions of sleep bring us new awareness of things we may have never seen or experienced before. The dream serves as a conduit to soul challenges for this lifetime and beyond.

### Jennifer's Dream

*"I had a dream about helping a man find a musical piece that he had composed in the 1800s. He explained that he had died before it was published and he showed me*

*the score on pieces of paper. The paper then played the music and it was beautiful. He kept saying it was a classical guitar piece composed in b flat. Once I heard the piece in my dream and acknowledged it was a work of genius, he and his whole family smiled and were at peace. I have no musical background, but I have asked if this composition is possible. The response from three classical guitarists says no, that it has never been done before. Why did I dream this?"*

Jennifer's dream exemplifies how the dreaming brain can illuminate in order to instruct. Her dream is one of profound creative genius, karma, and soul work. Her sleeping sight is allowing her to understand the complexities of music, something she has no knowledge of in her daily life. I love this dream because, in a sense, it relates to universal aspiration or the soul of humanity's dreams. We all can relate to the desires of completing a goal or creating a masterpiece. Jennifer acts as a bridge between this lifetime and the next. Why did she experience this dream? Is she aiding the spirit of a man who died before his dreams could be realized? Was it part of a karmic plan that she relay this musical information to someone today? Could it be that she is seeing a vision from a previous lifetime?

When I ponder the concept of reincarnation, I always like to remind myself that throughout most religious and spiritual teachings, the soul is valued as eternal. We will talk more about the soul purpose of dreaming in the last chapter, but for now, consider the idea that your soul has constancy and *concrete value*. Much like time, it is nonlinear, infinite. Taking this idea a step further, you can then embrace the possibility that your soul will transcend your own lifetime. Your deeds create results, good or bad, depending on your choices.

This spiritual perspective of cause and effect permeates religion and culture, taking us all into a divine order of humanity. Dreams parlay into this dynamic because they are sacred and sentient in nature. In a dream, our greatest visions can be sublime, our deepest fears frighteningly vivid. Our dreams give us the ability to reach the altar of faith and examine our growth on a spiritual plane. Much like prayer, dreaming allows us to reach beyond the boundaries of the known and to trust in the divine. As you continue to evolve with your dreams, know that they are the tapestries of your faith, the fabric of your life. They can bring information for the future or connect you to the past. The greater purpose will be determined by your survey of the dreaming scene and how you connect it to your waking odyssey.

### Michael's Dream

*"I think I am on some type of journey. It starts out with me looking ahead at a black woman with her hair cut very close to her head and she is wearing a brown or dark colored wrap that is torn and tattered and stops just above her knee. I am curious about who she is, and from behind me a woman tells me that she is someone who is upset with the world today. She looks like a slave from the Civil War. I ask why and she says that it's because the world has become too idealistic and materialistic. For some reason I want to follow her but I can't. It's like I want to go to the past, but I am stuck in the present. The other woman starts to show me around a huge plantation and explains how things should remain as they are. For some reason I think she is lying. Everything in the field is made with a white salt and the slaves toil away. Even the children play in it. I don't understand this."*

Michael, who is a history professor at an Ivy League university, spends a lot of time looking at the past and its relation to the present. As an African American, his dream explores the evil of slavery and racial division. He senses that he needs to reach into his own ethnographic timeline and help the oppressed woman in his dream. Yet, he cannot. The stark contrast between the white salt and the dark-skinned people represents the paradox in his mind. Salt is a symbolic element in the history of slavery throughout the world, being produced by the ancient Egyptians and the Indian people. Is Michael's dream revealing a past life or a glimpse into his own connection to slavery as a black man?

The answers to these questions can only be found in Michael's dream work. When I asked him if he knew his family history, he said that he had only been able to trace it back to his grandmother. He did not know if he had any lineage in the South, but was willing to pursue it. What struck me most about his dream was the soul determination of the vision, the hope of the moment. In his dream, Michael is connecting to a part of his heritage that has long been denied. If he can face the karmic past—be it his own, or that of others, he will create harmony and a better world for tomorrow.

## Celine's Dream

*"I keep having this dream of a man I know from work. I swear that I have seen him before. In the dream, it is the 1800s and I wear a huge satin dress. I can feel my waist being pulled in by the stays in my dress. Someone calls my name and it is "Madame Boulud." Roses and white doves surround us as we walk along the hallway of an old mansion, hand in hand. I cannot explain this feeling I have, but each time we speak, I know that he is my husband. The dream just repeats itself and I continue to awaken feeling wonderfully happy. This has been going on for several weeks. I told the man at work about part of the dream and he looked at me as if he had seen a ghost. His grandmother's name was Boulud. What do you make of this?"*

Celine is curious about the connection between her dream and a relatively unknown acquaintance from work. She cannot help but ponder the purpose of her life as it may relate to this man's past. The dream vividly parlays information revealing love, romance, and a soul connection that transcends time. White doves are symbolic of the peacemaking process. Celine admits that she felt a familiar connection to this man from work before the dream occurred. Did her outlook spawn the dream, or did the dream spring to life from a buried well of undone soul work?

When it comes to love and the bonds we share with others, our dreams can play a prominent role in parlaying a chain of events into material reality. If Celine feels drawn to this man, the dream may be asking her to explore her intuitive feelings along with her romantic ideals. The obvious conclusion that Celine may be sharing the same soul as this man's grandmother lends itself to the larger question of her future karmic choices. Should she let her dream guide her to a greater connection to the man from work? Is she meeting him in this lifetime to aid him in some way? Could the soul mission be about something entirely separate from the physical attraction? How do you go about defining the quantitative value of a dream based on an intangible element like the human soul and spirit?

### Elizabeth's Dream

*"My dream begins in an era long ago, such as the Renaissance era. I was lying down in a forest by a stream, and my best friend (I've known him since we were kids) was dressed in the Renaissance ensemble. Suddenly rose petals fell everywhere and he took me in his arms and I felt he knew I had loved him all those years and that he too had but had not wanted to disrupt our friendship. Suddenly, attackers (shadows, mostly) came and attacked us. We took out our swords, and it was a tough battle, but we defeated them. But one last swift sword stroke and I was down. As the shadows attacked each other, My love knelt beside me and made*

*a vow that our love would be bonded together eternally and that he would love me always. We would find each other, someway, somehow, and then the light came, a blinding light, and I thought I was in death. Then in flashes, like in the fire of a flickering candle, were different lives gone past, and he and I found each other and we loved, yet having no knowledge of that day so long ago. My dream ends with him taking my hand and saying, 'We will, in time.'" My dream ends. What do you think about this? I could feel every little breath of wind, blade of grass. Should I tell him? Is it real?"*

Proving the meaning of these profound dream couplings is a difficult task. In my experience, dreams are so inherently and internally connected to the dreamer that it is impossible to chart a course based on one model or set of rules—spiritual, psychoanalytical, or neuroscientific. Only the dreamer can understand the wisdom of the vision and how it relates to his or her life. Here lies the secret ingredient, the magic wand of the dreaming dialogue.

The power to create, design, and structure our future paths connects back to our own logic. When we trust in ourselves and let our internal sense of faith guide us, we cannot possibly fail. Action and reaction, karma and balance are inseparable from higher learning. The sentient and intuitive choices we make in our dreams create a new way of seeing things once we awaken. Simply put, it is our inner dialogue with life, our individual truth that functions as a tangible form of self-determination for future days to come.

## 7

# Beyond Discovery

*"Reach high, for stars lie hidden in your soul. Dream deep, for every dream precedes the goal."*
—Pamela Vaull Starr

T he realm of possibility exists within each of us. Creativity, determination, and emotional imagery all make up the language of our dreams. In science and politics, in business and fashion, in every bold human intention, the seed of the dream shines through. While we may not be able to peer through the veils of our own humble human doings, the truth is that we create and discover our own potential through our hunger for a more promising tomorrow.

I cherish my dreams and the years I have spent writing about them much like I do my own family tree. They are part of me. They are my heritage and destiny. They have shown me how to live, how to choose, and how to heal. My dreams have revealed themselves in my aspirations and achievements as well as my most profound tragedies and failures. What makes me complete in my trust of the dream is my knowledge that it will never fail me. I can count on my inner structure to lead me through any challenge. More importantly, I know that in dreams, I will always find resolution.

It's easy to think of dreams and their purpose as something outside of oneself. Many of us separate our lives from our dreams because we lack faith in our own abilities and inherent talents. Yet, time and again, great thinkers remind us of their infinite and tangible value. When Martin Luther King championed the Civil Rights movement in America, he built his greatest speech on the simple words, "I have a dream." This brilliant faith among the ruins of human travesty heralded the dawn of a new way of understanding truth. If you look at the dream in this way, you cannot separate the dream from the dreamer. The individual who designed the dream is indivisible from the wisdom of the idea.

Throughout this book, you have been given many examples, ideas, and new ways of looking at and working with your dreams. Hopefully, you have begun a journal and have been recording your insights and intuitive pursuits. Beyond the discovery of your dreaming landscape lies the world of your own purpose. If you find yourself unsure of how to move forward, ask yourself what you want from your life. What are your dreams? What would you like to achieve? How would you like to love? What would you like to learn?

As you answer these questions, realize that the intuitive heart offers us a grand opportunity for transformation. Whether it be the pursuit of a new romance, the act of giving, or the desire to discover new ideas, the seed of our own growth is born from our dreams. This birth of the soul's ultimate potential can only be found in taking the risk of finding enlightenment. At times it can be frightening, even paralyzing to glimpse the profound truth of your soul. Yet, here is where you will find the entryway to any path you choose. When you dare to dream, you dare to *find yourself.*

## DARE TO DREAM

*"Each of us has an inner dream that we can unfold if we have the courage to admit what it is."*—Julia Cameron

The courage to follow the message of the dream—be it a dream of sleep, or one of waking—is something that must be found in order to turn inspiration to reality. Once you begin to know and relate to your sleeping myths and rhythms, where do you go to find a practical role for your dreams in reality? How can you measure and use your dreams as a tool for better living?

Antoine de Saint-Exupery, the author of the famous story, *The Little Prince,* found himself stranded in 1937 by forced landing in the Sahara desert. Saint-Exupery was a formidable aviator who wrote extensively about the subject of flying. A thousand miles from help and without enough water, he asked himself how he would find his way out alive. In this moment of suspension and human paralysis, he found the determination not only to live but also to write this classic book carrying his vision of the meaning of life. "It is only with the heart that one can see rightly," he wrote. "What is essential is invisible to the eye."

Indeed, our blind faith in the ungraspable is what makes us question the idea, the *concept.* Humanity has discovered the earth's gravity, the atom, and the speed of sound without the knowledge of their physical existence. The bold heart of the dreamer also leads the search for discovery. Often it is our most crucial moments that propel us toward divine realization and salvation. The turning points in our lives are what define us. Like an intersection on a highway or a dividing trail near a mountain stream, we gaze intuitively down the road of possibility. Will my choices lead me to a better view? Does my journey have a purpose? Was it my destiny to arrive at this juncture in order to find out who I am?

## Robin's Dream

*"I had this dream after being diagnosed with cancer. I was standing in my livingroom and the front door was open. From the corner of my eye, it looked liked it was snowing. I opened the screen door and it wasn't snow; there were white flowers and petals falling everywhere. Ahead of me was a weeping willow tree, and an ancient woman was standing underneath. She was dressed all in white—she was very beautiful. There were white doves flying around her head. There was no sound, only the muffled light sound of fallen flowers. I walked up to the woman. She was saying something, but I couldn't hear her. That's when I realized the woman was me! I woke up with a total sense of peacefulness and serenity. No other words can really describe the feeling in this dream. It was the best dream I've ever had!"*

As Robin faces cancer, she finds her core belief in self. She is able to see beyond her illness and reach for a new definition of courage in this miraculous and peaceful dream. Her future looks bright on the morning she experiences the dream. Cancer is terrifying, but her mental outlook provides the right state of mind for the struggle. Instead of carrying frightening thoughts and anxiety, she has somehow found the will to go beyond the realm of the physical and explore the genius of her unknown.

You might feel awkward, even silly when you work on carving your future from your dreams, asking how you can allow your dreams to supercede your rational thoughts. Sure, we all want to improve our lives. But can we really do it by letting our dreams have a presence in our lives? Look at it this way: if you stop paying attention to your dreams, you may as well stop dreaming altogether. It's not enough to simply embrace the idea that your dreams have potential. You must also have the nerve and the resolution to act on them. When you separate your daydreams, the wishes and aspirations you carry in your heart, from the dreams you encounter in sleep, you sell your spirit short.

The dreams you have read in the pages of this book have shown you how grand and joyous the dreaming world can be. In writing your own dream journal, you now have the tools to work with your dreams on a focused and elevated level. Through association, metaphor, symbolism, as well as intuition, spirituality, and vision, you have the knowledge to carve a new path for your life, no matter how unlikely your future dreams may seem today.

The mystical union of your soul's purpose and your mind's ideas can take shape in any number of ways. Your dreams may be telling you to build a new business or to heal your heart through loving again. No dream is too grand for the dream creator—*you*. Coinciding with this truth is also the need for self–empowerment. You must be wise enough and also believing enough to take risks, to journey and find the inner mechanism of change. A good example from my own dream journal relates to the writing of this book.

### Suz's Dream

*"I dreamed that I was searching frantically for a book. This book is on the library shelf with a blue cover, green writing for the title, and smaller white writing underneath the title. When I finally found it, my name was on the spine. I realized it was my book! I felt surprise. I wonder if this will happen."*

In many dreams, I have seen myself as an author. However, my dreams of writing and publishing a book in the future were not a prophecy of my being an author today. My dreams have acted to propel me to a path of self-improvement. Through hard work, intuitive choices, and also personal courage, I found a way to make my dreams materialize. This book is my dream come true.

As you read through your dreams and question your ideas

and desires for the future, try using the following exercise to create a new dynamic for transformation. In your dream journal, write out the following sentences and your responses. Free associate and be true to your heart.

## I HAVE A DREAM: AN EXERCISE

1.  My most profound dream for the future is

_____

2.  The only thing holding me back from reaching my dreams is _____

3.  I have always dreamed of being _____, but I don't think it will happen because

_____

4.  I am afraid to share my dreams because

_____

5.  My dreams are unimportant because

_____


Now, choose people who have inspired you to go beyond your own expectations. They might be a gym teacher or a professor or even a person from history, like Joan of Arc or Jesse Owens. Answer these questions and compare them to your earlier answers.

1.  My greatest dream role model is

_____

2.  He or she is my inspiration because

_____

3.  I know that others have made their dreams reality. I can too
if I _____

4.  What inspires me most about dreaming is

_____

5.  All of my dreams are of value because

_____

Once you have completed this exercise you may be shocked by your own limitations. You might find yourself saying that money or family members are keeping you from reaching your goals. You may think that you can't achieve your goals of a dream home, a dream man, a dream job, or even your dream retirement because of circumstances or material roadblocks. Remember that the inspirations from your mind, your heart, and your soul are what create and define the dream. Let go of your old excuses and embrace the dreams that you have allowed yourself to neglect. In this small and simple act, you will feel a watershed of insight envelop you. Here is where you give birth to the material manifestation of all your wildest hopes and most profound dreaming desires. Daring to dream is the first step to happiness. You are now on your way.

## THE SOUL OF THE DREAM

*"If you can dream it, you can do it."*—Walt Disney

The soul purpose of life and dreaming is much like any spiritual component of our lives. Like oxygen, we need it to live, to be inspired, to breathe. The odyssey and experience of finding faith comes in many different shapes and sizes. While we all carry different definitions of religion and soul purpose, universal truth remains constant throughout humanity. Love remains love in any culture.

Thinking with your soul is not a new concept. Many creative

and scientific leaders have used their spiritual definitions as a launching pad for discovery. In essence, spiritual intelligence—the choices we make with our souls and our minds—matters because it gives us a place to lay the groundwork for life's design. Much like attending church or pursuing higher education, the critical step in seeing the future comes to life from knowing that we are guided toward a higher level of achievement, not only for ourselves, but also for humankind. The soul serves the function of intuitive radar, leading us to a chosen target.

This relates to dreaming because our dreams are a wellspring for our inner design. While they don't always offer a plan or even a concrete message, they usually relate to the sacred space of self, the part of each of us that we shield from others. Much like our bodies unclothed, our dreams are fragile and vulnerable to the outside world. Surely our inner truth, our most cherished personal sanctum, plays a large role in our dreams as we search for connection, familiarity, and destiny.

We all seek a truth that makes us feel we belong to a higher order. This is where your soul connection to the world around you comes into play on the dreaming stage. Think about it like this: You define your world in the same way you define your God. It doesn't matter which religion you practice, but it is important that you are able to conceptualize the concrete presence of the divine in your world. Like a recipe for bread, which combines water, flour, and yeast, the soul is a part of this spiritual make-up, a trinity of mind, body, and soul. When you define and visualize your soul on this level, much like you would define your sense of identity or even your own value system, you then ask for *divine guidance*. You put your *soul goal* into action.

### Dan's Dream

*"I had a dream that I was in a garden with my very good friend, an elderly Native American shaman. He was giving me guidance and answering issues for me, but I could not hear him. I then sat on a rock wall and as I*

*looked down at my dangling feet, I saw different types
of animals coming up from the ground. They all then lay
down at my feet as if asleep or dead. Then I found myself
on a rocky beach next to the ocean. The water was clear
blue and I heard a woman's laugh. It was the laugh of
a woman I had recently met and who kept calling me
until I asked her to stop. I then took her hand and walked
into the water. The waves washed over me and I began
to laugh with her and heard my own voice say, 'This is
where you belong.'"*

Dan's dream has many levels of soul purpose and definition.
He not only learns from his elder or shaman, his spiritual
teacher in the dream, but he is also able to lead another person
to a new way of knowing enlightenment and joy. The images of
the animals, the ocean, and the waves are all voices of cleansing
and healing. They appear in a variety of spiritual writings from
the Tao Te Ching to the Talmud. Dan, who is a police lieutenant,
is on a new path to helping others as he steps into a brighter day
of knowing and understanding his value on earth. No matter
what he undertakes as his mission, his soul is acting as a guide.
He has a bedrock way of viewing the world, and therefore, his
new journey as teacher and spiritual leader is in place.

### Nancy's Dream

*"I had this dream. I was walking down a beach lined
with rocks. It looked somewhat like my favorite part of
the Oregon coastline, where I love to go to escape. I was
looking at a large rock formation, when I looked down
and saw footprints in the sand. They walked toward me,
invisibly. I was so depressed at the time I had this
dream. I had lost my job and was drifting in my life. After
I had the dream, I went to that beach and bumped into
my ex-husband. We both lived miles from this beach, so
this was truly a miracle. We had a very bitter divorce. I*

*cheated on him and made a bunch of bad choices. I
knew this dream was telling me it was time to forgive.
Today we have reconciled, and I am so grateful for this
dream."*

Divine guidance plays a significant role in Nancy's dream
because it drives her to travel to her favorite beach. The manifestation of the dream thus becomes the mechanism for change.
Her dream is a lovely and defined statement about the soul and
its basic, intrinsic purpose on earth. The symbol of the footprint
is found in a variety of spiritual texts. Many Tibetans believe
that following Buddha's footprints will lead to enlightenment.
Feet symbolize security as well as freedom. Nancy, who is a
radio personality, found a way to make her dream work for her
life. The dream highlights the search for salvation and the feelings that awaken her to new ideas of self. Today, she hosts a
nationwide morning talk show on the topic of financial prosperity and personal empowerment. Nancy has reached beyond
her own expectations, using her dream logic to make the world
a better place.

Dreaming the future is not only a way to look at your dreams
and to make them come true. It's also a unique path to higher
vision in your creative and personal life. Don't be afraid to put
your arms around your dreams, to hold them, and to love them.
Be true to your voice, your story, your dreaming song. It's easy
to trivialize the idea that our dreams harbor a grand plan for our
lives. Yet, the truth is that time and time again, in each night that
we dare to see beyond our limits and fears, we dream of tomorrow, of better choices in time.

What counts in your dreams is the ability to know *individual
truth*. Within each of us is a landscape of personal experience
and dream source. Like individual snowflakes falling from the
sky, the combination of details and definitions in our dreams
are infinite. Don't sell yourself short if you have yet to reach
your goals or see your visions take fruit. Like any pursuit of

higher purpose, dreaming your future will happen over time. In your future writings and dreaming wonders, know that your life is something that deserves *mindfulness*, attention, and *care*. As you take this first step into the act of making your dreams become reality, know that the reins you hold on the unknown are what create a vision of your future. You are the master puppeteer, the painter of the mural, the inventor of the machine. *Believe it.* If you make dreaming your journey, finding your soul will be the destination.

## NIGHT CAP

*"Was it a vision, or a waking dream?"*—John Keats

I am a dreamer. I have always embraced the ways and wonders of what *could be*, what *might be,* and how we can use these two futuristic models of thought with *what is.* Time is the connective tissue in everything that life decision making has to offer. The approach we take to our own potential is what defines the dream itself. As a child, my ability to dream set me apart in the classroom. "She needs to pay attention more," wrote my eighth grade teacher. Today, however, these visions of idealism bring me abundance and joy, not only in my career but in my personal life as well. Better still—I am not alone in being a dreamer. We all carry that deep and profound space of desire and aspiration.

Dreaming your future is not about mind control or wishing your dreams into reality each night. The act of creating, defining, and dreaming the reality of tomorrow comes from emotional integrity. It's about having the courage to be who and what you want to be. It's about living out your own ideas in application and design. We do our learning through our dreams. In our waking lives, we either apply the vision of our aspirations or we live in a world of limited possibilities.

## Andrea's dream

*"My dream happened two nights in a row. The first night I woke up sweating and shaking and couldn't remember the dream but as soon as I fell back to sleep I picked up on the dream like I never woke up. A woman just keeps reappearing in every mirror I pass or look into and she keeps telling me I can find all the answers to my questions. All I need to do is look to the mirrors for the answers to all my questions, problems, and fears. I have never had a dream like this and I really can't understand it. I wonder if, when I go to sleep tonight, I'll have the same dream. This morning I felt so at ease and rested."*

Andrea's incredible dream relates a simple message of individual truth. The main message is, of course, the words of the mysterious woman, "Look in the mirror for the answers." When she tells Andrea to look at herself to eliminate fear, she is really telling her that the secrets to her problems and her joys are all found in the internal kingdom of self. This is the ultimate nocturnal metaphor for the journey of self-discovery and personal awareness.

The obvious message within this dream is that we all need to begin with self in order to grow and change. As you finish reading this book, ask yourself the big questions about your world. Are you seeking out changes and unable to ask for help? Do you fear the journey because you are concerned about how others perceive you? How do you define your own limitations and beliefs? What is *your dream?* Whatever the answers may be, you will surely find your own truth if you can have the courage to speak your dreams aloud and follow them as you would any goal.

Say it. *I have a dream.*

Billionaire Richard Branson, who is a high school dropout, once said that he awakens some days and wonders if his life is just one big dream. "I suspect it is just one big dream," he said, "but I hope I never wake up." Branson's Law is one we might all benefit from employing. When we realize the fragile wonder of soulful living, in all of the abundance of the days we have already experienced, we gain tenfold in the act of our future pursuits.

Throughout my life, I have thought a great deal about my dreams, my hopes, and my idealistic visions for years to come. In completing this book, one dream ends and another dream begins. The message I impart and relate to you is that of your own self-discovery. As you put your head to the pillow each night, remember that your dreams are a part of your life. Don't deny yourself the sacred space of dreaming. Instead, use the time of nightly flight to explore and renew your deepest passions. Remember always that if you can dream it, *it can happen*. In the land of dreams, the human heart usually brings the answers, telling the larger story of offering and redemption. Let your dreams be your daily bread. Integrate your dreaming story with your daily truth. Divine desires are fragile and it's vital to keep them safe and alive in your heart. Dream tough, dream loud, and dream big. After all, the future is anyone's dream.

# Dictionary of Words and Symbols

These definitions were created based on cultural, mythological, spiritual, psychological, biblical, and religious symbolism. The goal of this dictionary is to offer a concrete combination of symbol systems from cultures throughout the world. Our dreams are often defined by the images we feel most comfortable with. Many symbol systems connect and overlap with one another, giving the dreamer an opportunity for new avenues of multilayered understanding and awareness. As you use this dictionary for dream work, be sure to acknowledge your own personal symbols and what they represent to you. *Context* and individual *frame of reference* must act in concert with the symbol to define the dream and its meaning.

**Abandonment:** The sensation of being left behind or abandoned can often relate to a loss or lack of emotional control. Ask yourself how you can face your fears. Work on associations from your own personal history.

**Aborigine:** Aboriginal culture is the oldest living culture still in existence today; if your dream relates to the culture itself, explore the symbolism of the dream. If it connects to an Aboriginal person or to *Dreamtime*, you may be on a spiritual journey.

**Abortion:** The act can relate to death of self or the loss of personal history. Abortion dreams often occur in women from fear or anxiety. Place this dream in your own perspective. Work on overcoming internal pain.

**Abuse:** The theme of abuse relates to extremes of emotion or addiction. Has violation occurred in your daily life? Are you abused or abusing? Balance is essential in further exploring this dreaming metaphor of polarity and dependence.

**Abyss:** A vast space or abyss in a dream usually connects to the context in which it is placed. If there is an emotional conceit to the void, ask yourself how you felt and what you are searching for.

**Accident:** Accidents can relate to loss or lack of control. Work on integrating the nature of the accident with your waking reality. Depending on the type of accident and who was featured, context will define this dreaming story line.

**Acorn:** Symbolic of harvest and the results of our efforts, the acorn is represented in almost every culture. As a small seed which falls from a mighty tree, the acorn presents an image of the natural order of life.

**Acting or Actor:** Illusion, fantasy, and role playing all connect with this dreaming occupation. Depending on the associations of sleep, this dream can indicate a need for greater or lesser expression. Work on understanding who is doing the acting and what message is being communicated.

**Addict or Addiction:** Themes of addiction connect to concepts of need and obsession with a person or an object. Depending on who was addicted and the nature of his or her dependence, the dream may relate to a number of emotional, physical, or psychological components such as desire, anxiety, and fear.

**Adopt or Adoption:** The act of adopting a person or an animal can represent the act of parenting. Some dreams may symbolize the legacy of identity or the altruistic nature of teaching and leading other people.

**Affair:** Dreams that carry the theme of love and passion in a romantic or sexual affair represent the deeper components of human love. Many people dream of having affairs even though they would never consider the act in their waking life. If there is betrayal in the event of pursuing an affair, the dream may relate to a need for greater self-empowerment or self-awareness.

**African or African American:** Race and definition of social standards play an important role in our lives. Depending on your own racial or ethnic origins, a person of black heritage can play varying roles. Integrate who you are with how you define others.

**Agate:** These stones represent the physical body on the natural plane. Agates assist in balancing, energizing, stabilizing, and in strengthening and bringing sympathy to the wearer.

**Age:** Changing age relates to identity and physical mortality. Depending on the context of the dream, you may be probing your own value in life. Ask yourself how you define age instead of how it defines you.

**Agreement:** Being in agreement is a positive message about human understanding and compassion. Simply put, agreement relates to empathy and intuitive strength.

**AIDS:** Humanity and mortality connect with this disease of the twentieth century. Context is vital in a dream about AIDS because it relates to the associations of the dreamer. Ponder your own connection to this illness or any other.

**Air:** A fundamental element, needed for living and breathing. Eastern philosophies believe that *prana* or *chi* is the source of the body's vital energies. Air is symbolic of natural forces relating to health and spirit.

**Airplane:** Airplanes are connected with the avenue of flight. Depending on the placement of the plane and how it was flying, the dream can have many meanings. Ask yourself how movement, travel, and flight parlay into the larger dreaming picture.

**Alcohol:** Depending on your associations with alcohol, the dream may take on a variety of meanings. Drinking alcohol relates to escape and the desire to forget reality. Journey into the heart of the drinker or pursue the context of alcohol for the meaning of this dream.

**Alley:** Narrow enclosures and passageways relate to a finite path. How does the alley connect to other parts of the dream? What is the prevailing emotion? Context will define this dreaming story line.

**Alligator:** Akin to the serpent, the alligator has a long life span and can be found in some Pacific myths, mainly from Thailand, illustrating the combination of power and force. The jaws of the animal can devour with swift speed, thus giving it a place of high regard in hunting lore. Alligators can often symbolize ferocity and power.

**Altar:** This wonderful representation of spiritual striving and attainment can be a key symbol in any dream. It relates to an inner need for divine truth. Altars represent the religious universe as a whole and how we perceive our lives.

**Amber:** This fossilized resin formed from tree sap holds important significance in the Baltic regions of the world. It is prized for its longevity, as well as its electric properties, known to aid with meditation.

**America:** America has always been colloquially known as land of the free and home of the brave. America often represents the New World and the discovery of new lands. What are your associations with this country? Context and association will define this dream.

**Amethyst:** This purple stone, which is also a form of quartz, was known in ancient Greek mythology as a symbol of beauty, modesty, and purpose. In healing traditions, it is known as nature's grand cleanser and also functions as a spiritual stimulant. It is folklorically believed to enhance the dream state, thus the name "dream stone."

**Ancestor:** Heritage, definition, and identity all connect to the image of an ancestor of ancestors. The dream may connect to a transitional period of life. Explore lineage and probe what defines family life.

**Anchor:** This seafaring symbol relates to the cross as it was first created in Italy, in order to help guide sailors safely home. It is attributed to many saints and acts as an emblem of protection.

**Angel:** Divine energy, source, and guidance. In Christianity and Catholic traditions, angels play the roles of both guide messenger and merciful healer. This symbolic figure could relate to a newfound sense of soul or spiritual renewal.

**Anger:** Rage and anger in dreams can connect to pain and unhealed wounds. If you are acting out your anger, you need to face the source. If anger is directed at you, ask yourself what makes you feel shame. Anger dreams are dreams of growth, either positive or negative.

**Animal:** The animal kingdom acts as a mirror of the human world. The Egyptians believed that many animals embodied a creative force or spirit. In Native American traditions animals are seen as parallel beings. Often considered a source of wisdom greater than humans, animals are connected to raw spirit and the simplicity of the natural world.

**Ankh:** The Ankh is an ancient Egyptian symbol, carrying the representation of immortality. The T cross and the oval symbolize the connection between heaven and earth.

**Ant:** The ant, found in passages of the Bible (Proverbs 6:6), is like the bee, a symbol of diligence. The Greeks view this tiny creature as a creator. Association is essential in interpreting a dream of this worker creature.

**Antique:** Dreams of antiques can relate to anything that has value, purpose, or a lasting impression. Depending on the object, the dream will correlate to an exploration of a given element.

**Anxiety:** Dream anxiety is a common emotion and theme. The dreaming story must be analyzed in relation to daily motivations and ideas. Stress must be looked at when deciphering the messages of an anxiety-related dream.

**Apartment:** Typically, apartments and houses relate to the various components of our waking lives and minds. If you reside in an apartment, your dream connects to your home. How did the apartment connect to the dream? Probe the scope of this symbol's placement.

**Ape:** In India and parts of Africa, the ape is revered as a holy symbol of power, representing strength and loyalty. In the west, the ape is often portrayed as a creature of lesser intelligence. Ask yourself how you view the ape and how experiences from your life connect to the dreaming story.

**Applause:** Applause in a dream can relate to a rush of acknowledgment or a need for recognition. Applause often has a positive message of embrace and human understanding.

**Apple:** Apples can be found in many theological and symbolic systems from the story of Adam and Eve to Aphrodite to Norse gods and Avalon. This hard fruit with a sweet core relates to abundance, youth, and the earth. Look at the placement in the dream and how it relates to life's offerings.

**Aquarium:** Aquariums harbor the world of the sea. Depending on personal associations with the ocean and tropical creatures, you may find the aquarium relating to personal associations and ideas. Often, aquariums represent a Pandora's box of the watery kingdom.

**Arch:** Much like a bridge, an arch in a dream can relate to areas in life that are in transition or an awakening from effort. Depending on context, the arch can portend a wonderful discovery or a mystery in the offing. Integrate the emotions of sleep with the choices of waking.

**Arctic:** Polar regions are often seen in dreams as icy imaginary lands or landscapes of infinity. Ice and snow can relate to things that are fixed or immovable. Was the arctic vision a positive one? How does the symbol of the dream connect to your mental assumptions? Association will bring the dream meaning to light.

**Arena:** Huge theaters such as stadiums, coliseums, or amphitheaters carry a landscape of cumulous experience or collective reasoning. They often provide a context of excitement or anticipation, but the dreaming story will likely determine the importance of this symbol.

**Argue or Argument:** If you were quarrelling in your dream, you are likely quarrelling with yourself or the person you dreamed of about an issue of relevance. The act of arguing connects back to hidden fears and frustrations.

**Ark:** The word *ark* is derived from the Latin word "arca," meaning chest. It represents a vessel for transport or a ship of goodness. In Christianity, we have many illustrations of the ark of the covenant and Noah's ark representing a holy protector. In some symbol systems it represents God or a temple of oneness.

**Arm:** Parts of the human body usually connect back to self. An arm is a key player in the world of dreaming because it is a purposeful tool we all use. It connects to the hand, a symbol of giving and truth. Depending on the nature of the arm and its use, your dream could connect back to your own pursuits.

**Armageddon:** *See Doomsday*

**Armor:** Armor was used for battle in many early civilizations. It acts as a shield between humankind and danger. If the armor was protecting you, your dream story could connect back to fear or personal protection. If you are viewing armor, you may be asking yourself about purposeful boundaries.

**Arousal:** Sexual and sensual dreams are fairly common, and the theme of arousal can relate to a psychophysiological state or an inner desire. Ask yourself what you want, need, and crave; and your dream will take on a new meaning relating to your inner fire of yearning.

**Arrest:** Arrests connect to the idea of being stopped in an action. Often arrest dreams relate to stress or anxiety. Who was being arrested and for what reason? Look at the emotional connection to this dream.

**Arrow:** While the arrow has a close mythological association to Cupid or Eros and the god of love, it also relates to reaching a destination or hitting a given target. Since it is a weapon, its image can be found in many symbol systems relating to the hunt. Work on understanding your ideas about the arrow and the way that it connects elements in your dream.

**Art or Artist:** Art relates to fantasy and dreaming in its very essence. The creative force has many spiritual overtones because it asks us about soul purpose and definition. If you have a personal connection to a piece of art, your dream is leading you to a higher awareness of your own creativity.

**Ashes**: Ashes often connect to the afterlife, or the effect of fire on what it consumes. Depending on what was burned, the ashes can relate to spiritual choice or bridges burned. Look at the history of the dream and how the past brings you to the future.

**Asia or Asian:** This rich and vibrant land has many cultures and traditions. Often associated with mystery, Asia is known as the birthplace of Buddhism and many ancient traditions. Association, context, and ideology will play a role in your dreaming definitions.

**Astrology**: In the twelve signs of the zodiac, the system of astrology relates to individual personality traits or emotional ideas. Define the message and key symbolism of this dream and integrate it with the context of the dream's message.

**Athlete:** Athletic prowess connects to vitality and physical pursuits. If you were the athlete, you may be journeying to a more connected physical state. If you were viewing athletes, you are probing the definition of the physical in your world. Focus on material awareness and how it relates to the soul.

**Attack:** Conflicts in dreams are typically about problem solving. Depending on the nature of the attack, you may be searching for the answers about someone or something. Ask yourself what things are out of balance in your world and work from a point of integration.

**Attic:** Attics can often represent a higher level of learning or an undiscovered country of ideas. Depending on the feeling about the attic, the dream may be directed to new vistas of soulful experience.

**Attorney:** Legalities can be frightening for many in the land of dreaming. The law is about balance and justice. If you dreamed of an attorney or someone you know with this profession, ask yourself about personal association and how the dream connects to your waking story.

**Autumn:** Season of harvest and change. Autumn connects to bounty, abundance, and also reservation of strength for the winter months ahead. A dream of autumn can reveal an inner planning process, a new awareness of unfound strength, and the healing journey.

**Avalanche:** A destructive force of overpowering nature, an avalanche in a dream can connect to many forces beyond one's control. Context plays a large role in this dreaming scene. Much like a dream of a tidal wave, it is vital to explore how you perceive control in your waking reality.

**Axe:** The axe has a dualistic nature, being used for battle and also for productive works. Many people have no tangible connection to an axe and yet dream of it. How did it fit into the dreaming story? What was it being used for? Context will tell the story of this dream.

**Baby:** The raw unencumbered essence of the infant spirit can connect to many aspects of life. The dream may be connecting to ideas of innocence or newness. In dreams, babies often represent a blank slate, raw and vulnerable to the world.

**Back:** Viewing the back of someone or something often brings a sense of being unable to move forward. Dreams featuring this theme often serve the purpose of omniscient viewership or seeking new awareness, relating to concepts of identity and boundaries.

**Baggage:** Baggage often represents the preparation or containment of an idea or a purpose. Like the bags we pack when we travel or the concept of departure, our perspective can be found in this dreaming vista. The context of the baggage in the dream will tell the greater story.

**Balcony:** Depending on the view, a balcony can offer new insights on relationships or points of view. If you are on the balcony looking down, you may be integrating new ideas of purpose in your life. If you are gazing upward, you may be working with attainable goals. Balconies can also associatively connect to romance and creativity.

**Bald:** Losing one's hair often connects to anxiety or other stress-related issues. If you are already bald, your dream may relate to a well-established identity. If you view someone who is bald, you may be questioning longevity and human mortality. Association is essential in interpreting this symbol in a dream.

**Ball:** The ball is an ancient symbol associated with gaming and adventure. In Aztec civilization it represented the sun and its phases of movement. Since this symbol is so highly relative to its use and representation in a dream, focus on the larger message of the dreaming story.

**Ballet:** Dance is connected to freedom of spirit and movement. While ballet is a traditional form of dance, the act of sentient movement and connection tells the larger story of dreams featuring ballet and the tribal joy of dance.

**Ballgame:** No matter the game, be it baseball, basketball, or tennis, games can be associated with fun, sport, and revelry. Association is essential when exploring a dream of a game as well as the rules and principles of the given sport.

**Balloon:** Balloons are wonderful and elusive symbols connecting us to the material aspect of freedom of thought. The concept of the thought bubble is a good symbol for the childlike representation of a balloon and how it connects to our dreams. How was the balloon featured in the dream? Did it take flight? How did it make you feel? Context will help in unraveling the meaning of this dream.

**Bamboo:** The ancient root has a profound place in spiritual symbolism in Asia where it represents many things, including an empty heart and also formidable strength. Bamboo itself is a very sturdy and indestructible force akin to a diamond. Depending on the source of this dream, the bamboo can have a variety of meanings.

**Bandage:** Dreams of being bandaged can reveal a sense of healing or repair. Depending on the nature of the wound and why the bandage was featured, the dream may relate to themes of vulnerability, fragility, and also healing.

**Bank:** Financial institutions and other houses of money can reveal a sense of security or fear, depending on the dreamer. Probe the associations of sleep and work on understanding what a bank represents in your world.

**Banquet:** Feasting is an old tradition that goes back to the dawn of humanity. Partaking in a grand banquet can connect to themes of reward and well-being. Dreams with this symbol should be explored in terms of abundance and reward or, alternately, gluttony.

**Bar:** Bars or watering holes relate to alcohol and its place in the dreamer's world. If you spend a lot of time in bars, this landscape will be a familiar one. If you dislike bars, your dreaming backdrop is a setting of mistrust. Context will provide the larger dreaming picture along with emotional connection.

**Barn:** Barns are a haven for the animals and tools of the farm. They often house hay and food along with other hidden secrets. Like any other house, the barn might represent a higher form of thinking or undiscovered emotions. Explore your intuitive programming in this natural house of understanding.

**Basement:** Parts of homes typically connect with parts of our minds or our emotions. A basement in a dream could act as a basis for a new foundation of thought. However, association plays a defined role, depending on what the dreamer experienced in the basement and how he or she felt about the individual legacy of the dream.

**Basket:** A northern European symbol for the harvest, a basket can be an object to symbolically carry any number of things. Examine the purpose of the basket in the dream as well as your intuitive feelings.

**Bat:** This nocturnal creature has a wide array of symbolism throughout many cultures. It is often connected with the souls of the undead or the mysteries of night. In the West it is seen as evil and in China it represents happiness. The exploration of individual associations will aid in understanding this highly dualistic dreaming symbol.

**Bath or Bathing:** From ancient Roman baths to the town of Bath in Great Britain, this watery wellspring of human cleaning is known to be a part of healing traditions. In Christianity, John the Baptist made the act of bathing a spiritual resurrection or cleansing of sin for anyone who became baptized. In Buddhism, baths are used as a ritual for each phase of life. This strong symbol should be explored in the context of the dream using intuitive reasoning and associative understanding.

**Bathing Suit:** Often associated with the beach or summer, this item of clothing can carry associative meaning depending on the dreamer and how the bathing suit played a role in the dream. From bikinis to surfing gear, bathing or swimming apparel is usually equated with the water, but it can also have an image of sexuality and the adornment of the human body. Context will define the meaning of this dreaming symbol.

**Bathroom:** Many people experience dreams featuring bathrooms, relating to bodily functions or other acts such as brushing teeth or taking a shower. Bathrooms are often associated with the more sterile part of the home and can be found in anxiety-related dreams. However, association is essential in interpreting a dream with this landscape.

**Battle:** Battles are scenes of conflict, and depending on the result they can have a profound symbolic meaning in a dream. The obvious association of division and war remains important. However, a historical reference may take part in the dreaming landscape. Context, association, and intuitive design will aid in interpreting a dream of battle.

**Beach:** Because they are a partner to the sea, beaches have a tranquil and blissful quality, and many people associate them with sunshine, happiness, and ease. Their other symbolic connections to the marine world also offer varying mythological traditions. In Thailand, the beaches are considered the sleeping place of the gods. In Hawaii, beaches are known to be owned by the natural world and therefore a gift to humanity. If your dream featured a beach, it may also relate to a spiritual journey or awakening.

**Bear:** Important in Norse and Russian mythology, the bear is a symbol of strength as well as compassion. Much like the St. Bernard, it is an animal that can harm or help. This dualistic construct offers parallels in dreams. Bears hibernate and can also be associated with sleep or wisdom. To Native Americans, the bear represents the uncharted intuitive mind. Probe the nature of the bear's appearance and journey into the untamed heart of the bear symbol.

**Beard:** An early European symbol of power or status for men, the beard can be seen on portraits of kings and noblemen. In Asia, a beard represented strength in battle and, depending on length, protected the warrior from evil. Modern associations have offered a different twist, seeing the beard as sharing the general symbolism of hair and linked to vanity and ego. Association and context will define a dream featuring a beard as a primary symbol.

**Bed:** Associated with sexuality, the symbol of the bed is also connected with sleep and dreams. Beds are a common comfort zone and often appear in dreams as the central point of a story line or a mirror of the dreamer's sleeping actions. Probe the nature of the symbol's placement in order to interpret a dream featuring a bed.

**Bedroom:** Much like the symbol of the bed, the bedroom carries specific associations and environmental representations. This room is central to themes of individuality, love, and relationships. Depending on the dreamer's associations with this room, any numbers of meanings can be purposeful and important.

**Bee:** These tiny creatures with a powerful sting have a dualistic association and historical symbolism. Because they are associated with honey, they can represent abundance and also joy. Their hive existence represents themes of working or communal life. In Chinese folklore, the bee represents a woman's soul. The bee is also a royal symbol because of the Queen bee. Bees in dreams can appear as fearful creatures who chase the dreamer. It is important to place the symbol within the context of the dreaming message in order to understand this highly complex mythological image.

**Beggar:** Connected to class and social order, this archetypal figure representing the needy can appear in a dream as part of a story line or a symbol of an element of the dreamer's world. Other associations are charity, compassion, social order, and the dualistic construct of selfishness and generosity.

**Beige:** The color beige has an earthy tone and is often associated with peace or tranquillity. Since it is often found in the natural landscapes of deserts and beaches, the connection to the earth is also part of its symbolic legacy.

**Bell:** Bells have been used in many cultures through most of history. These instruments of sound and also alarm have mythological and also spiritual connections. Of course, the bells of a church are commonly connected to the image, but there is also a rich history of bells and freedom or the sounding of a new day. In modern iconography, bells have become associated with ideas and awakening, with phrases like "A bell sounded in my head."

**Berries:** Often associated with other fruits, berries can also be connected with themes of innocence because of their presence in fairy tales and folklore. No matter what type of berry was featured, blueberries, strawberries, or raspberries, the theme of sweetness of taste may also be part of the larger dreaming story.

**Bicycle:** Often associated with speed, movement, travel, or leisure, the bike is also equated with the basic learning skills of youth, hence the expression, "It's like riding a bicycle." Depending on the dreamer's personal connections to the bicycle, the dream symbol may play any number of roles.

**Big:** Changes in size often occur in dreams and reflect transition or transformation. The surreal world of dreams can create anything from a giant paperclip to a tiny elephant. Look at the dreaming symbols as they connect to the larger story and explore the element of transformation in daily life.

**Bill or Bills:** Part of the human landscape of life and survival, bills are a paper representation of dues or legal concepts. Often dreams featuring a pile of bills or a bill that is unpaid indicate anxiety within the dreaming story. However, the nature of the bill and its placement in the dream will reveal the larger picture.

**Billfold:** *See Wallet*

**Bird:** Associated with flight and perspective, birds have a highly positive connection in mythological traditions and symbols. Of course, there are birds of paradise and also birds of prey. The legend of Icarus is a tale of a winged creature making its way to the sun. Birds are also connected to the concept of heaven, as their wings enable them to reach beyond the human dimension. In dreams, birds can take on any number of roles from deliverer to messenger, but almost always involve flight and the passage of a dreaming element.

**Birth:** The gift of life, newness, and the theme of emergence all relate to the symbol of birth. Whether giving birth or observing some form of birth, dreams relating to this theme are intertwined with the dreamer's ideology and perspective on beginnings.

**Birthday:** Birthdays are very personal events relating to identity, growth, and the passing of time. They not only reflect the day of being born but also the calendar of an individual life. Dreams featuring a birthday can have varying associations depending on the dreamer's connection to the event and the concept of this yearly anniversary of life.

**Black:** The polar opposite of white, black is an absolute color or noncolor. Many people equate it with darkness or blackness. Dreams featuring a black landscape or object often relate to the dreamer's associations of these themes. Mythologically, blackness was known as a symbol of metamorphosis and often used in designs of deities in India, Polynesia, and Eastern Asia.

**Blanket:** Security and comfort are connected to this household symbol of warmth. Since blankets are used in sleep, they are often featured in dreams about sleep or other forms of relaxation and comfort. They can also be perceived as blanketing an issue, persons, or an idea. Context will play a vital role in interpreting this dream.

**Blind or Blindness:** Symbolizing both truth and ignorance, blindness is often dualistic. It also appears in dreams connected to fear and an inability to find an object or a person. Emotional sensations and the inner journey of the dream will reveal the meaning.

**Blood:** While blood has a great significance in Christianity and other religions, representing purity, salvation, and the regenerative powers of spiritual life, it is also a basic symbol of a biological life-giving force. Used in ritualistic traditions, it can connect to the concept of taboo or sacrifice. The overall intuitive feeling along with the context should be used in interpreting a dream featuring blood.

**Blossom:** An open flower or a blossom is a symbol of new life or the image of natural potential. This image featured in dreams will have a contextual meaning and may interconnect with a specific story line. Probe the intuitive meaning of the symbol, coupled with the larger dreaming message.

**Blouse:** This piece of clothing is often connected with femininity and womanhood. As apparel, it is also closely associated with themes of identity and outward appearances. Context and personal association are vital in interpreting a dream featuring this article of clothing.

**Blue:** Known as a symbol of ideas and of the mind, the color blue has a rich mythological history in many symbol systems. It is often associated with creativity and imagination. This color is mentioned in every spiritual text from the Q'uran to the Old Testament. Its representations are that of substance, truth, eternity, immortality, and illumination. It is connected to water-symbols systems, and in modern use the term "I am blue" has come to be equated with pathos and sadness.

**Boat:** Vessels for navigating on the water, boats are often found in dreams as part of the dreamer's journey from one destination to another. Depending on the sturdiness of the boat or the nature of travel, the dreamer may have any number of impressions. Boats are also highly symbolic in Oceanic traditions and water mythology, representing survival and the soul of the fisherman.

**Body:** The human body is much like a vast landscape. In its entirety, it is often associated with the varying parts of the human mind or spirit. It is also closely connected to health and well-being. Many dreams feature parts of the body or actions of the body and how they relate to the dreamer. Context, association, and intuitive reasoning must be used in interpreting a dream relating to the human body.

**Bomb:** Because of modern iconographic symbolism using the atom bomb and other forms of bombs, this symbol has become part of dreaming lore and is usually equated with mass destruction or a doomsday scenario. Bombs often act as scene-changing actions in dreams and should be interpreted in context of the dreaming story.

**Bondage:** Dreams of bondage or other forms of restriction are much like dreams of being enslaved, kidnapped, or having part of one's identity stolen in some way. Bondage dreams often ask the dreamer to probe his or her ideas of restrictions or other unchangeable elements of life—emotional, physical, or spiritual.

**Bone:** Often connected with the desecration of the human body and the symbol of death, bones are found in many symbol systems and mythological stories. Many cultures buried or stacked bones as a way to remain in spiritual contact with their ancestors. Bones in dreams can be terrifying or confusing depending on their placement and context. Their rudimentary representation is the structural or skeletal building bocks of the human body.

**Book:** This symbol of higher learning has many facets to it. Often dreams featuring books relate to a search of some kind or a need for knowledge that parallels the dreamer's daily life. Books in dreams can also surrealistically offer some sort of message or give the dreamer a chance to "read" the message of the dream.

**Bookstore:** Bookstores are a dreaming landscape relating to knowledge, learning, and also literature. Much like a supermarket, the setting offers the dreamer a large selection of choices. Depending on the intuitive desires of sleep, the dream may have a unique message or story.

**Boots:** Much likes hats, boots are typically symbolic, related to identity. They can also represent industry, work, or grounding depending on the dreamer's associations and ideas about these crafted and unique shoes.

**Border:** Borders in dreams appear in various forms. Sometimes they can be a line in the sand, or they can be featured as bordered maps or other boundaries. If you dreamed of a border, probe the nature of how it integrated with the dreaming story for higher meaning and understanding.

**Boss:** Dreams that feature a boss or an employer have a multilayered symbolic connection. Issues of emotional and intellectual connection to a superior along with career identity and purpose all come into play. Probe the intuitive and emotional connection to the symbol in order to unravel the dream in message and story.

**Boulder:** These giant rocks can represent a blockade or an icon, depending on the dreaming story line. Boulders are symbolically connected to mountains and western motifs, but they also have meaning relative to their placement in dreams.

**Box:** Boxes, containers, and packages are often defined in dreams by their contents. The act of opening the box can also be relevant on a symbolic level, relating to searching for answers or the act of discovery on a parallel level to the dreamer's waking reality.

**Boxing or Boxer:** Physical and combative activity both connect to a dreamer about a boxer or the act of boxing. Associations to this aggressive sport are highly personal. Context and emotional connection must be used in interpreting a dream with these symbols.

**Boy:** Much like the symbol of a girl, boys are the masculine counterpart representing male youth and identity. Context and association will define a dream featuring an unknown boy or archetypal symbol of a young man.

**Boyfriend:** Boyfriends, admirers, spouses, lovers, and friends connect back to basic questions or searches of the dreamer. If you dreamed of a boyfriend, probe the nature of the story line and context in order to unravel the larger message and purpose of the dream.

**Bra:** Lingerie and other undergarments are often associated with sensuality or the hidden identity of an individual. Many dreams feature the act of undress or the type of bra worn. Context and placement must be used in unraveling the emotional and associative connection to this sleeping image.

**Bracelet:** Unlike rings, bracelets don't have a large history in symbols systems, although they are associated with the ring because of the circular nature of their shape and the concept of keepsake and unity. Often bracelets in dreams are connected to the wearer or owner and are an associative symbol of identity and adornment.

**Brain:** The center of all thought and the organ of mental activity, the brain is a powerful anatomical symbol of mind, intellect, wisdom, and idea. Dreams that feature the brain and its powers are often about psychic or spiritual pursuits and have mind/brain story lines. Use intuitive reasoning in exploring dreams featuring the brain or the human mind.

**Brakes:** Many dreams feature the act of brakes failing in a car or the act of slamming on the brakes in order to avoid disaster. The emotional mechanisms of these dreams will define the dreaming message in theme and in story.

**Branches:** Branches of trees, bushes, flowers, and other plants are often found in dreams as extensions of larger symbols in nature or in life. They can act as supportive structures, as in sitting on a branch of a tree, or they can act as symbols for reaching out, as in hanging on to a branch of a tree. Context and emotional sensation are vital in defining the meaning of a dream featuring this symbol.

**Brass:** A metal used mainly in the construction of useful objects, brass has an association with music because of the instruments that are constructed from this material. It represents purposeful value and the working class.

**Bread:** From ancient Egyptian myth to biblical stories to Native American lore, bread is a valued and important symbol relating to sustenance, spirituality, giving, and fundamental goodness. It is used in Christian communion as well as Arabic rituals of community. Dreams of bread are typically positive and can relate to unity, sharing, and soulful nourishment.

**Breaking:** In many dreams that feature breaking objects or elements, the meaning depends on what is being broken. The concept of fragility relates to impermanence, crisis, and also transition. Emotional impressions and intuitive reasoning will determine the main message of dreams featuring this theme.

**Breast:** Beyond the obvious association to sexuality and femininity, breasts are also represented in religious and spiritual art as the image of the mother goddess. In Greek mythology, breasts represented a highly developed sense of faith. Because breasts also provide milk, they are also equated with nourishment and a universal connection to humanity.

**Bricks:** Formidable in weight and construction, bricks are often symbolic of an earthen iron and a building material. Houses and other structures built from brick are associated with permanence, and modern phrases like "made of brick" relate to sturdiness and hardiness. Context is vital in interpreting a dream with this versatile symbol.

**Bride:** The female counterpart to the groom, a bride is traditionally equated with virginity, purity, and innocence. In varying cultural traditions brides are veiled in order to keep them pure before their wedding night. Dreams featuring a bride or becoming a bride are highly personal and will usually relate to the dreamer's ideology and vision of marriage and matrimonial union.

**Bridge:** Bridges are wonderful symbols in dreams, connecting to crossing barriers, transition, and right of passage. Often they are featured as a point of destination or arrival and can connect to themes of spiritual ascension, intellectual evolution, and self-awareness.

**Briefcase:** Much like a purse, wallet, or other personal effects, the briefcase is a compartment or element of containment. It is often associated with the workaday world and is a modern iconographic symbol of the working man or woman.

**Broom:** A basic household object for cleaning and sweeping, brooms have a strong cultural and mystical history from Celtic traditions to the Mexican broom festivals. Their association is usually connected to the ability to reach beyond the simple and basic elements of the human plane in flight or in other forms of ritual magic. In ancient Greek traditions they were used to summon the rain.

**Brother:** Familial connections are important in dreams because they feature human connection and, depending on the nature of the relationship, a clear and emotional message. Brothers are archetypal representations of brethren or brotherhood and symbolically represent the union of manhood.

**Brown:** The color brown is representative of the earth, the soil, and other elements of the natural world. Though not a striking or vibrant color, it is found in many dreams and usually connects to the dreamer's personal associations with this subtle and natural hue.

**Bubble:** A bubble is unusual because it is rather surreal and when featured in dreams can portray many meanings. The basic form of a bubble is fragile and translucent and yet, like a balloon, able to hold air. Bubbles can carry anything in dreams, and the placement along with the story line should be explored in order to interpret a dream featuring this symbol.

**Bucket:** Devices for holding water, buckets are connected to the transportation of objects or physical elements. Their symbolic meaning depends on how they are used or featured. If they are for holding water, they may have a spiritual connection. Context will provide a better picture of the dreaming message.

**Buddha:** The Buddha is a God figure representing happiness and enlightenment for Hindus and Buddhists alike. While the Buddha has many forms, it is known as the father of compassion and, much like Jesus and Christianity, the foundation of the Buddhist religion in India, China, and Japan.

**Bug:** *See Insect*

**Bull:** With the use of modern terms like "bullheaded" this ancient symbol is actually a Paleolithic image often associated with horses and infinite strength. In astrological symbolism, the bull is the image for the sign of Taurus and represents earthy tenacity and determination. Bulls are also connected with the modern image of finance and the "bull market." Association will tell the story of this misunderstood and important symbol.

**Burial:** Dreams of funerals and burials often connect to undiscovered parts of self or the concept of an afterlife. If you were viewing a burial, you may be working on understanding your own views on the purpose of afterlife. Burials also relate to the act of resolution, finality, closure, forgiveness, and healing.

**Burning:** Fire is a common dreaming theme and can bring a dichotomy of either fear and peril or illumination and wisdom to the dreaming mind. Dreams of burning fires, objects, or people are related to the concept of consumption, energy, death, and regeneration. Probe the nature of what was burning and how the dreaming story interacted with this fiery symbol for action, illumination, or destruction.

**Bus:** Buses are a modern representation of a moving house. Many people relate them to their school days or other forms of collective movement. The key component to understanding the dream will be where the bus was traveling and why.

**Butter:** Butter is a milk product that some consider decadent and many associate with richness and smooth delight. Depending on how you view this mainstay in food lore, butter may connect to a higher force of renewal. In Tibet, for example, Yak butter is still used to cleanse and bless.

**Butterfly:** This miraculous creature can be found in many symbol systems. Usually, the butterfly symbolizes metamorphosis or the transition from one stage of life to another. In Japan, it connects to femininity and womanhood. In Greece, it represents the soul's evolution. In Pacific cultures, it reveals the force of natural order.

**Cabin:** A rustic example of a house, the cabin is usually likened to a nature retreat, representative of home and peaceful structure. Cabins can also relate to family and the placement of individual identity within a given structure. Context and the emotional sensation of the dream will integrate the landscape with the dreaming story.

**Cage:** Much like prisons or jails, cages often reflect a loss of freedom or the dreamer's emotions relating to loss of control. Context and association, as well as the way this symbol was featured, will reveal the larger dreaming story.

**Cake:** Often a symbol of sweetness and decadence, cakes also have folkloric representations of harvest and, much like bread, nourishment. Wedding cakes are highly representative of love and romance and are often connected to the act of bride and groom feeding each other in spiritual union.

**Calm:** Dreams can often have a calming effect, providing the dreamer with an emotional stage for insight. Dreams featuring calmness or a sense of peace are usually positive in and may represent a higher level of understanding in theme and story.

**Camel:** This unusually shaped animal is typically associated with desert lands and peoples, yet it also has a rich symbolic history. In both the Bible and the Talmud, there are references to the camel's ability to achieve the impossible, making it a symbol of steadfastness. Since these creatures are able to survive without water for long periods of time, they also carry a modern representation of survival in harsh conditions.

**Camera:** Optical and also industrial, cameras are devices which create an image through the process of reflecting light. Symbolically, they can represent illusion, fantasy, clarity, polarity, and also vision. Personal association and metaphor will likely play a defining role in a dream featuring a camera.

**Camp or Camping:** Rustic and natural, campgrounds or the act of camping relates to landscapes or structural environments. Objects of necessity, like tents, pots, and outdoor gear, may be featured. Context and metaphor are pivotal in interpreting a dream featuring these elements.

**Cancer:** A modern disease of death and suffering, this illness usually has very personal associations. Often people dream of having cancer themselves and awaken terrified. Explore the symbolic meanings of illness and crisis for understanding, as well as using contextual analysis.

**Candelabra or Candlesticks:** Candleholders of any kind have been around since ancient civilization, providing people with the ability to see during night hours. In Jewish traditions the menorah, a seven-pronged candleholder, represents the eight days of eternal light from which faith cannot be extinguished. In modern lore they carry an association of mystery and romance with folkloric tales like "The Phantom of the Opera." Probe individual connections and references to interpret the meaning of a dream featuring these symbols.

**Candle:** Candles are related to light and the symbol system of the flame. Since they are used in almost every religious tradition, they often take on the meaning of the light of God or the oneness of human soul and divine spirit.

**Candy:** Sweet, decadent, and often connected to perceptions of childhood, candy is typically found in dreams relating to sensation of taste or the desire for nourishment. Probe the placement of the symbol along with the emotional sensations of the dream for interpretation.

**Cane:** Canes or walking sticks can be decorative and status-oriented symbols. Or they can represent dependence and physical weakness, depending on the dreamer and the use of the cane in the dream. Since canes are also used in magic acts, many associate them with illusion and mystical powers. Association will define a dream with this symbol.

**Canyon:** Much like valleys, canyons are vast in expanse and have a spiritual relationship to the dreamer's journey. They are symbolic of a void or a divide and yet also a place of rest and meditational retreat from the active world.

**Cap:** *See Hat*

**Cape:** Capes and cloaks worn as vestments are usually a covering and can represent that which is hidden from view or a protective disguise. Because cloaks and capes are much like king's robes, they can also relate to regal position and authority. The meaning of the cape, the way in which it was worn, and how it felt will all be components of interpreting this dreaming symbol and its connection to the dreaming story.

**Car:** Vehicles of any sort usually take the dreamer from one dreaming framework to another. Cars, since they are the most commonly used driving vehicle, can act as a method of transport or a backdrop for a given story or event. If a specific type of car was featured, personal association will likely tell the larger dreaming story.

**Cards:** Used for magic or as games of chance, strategy, and skill, cards can represent any number of things, being that they also carry their own unique individual symbol systems. Within each type of deck (Tarot cards, playing cards, and medicine cards) are representations of number systems as well as imperial images. Context and intuitive reasoning must be used.

**Carnival:** Much like fairs and festivals, carnivals are landscapes of magic, illusion, fun, and adventure. While they are more commonly associated with early twentieth-century themes, they are known in modern thought more like the circus—a place of amusement and childlike dimensions of symbolism.

**Carousel:** Found in amusement parks and public parks around the Western world, carousels have a circular motion and are often connected with a whirling sensation as well as the element of time. Since this ride features horses or other animal imagery, there may be symbolic association in theme and content. Explore both the symbols and the emotions relating to a carousel or carousel ride.

**Carpet:** Any flooring, be it wood floors or carpeting, typically will connect to the dreaming landscape and its relevance to the dreaming story. However, many people dream of stained carpet or the sensation of walking on carpet. Intuitive reasoning as well as placement of the symbol will determine the importance of this symbol in a dream.

**Cartoon or Cartoon Character:** This modern celluloid creative form often lends itself perfectly to the world of dreaming because of the fantastic nature of the cartoon character and the surreal ability to override reality. Dreams of cartoons or their characters are fairly common and usually connect back to the dreamer's ideas and representations of the given stories and symbols.

**Castle:** Known more in folkloric and fairytale traditions as a symbol of romance and regal stature, the castle is a basic symbol of a fortress or a large imperial domicile. Since castles are found in many children's stories, they may take on a fantastic role in dreams, but context and placement will offer a more purposeful meaning of how this symbol integrates with the dream.

**Cat:** The cat can be found in almost every mythological and spiritual text and is often associated with symbol systems of mysticism, awareness, keenness, insight, spiritual evolution, and intelligence. The belief that cats have nine lives also connects to the basic concepts of reincarnation and the evolution of the soul.

**Catalogue:** Much like magazines and newspapers, catalogues offer the dreamer an option to choose a given topic or to "read between the lines" of a given dreaming subject or theme. This symbol may also relate to shopping or material wishes and concepts.

**Cave:** Although caves are typically associated with primitive humans, they are dualistic in symbolism because they can either appear foreboding, empty, and dark or act as a place of shelter and retreat. In Hawaiian spiritual traditions, caves were used as burial grounds for fishermen and acted as soulful shelters from the sea.

**Cedar:** This prized wood is found in many areas of the world and is commonly valued for its scent. In ancient Egypt and biblical traditions, it was known for its durability. It is also known as the national tree of Lebanon.

**Ceiling:** Related to themes of perspective, ceilings are usually featured in dreams as a component of a higher representation or point of view. Probe the context and emotions associated with the ceiling and its placement in the dream.

**Celebrity:** Symbolic of glamour, beauty, and fashion, celebrities or movie stars in dreams are common and usually connect with the dreamer's ideas of self or an associative message relating to the given personality. Work on understanding what the movie star or celebrity represents and integrate it with the larger dreaming story.

**Cellar:** Damp and dark, cellars are part of houses and homes and are associated with a component of the dreamer's thinking or spiritual ideas. Depending on how you felt about the cellar or what role it played in the dream, it may reveal underlying themes or events not yet realized.

**Celtic Cross:** The Celtic cross predates Christianity by many centuries. Its early origins gave it a symbolism of fertility. Its design and structure is unique and is known among scholars as the inception of many symbol systems we know today. Today, it represents the union of heaven and earth, much like the Ankh.

**Cemetery:** Mainly connected to the burial of the dead and the concept of the human "final resting place," cemeteries became more common during the sixteenth century. In dreams, cemeteries are often haunting landscapes relating to the metaphysical or the mystical concept of an afterlife.

**Centaur:** The legend of the centaur goes back to Greek mythology and is often representative of the dualistic struggle between human and animal. This half-man, half-horse creature is also the symbol of the astrological sign Sagittarius and can symbolize freedom, strength, and honesty.

**Center:** Many dreams feature scenes, objects, and landscapes that contain a central area or definition. The meaning of central placement relates to the concept of oneness in Taoist thought and is believed to be the human area of insight and enlightenment. Context and association must be used when interpreting a dream with a central theme.

**Ceremony:** Pomp and ceremony are common in dreaming stories because they often connect to life themes like winning awards or cultural achievements. Ceremonial aspects were highly important and symbolic in ancient cultures, and dreams carrying this theme should be explored relating to the nature of the ceremony and the underlying message.

**Cesspool:** Dreams of cesspools, sewers, and gutters connect to the underside of life or the concept of human waste. Many dreams carrying these images can reveal emotions of anxiety or feelings of filth and shame. Context and personal association must be used when interpreting the importance of this dreaming symbol.

**Chain:** Chains are dualistic objects because they represent collective infinity and are often used in jewelry and other objects of adornment, and yet they are also symbolic of slavery. In ancient symbol systems and Christianity, chains are either featured as golden paths to heaven or links to hell. Depending on how the chain was featured in the dream, it may either symbolize a form of unity or, alternately, bondage.

**Chair:** Chairs are typically associated with the material representation of humankind because of their design and form. Chairs are found in dreams connecting to rest and relaxation and often reflect that which is stable and secure. If a specific chair was featured, personal association will determine its meaning.

**Chalice:** As a basic symbol of the grail, the chalice represents a spiritual offering or a higher journey. Chalices were used in medieval Europe to offer purpose and true faith for a given mission.

**Chandelier:** This lighting fixture is often equated with opulence and privilege. The origin of the chandelier came from a Byzantine design and the need for lighting within a vaulted structure. There are also Celtic origins of this design, and while modern use is associated with wealth, chandeliers are also featured in many fairy tales. Personal association will reveal the dreaming importance and message.

**Channeling:** The concept of channeling, much like levitation, is one that relates to higher levels of metaphysical study or transcendence of the physical plane of being. Channeling involves the ability to reach into the spirit world in order to make contact with souls who have departed; the term "channeling" came into use in the late twentieth century. Since dreams and the soul are so closely intertwined, the dreaming story and intuitive message will reveal the dreaming meaning.

**Chariot:** The symbol of the chariot is closely connected with the invention of the wheel and can reflect the basic concept of unity or the circular essence of life. Chariots are also found in many ancient spiritual systems like Greek and Norse mythology. They can represent speed, force, and the path to other worlds.

**Charity:** Dreams featuring acts of charity or compassion are usually very positive and can connect to the dreamer's concepts of goodness and human understanding. Many emotions of faith, spirit, kindness, and empathy are found in dreams carrying this dreaming theme.

**Chasing:** Many dreams feature the act of chasing a person or a thing, or the alternative of being chased and pursued. Often these dreams carry a strong emotional impact with sensations of elation and power or anxiety and fear. The intuitive essence of the dream should be used in interpreting dreams carrying this theme.

**Cheating:** Acts of betrayal or cheating are common dreaming themes. Many people dream of being betrayed by their lovers and friends only to awake in anxiety and fear. The emotional legacy of the dream, along with the story and theme, should be probed for understanding and self-awareness.

**Check or Checkbook:** Relating to money, banking, or the act of payment, checkbooks are modern symbols of finance and balance. Depending on how the check or checkbook was featured, the dream may relate to debt or abundance, and context as well as waking parallels must be explored.

**Cherry:** This highly associative symbol has diverse meanings. In ancient traditions, the cherry was a prized and valued fruit used in many foods and often symbolic of sweetness and goodness. In China, the cherry blossom represents an ancient myth of a beautiful maiden and her immortality. In nineteenth-century England, cherry wood was known to drive away evil forces, and the cherry tree is also connected in the American folkloric tale of George Washington and his famous cutting down of a cherry tree.

**Cherub:** Cherubic figures are often found in Renaissance artwork and lore and relate to the Greek myth of Cupid *(see Cupid)* and the theme of unconditional love. These tiny angelic creatures connect to the dreamer's concepts and definitions of innocence, spirituality, heaven, and earth.

**Chest:** Chests or other caskets to hold objects are found in many folkloric stories relating to treasures. Originally connected with the Ark *(see Ark)* and other mythological lineage, Caribbean and English pirate stories of hidden treasure chests are symbolically linked to the discovery of wealth and hidden bounty. A dream about a human chest may relate to symbols of comfort, love, or the heart *(see Heart)*.

**Chicken:** While the chicken lacks a connection in ancient symbol systems, it is often connected with the modern-day concept of fear or weakness. The act of being "chicken" is associated with spinelessness. The chicken is also a farm animal connected with the laying of eggs and can be identified with femininity. Association should be used when probing the meaning of this complex and yet common animal.

**Child or Children:** Many dreams feature unknown children and are often reflective of innocence or childishness. Depending on the acts or intuitive associations to the given child or children, the dream may have many varying meanings.

**China:** Fine and delicate porcelain, china is often connected to the concepts of breakability and fragility. Depending on how it was used or featured, symbolic representations will be important. China, the country, is also featured in dreams and is related to the mystical and ideological notions of the East *(see East)*.

**Chocolate:** This decadent and delectable treat is often associated with divine pleasure or hedonistic desires. Chocolate can also relate to the idea of temptation and is typically a positive symbol in dreaming lore.

**Choking:** Many dreams feature the sensation of being unable to breathe or the act of choking. These dreams are the physical representation of limits, restraints, or other anxiety-related themes. Probe the emotional context as well as the symbolic meaning in order to define the larger message of the dream.

**Choosing:** Dreams carrying a theme of choice often reflect our connection to a time, a place, or a person. Dreams of choosing can also relate to themes of balance, connection, and the motivation of individual choices.

**Christ:** *See Jesus*

**Christmas:** This seasonal holiday of giving and love is traditionally related to the Christian story of Jesus' birth and the holy nativity. Varying cultures embrace it in different ways, but it is an archetypal and universal symbol of giving, joy, bounty, humanity, and compassion.

**Church:** Churches, mosques, and temples relate to the physical landscape of a place of worship. Often churches in dreams relate to the dreamer's basic history or association of spirituality and religion and should be explored when interpreting the larger dreaming message.

**Cigarette:** While Freud believed the cigar to be a symbol of oral fixation, this modern version of the cigar is a symbol that will almost always relate to the dreamer's personal ideology and associations about smoking.

**Circle:** This ancient geometric symbol of infinity, limitlessness, and unity is connected to almost every religious and spiritual system around the world. In Celtic and early Roman symbols it is found in the design of temples and coliseums. It represented the sun or the moon to many Oceanic and Latin American cultures. In Buddhism the circle represents enlightenment *(see Mandala)*. Circles are also found in modern symbols like the ring and the fountain.

**Circus:** Often associated with amusement and surreal entertainment, the featured components of the circus—animals, clowns, and amazing acts—make it a symbol of imagination and fantastic creation. Personal association and history will determine the meaning of this dreaming landscape.

**City:** Cityscapes and other modern landscapes can connect to the dreamer's ideas of population or culture. Often, specific cities can represent ideals, images, and impressions, and context is vital in interpreting a dream about a known or unknown city.

**Class or Classroom:** Dreams about being in class or classrooms are fairly common. They can reflect parts of the dreamer's personal history or other associations of learning, study, understanding, and instruction.

**Claw:** Much like a hook, the symbol of a claw is connected to the animal or biological form of something that can scratch or ensnare. Many people have a fear of claws and associate them with phrases like "claw your eyes out." Dreams featuring this symbol should be explored by using constructive reasoning as well as symbolic interpretation.

**Clay:** Derived from the earth and often gray or russet in color, clay is symbolic of that which is pliable or connected with the concept of natural metamorphosis. Found in the Bible in Genesis, it can spiritually represent creationism. In Hawaii, many early shrines were formed from volcanic clay, and it was believed to have a restorative power.

**Cleaning:** The act of cleaning is often featured in dreams and can relate to organizational skills or spatial concepts. Depending on what was being cleaned and how the dreamer felt, the dream may illustrate themes of control, perspective, and renewal.

**Cliff:** Often representing a unique point of view, cliffs can be featured in dreams as relating to the sensations of elation and clarity or fear and insecurity. Many people dream of falling off a cliff, which can relate to loss of control. The symbol of a cliff in Taoism is that of a place of higher awareness. Context and association will define this dreaming symbol.

**Climbing:** The act of ascension is usually a positive one unless the dreamer feels burdened by the climb or is unable to reach a given destination. Climbing in dreams is fairly common, and the meaning can be found in the dreamer's ideas on goals and aspirations, as well as in the dream story line.

**Cloak:** *See Cape*

**Clock:** Clocks are highly elusive symbols relating to the passage of time and its relevance to the dreamer's life. Clocks have been around since ancient days and have a spiritual representation of the passage of the soul as well as the connection between humanity and the solar system. Probe the intuitive resonance as well as the emotional sensations in order to interpret a dream featuring a clock or timepiece.

**Closet:** While closets have a modern reference to the theme of sexual repression, they are also symbolic of a place to house clothing and basic individual identity. Often closets are found in children's dreams because of the size and number of closets in a home.

**Clothing:** Closely connected to identity, clothing is often found in dreams and typically symbolizes a given aspect of the larger dreaming story. Depending on which type of clothing was more prominent, many different interpretations can be found. Explore personal ideology and material identity for a greater dream meaning.

**Clouds:** Lofty and elusive, clouds reflect the concept of unknown potential, because they form in infinite shapes and sizes. They are also associated with themes of flying and the heavens. Chinese mythology portrays clouds as symbols of peace. Dreams of clouds usually offer a unique perspective and a greater journey toward a new wisdom.

**Clover:** This Celtic symbol of good luck is found throughout the British and Irish cultures and is formally referred to as the shamrock. Because it has three leaves, it is representative of the Holy Trinity and, in modern thought, a symbol of good fortune if found with four leaves.

**Clown:** Traditionally connected to the ridiculous and the foolish, clowns date back to the medieval form of the jester. It was then believed that these individuals or entertainers had greater insights on humanity and its flaws. Personal association will define a dream featuring this perplexing symbol of human imperfection.

**Coal:** Black and gritty, coal is a fuel and a way to create fire. It is also symbolic of blackness on a general level; because of its modern associations to the Christmas traditions, "coal in your stocking," it can be associated with negative behavior or shame. Intuitive reasoning and personal association will define this dream.

**Coat:** Coats worn to shelter from the cold are found in many dreams, and yet coats for dress or other forms of occupation, such as military coats, are symbolic of identity and cultural placement. Context and association will define a dream featuring a coat symbol.

**Cobra:** An ancient Egyptian symbol of regal position and power, the cobra has modern associations of fear and a venomous bite. Cobras are also connected to the folkloric and cultural concept of the snake charmer and that which can be tamed.

**Cobweb:** Because cobwebs are connected to spiders, they are often feared and can appear in dreams as surreal traps for the dreamer to fall into. Depending on how the symbol played a role in the dream, intuitive reasoning will most likely define the larger dreaming message.

**Cocoon:** A symbol of life, death, and rebirth, the cocoon is much like the womb in that it houses life until it is ready to be born again. Because it connects to the butterfly, it can also represent reincarnation or the act of personal transformation.

**Coffin:** Found in modern horror films as a symbol of the macabre, coffins are often viewed with fear and trepidation in the dreaming landscape. However, they can also be reflective of a place of rest and resolution, depending on the larger dreaming story line. Context and placement will define this dreaming symbol.

**Coins:** While coins are representative of monetary and financial associations, they are also symbolic of time and the numeric value of the given coin. Since they have been in existence from ancient cultures to the present day, they have a connective symbolism of history, antiquity, and value.

**Cold:** Differences in temperature such as extremes of heat or cold often reflect the dreamer's connective associations within a given framework. Cold or frigid dreaming landscapes can also represent the concept of being "frozen" in a given situation or event.

**College:** Much like a dreaming environment of high school, college represents a place of higher learning and will usually reveal aspects of the dreamer's personal experience in the given landscape.

**Colors:** Color systems are very important in dreams because of the emotional and intuitive symbolism they provide within the dreaming story. Because color systems relate to elements like earth or water, they have huge symbolic connections and should be explored on an individual basis, as well as in their dreaming context *(see specific colors)*.

**Comet:** Much like meteors, comets are usually associated with the fantastic or planetary forces of speed. Comets have a common association with enlightenment or exceptional circumstances with phrases like "hit by a comet" and usually relate to idea, insight, and new concepts of awareness.

**Compass:** This ancient drafting tool has modern representations relating to direction and the concept of "finding one's way." Compasses symbolically represent direction, knowledge, intuition, and also orientation. Depending on how a compass was used or featured in the dream, it could represent a new journey or path.

**Computer:** A modern, everyday device for work, play, and learning, the computer is a common element in dreams. Computers can represent the ulterior ideas of self or concepts of study, work, industry, and intellectual pursuits, depending on how the dreamer uses this technical wonder in his or her daily life.

**Concert:** Dreams featuring concerts and music are usually positive experiences and can represent creativity, enlightenment, joy, and also other emotional connections related to the dreamer's life and experiences.

**Conch:** While the conch has a great mystique to Oceanic and Caribbean cultures, it is often associated with the bounty of the ocean or music. In Hindu and Buddhist traditions, however, it is a spiritual symbol of the call to enlightenment.

**Construction:** Dreams of construction and debris connect to concepts of building, organization, repair, and also industry on a general level. Depending on what was being constructed and how the dreamer felt, the dream may relate to new avenues of awareness or ways of approaching goals in life.

**Contest:** Contests are fairly common in dreams and, much like winning awards or other pursuits of accolades, relate to the dreamer's emotional legacy and impressions during the dream. Dreams featuring contests carry a basic symbolism of human worth, value, and competition.

**Convent:** The female order or version of a monastery, a convent is a place of learning and monastic life in the Catholic faith. Personal association and ideology will determine the meaning of this spiritual and religious dreaming environment.

**Cook or Cooking:** The act of cooking is a creative and personal pursuit relating to nourishment and care. Depending on who was cooking and what was being prepared, the dream may carry many different meanings. Context, association, and intuitive understanding should be used in interpreting a dream about cooking.

**Cop:** *See Police*

**Copper:** This metal used in many ancient cultures is often associated with hearth, home, and femininity. Because of its rich, warm color, it is valued highly in Celtic symbolism and also represents undiscovered truth.

**Coral:** Found in the Greek myth of Medusa, coral has an ancient legacy relating to preciousness and an oceanic rarity. Coral is valued in Hawaii relating to its color (red, pink, black, and gold) and has a symbolic resonance of that which is pure or genuine.

**Corner:** Dreams of rounding a corner or sensing something around a corner are highly intuitive in nature and design. Dreams featuring this symbol may feel frightening or exciting and act as a metaphor for undiscovered truth or new vistas of awakening.

**Cornucopia:** In Greek mythology, Amalthea nursed Zeus to health by providing him with a horn of plenty. This symbol has become known in our modern day with connections of bounty, abundance, and offering.

**Corridor:** *See Hall or Hallway*

**Costume:** Costumes and disguises mask the true self and, featured in dreams, they can relate to varying themes of identity, perception, and human approach. Context and type of costume will likely determine the importance and also intuitive message of the dream.

**Cottage:** A small and cozy version of a home, cottages are highly associative depending on the dreamer's personal history. Many people think of them in terms of fairy tales, such as "Little Red Riding Hood," and therefore there may be a childlike link to a dream featuring this symbol.

**Country or Countryside:** Dreams featuring the countryside or a landscape that is natural offer a unique perspective because they are unencumbered by the modern world. Probe the associative emotions to the given backdrop in order to integrate it with the larger dreaming message.

**Court:** Being in court or on trial is a common dreaming motif that can relate to balance, justice, fairness, and human laws. Often these dreams are anxiety-oriented; however, personal association will tell the larger dreaming story.

**Cow:** This wonderful bovine creature is considered sacred in the Hindu culture, while in the West we view the cow as a symbol of nourishment because of its milk. Ancient Sumerians believed that the cow was a symbol of femininity and the moon. Many Nordic cultures accept it as the forceful and powerful female equivalent to the bull.

**Cowboy or Cowgirl:** The western motif of a cowboy or cowgirl is an American symbol and is often associated with the pioneer or maverick spirit. Depending on how this archetypal figure was featured in the dream, the dreamer may be exploring themes of discovery and new ideology.

**Co-Worker:** Dreams featuring office mates or co-workers can reveal issues pertaining to career, employment, identity, and also basic themes of industry and advancement. Much like dreams featuring family members or friends, these dreams relate to our perceptions of self within a working environment and should be interpreted using context, association, and intuitive reasoning.

**Coyote:** This Native American symbol of cunning is often equated with archetypal human qualities of being a wanderer, glutton, outlaw, pragmatist, and a survivor. Because this desert creature is tenacious, it can also represent internal will or purpose of resolve.

**Crab:** This dualistic sea crustacean has a rich mythological and spiritual history. In astrology it is associated with the sign of Cancer and represents femininity, emotion, and tenacity. It is also closely connected to the planetary symbolism of the moon. In ancient Greek myth the crab took on the role of philosopher and symbolized new awakenings of consciousness.

**Crash:** Dreams featuring crashing or viewing some type of crash often relate to the basic concepts of time, disaster, and outcome. While many of these dreams are frightening, they also ask the dreamer to explore the larger scope of the dreaming message. Depending on the crash experience, the dream may connect to problem solving, conflict, or themes of endings and beginnings. Context will define this dream.

**Crawling:** Many people dream of crawling to and from places or in and out of tiny spaces. The act of crawling connects to infancy and the sensation of vulnerability, weakness, or lack of individual strength in a given context.

**Crazy:** Dreams of insanity or of crazy individuals and situations are fairly common and can carry emotional legacies of fear, euphoria, concern, anxiety, and also shame and lack of understanding. Explore the symbolic imagery along with the greater dreaming story for understanding.

**Creek:** Creeks, brooks, and streams carry the basic symbolic association of water *(see Water)* and yet also are associated with rivers *(see River)*, the flow of movement, and the concept of the journey. Explore the placement of the symbol along with individual associations for the dreaming meaning.

**Crescent:** The shape of the crescent is associated with the moon and its phases. It reveals the changing form of the world we know. It is also the emblem of Islam and, coupled with the star, it can represent divinity.

**Crime:** Crime story dreams can be terrifying or intriguing depending on the story and on the emotional legacy of the dream. Often the act of a crime being committed is a symbol for guilt, shame, fear, or doubt, but context will likely define a dream featuring a crime.

**Criminal:** The archetypal personification of the crime itself, a criminal is a more personal symbol of human failure or imperfection. If the dream featured a threatening criminal, the emotions and feelings will play a more prominent role than the character or symbol.

**Cripple:** *See Disabled and Handicapped*

**Crocodile:** Connected mythologically to the dragon in ancient symbol systems, the crocodile is also found in the Bible as a symbol of chaos or conflict. Because of its large jaws and teeth, it is viewed by many symbol systems as the devil or a creature of fear and terror. Explore how the emotions of sleep connect to waking realities.

**Cross:** A universal symbol for Christianity, the cross is found in many sects including Celtic, Greek, and Eastern European orthodox traditions. It represents compassion, humanity, divinity, God, Christ, spirituality, and the quest of the human spirit and eternal soul.

**Crossroad:** Crossroads or intersections are highly symbolic images in dreams, and they represent a point of decision—a fork in the road or a turning point—in the dreaming story or, perhaps, in the dreamer's waking life.

**Crowd:** Dreams of crowds or overwhelming gatherings of people can carry either a positive or negative association, depending on the dreamer and his or her perceptions of the crowd. While some crowd dreams relate to being part of a greater human whole, others are suffocating and claustrophobic. Association is vital in interpreting a dream with this symbol.

**Crown:** An imperial symbol of higher order or regal stature. The crown is also found in almost every culture and usually signifies the wearer's achievements in life. Crowns can also represent a higher spiritual order of attainment or material bounty, depending on how it was placed in the larger dreaming landscape.

**Crutches:** The act of using crutches is symbolic of dependence or reliance and, depending on placement, can relate to issues of purpose, survival, and human fragility. Association, metaphor, and context will determine the larger dreaming message.

**Crying:** The emotions of pain, fear, anxiety, and joy can all accompany the act of crying in a dream. Many people awaken from dreams of crying only to realize that no tears have been shed. This powerful symbol relates entirely to the emotional construct of the dream and should be explored from that point of view.

**Crystal:** Often a symbol of ancient alchemy or science, the property of crystal has great symbolism relating to illumination, light, ideology, spirit, and invention. If crystal objects were featured, the same symbolism applies and should be interpreted within the context of the entire dreaming story.

**Cube:** This three-dimensional geometrical formation is a part of many ancient symbol systems and can indicate completion or purpose and wholeness. Connected to dice and the square, the cube is also a symbol of stability and balance.

**Cup:** Cups are a modern representation of the chalice or the Holy Grail *(see Chalice and Grail)* and are objects that hold or contain things. Depending on how the cup was used, it may indicate abundance or completion, but association will likely reveal the larger dreaming message.

**Cupid:** Also known as the Greek god Eros, Cupid is the god of love and is known in modern representation as the symbol of St. Valentine's Day. This ancient symbol is an archetypal image representing love, romance, passion, and bliss.

**Cupboard:** Since pantries and cupboards are used to store food, they can relate to nourishment or other acts of preservation and containment. It is vital to explore what was contained in the cupboard and how it related to the overall dreaming experience.

**Curtain:** Much like a veil or a closet, curtains are representative of the enclosure of the material world. They can either reveal or conceal depending on their placement in the dream. Metaphor and context will define this dreaming theme.

**Cut or Cutting:** Many dreams feature the act of cutting an object or the fear of being harmed and cut by a knife or other sharp tool. Dreams of being cut are often frightening and relate to physical vulnerability. Dreams that illustrate cutting paper or other objects can also connect to creative acts or problem solving.

**Daisy:** This beautiful spring flower comes in many differing sizes and colors; however, it is typically symbolized in the traditional white and yellow formation. It can represent youth, innocence, luck, and joy and is often experienced as a positive dreaming symbol.

**Damage:** Dreams of damage or ill-repair can be complex in form and meaning because they relate to problem solving as well as to structural definitions. Depending on what was damaged and the emotional legacy, the dream may have many meanings. Association and metaphor will play a large role in defining a dream of damage.

**Dance or Dancing:** Dreams of dancing or watching others dance are often illuminating and joyous experiences. Much like dreams featuring themes of flying, the act of dance is found in many cultural traditions relating to celebrating, spirituality, and human potential.

**Danger:** Dreams that carry a message of terror or danger often represent other emotional themes. Depending on the severity of danger felt and the overall dreaming story, the dream may connect to aspects of anxiety, worry, stress, panic, fear, and also vulnerability. Context is vital for interpreting this dreaming theme.

**Dark or Darkness:** The opposite of light or lightness, darkness in dreams can reflect the mysterious and has many emotional associations such as fear, doubt, and confusion. In Hindu, Christian, and Buddhist religions, darkness represents a fall from grace, disillusionment, lack of purpose, or being spiritually lost.

**Dawn:** Symbolic of illumination, rebirth, rejuvenation, and newness, the dawn of a new day is spiritually represented in many ancient mythological systems. Dawn is also reflective of the lunar and solar cycles and their connection to universal themes of light, vision, and discovery.

**Deaf or Deafness:** Many people dream of being unable to speak or hear and awaken terrified. The meanings of these dreams often relate to basic internal conflicts or metaphors of change and disability. Themes of communication and understanding should be probed to define this dreaming symbol.

**Death:** While death is a universal symbol often carrying negative connotations, it represents rebirth in many religious and spiritual traditions. Symbols of death, like the skull or the coffin, can be terrifying to the dreamer. Dreams of death should be explored in terms of how they relate to change, transition, and new ways of thinking.

**Deer:** In the animal kingdom, deer are one of the few species that mate for life. Because of their beauty and striking antlers, they are found in ancient Nordic and Christian iconography representing rebirth, strength, and divine blessing. In Celtic myth, deer are messengers to the other world of spirit and God.

**Defense:** Dreams of defending oneself or others are fairly common and usually carry themes of reaction, strategy, and the emotional legacy of anger, fear, or altruism. Dreams carrying this theme should be explored in terms of the overall emotional message along with the greater story line and meaning.

**Deformed or Deformity:** Dreams of deformity are often surreal and can feature a person or a material object in transition or unusual form. These dreams relate to transformation or identity but should be interpreted in terms of basic symbolism and context.

**Demolition:** Dreams of destruction or demolition can be paradoxical. If the thing being destroyed creates a positive experience for the dreamer, the dream will have an entirely different meaning than the ruin of a valued item. Context and association will determine the significance of this dreaming action and theme.

**Demon:** Demons, while somewhat comparable to the devil, are often a folkloric version of threat or danger. In dreams, they can take on any form, from an evil giant to a demonic snake, and should be explored in terms of intuitive experience and the larger dreaming message.

**Dentist:** This modern occupation has an often anxiety-ridden association in dreams. Many people fear going to the dentist and this waking trepidation can bleed into dreaming story and theme; however, association will define this dreaming symbol.

**Depression:** Dreams of depression and extreme sadness typically relate to a part of the dreamer's waking reality. The theme of depression in a dream or the overall sense of loss should be explored by coupling daily parallels and dreaming insights.

**Desert:** Vast landscapes of barren or desert plains often reflect an openness of thought or a spatial association of separateness. Depending on the role of the landscape and the experience, the dream may take on the context of discovery, challenge, or exploration.

**Desk:** Often connected with concepts of work, industry, and creativity, desks are usually very personal symbols in dreams and can also relate to organizational skills, higher learning, or education.

**Dessert:** Sweet and tempting, desserts in dreams are also connected to basic themes of food and nourishment. They can symbolize decadence, reward, or even sensuality depending on the dreamer's personal association and the particular dessert.

**Detour:** Dreams of being detoured or derailed from a given mission or journey are often indicative of change and conflict within the dreaming story. Meaning will depend on how the element of problem solving and the challenges were handled in the dream.

**Devil:** Also known as Lucifer, Beelzebub, and Satan, the prince of darkness is largely connected to Christian traditions, although many spiritual traditions carry a similar symbolism of evil and hatred. Because the concept of the devil is highly symbolic, in dreams the basic elements usually become images that represent hatred, lies, evil, deceit, and horror. Spiritual definitions and personal ideology should be used when interpreting a dream featuring this symbol.

**Devotion:** Dreams featuring themes or emotions of devotion are usually euphoric and sentient in nature. These dreams can be very powerful, and the larger story and dreaming message should be explored as the concept of devotion can relate to spiritual enlightenment and soulful attainment.

**Dew:** *See Mist*

**Diamond:** This powerful and valuable gem is symbolic in many cultural traditions and spiritual systems. Because of its hardness, it is often associated with permanence or indestructibility. Because the gift of a diamond is connected to marital tradition, it can also symbolize love, infinity, and romance. Diamonds were treasured by early Christian societies as a symbol of Christ, and the stone, because of its brilliance and ability to trap and reflect light, represents illumination of soul and being.

**Dining Room:** The various rooms within a house play different roles in the dreaming landscape. Dining rooms usually are associated with family, eating, and collective gatherings. Context and metaphor should be explored when interpreting dreams with a dining room as a backdrop.

**Dinosaur:** These ancient and extinct creatures hold a great fascination in the modern framework of thought. Because these creatures are intangible to us, they often represent the mystical, mythical, and unknown. They can also be connected to concepts of being outdated as well as fantasy themes of monsters or wildness.

**Dirt:** Dirt, much like filth, often connects to our ideas of its association and how it was featured in the given dream. While traditional interpretation correlated the presence of dirt to emotions of shame, dreams of being dirty can also connect to self-image and identity.

**Disabled:** Dreams of being disabled or wounded can indicate a symbolic representation of a larger waking issue. Many people dream of being crippled or viewing others who have been harmed, and these dreams offer emotions of compassion, pain, longing, and reflection.

**Disguise:** *See Costume*

**Dishes:** A basic household object, dishes relate to domesticity, food, eating, and nourishment, but they can also be associated with breakability or housework, i.e., "doing the dishes." Focus on how the symbol was integrated within the larger dreaming story.

**Diving:** Dreams of diving are akin to flying dreams because they capture the power of possibility and promise. If the emotion of fear was felt, the dive may relate to time passing too quickly or being out of control. Context and intuitive experience will determine the integration of this powerful dreaming symbol.

**Dock:** Because docks are found in harbors and connect to the stationing of a vessel, they can represent safety and a haven from the open water. If a dock was featured in your dream, explore the role it played in the larger dream message.

**Doctor:** Much like a dentist, the doctor is an archetypal symbol that causes fear for many dreamers because of the concept of examination. However, the symbol of the doctor is essentially one of the healer or a persona who can aid in physical crises. Personal association and ideology will aid in capturing the relevance of this dreaming symbol.

**Dog:** This domestic creature is connected to modern traditions of loyalty, honesty, and purpose. In many ancient cultures, including Egyptian, Nordic, and Aztec societies, dogs were valued as symbols of the afterlife or spirits of the dead.

**Doll:** A toy of childhood, dolls are usually connected to feminine maturation and play. They also carry a great deal of symbolism in specific cultures representing human form and identity. Depending on the intuitive connection to the doll, the dream may relate to self-discovery or the exploration of internal innocence, but association will define the dream.

**Dolphin:** These wonderful sea mammals are highly intelligent and sentient in their movement. In Greek mythology, Apollo was known to have taken the form of the dolphin at sea. In modern traditions, dolphins are seen as insightful symbols of the ocean and carry a mystical association to intuitive healing.

**Donkey:** This ancient symbol of foolishness and pride has many differing meanings from varying cultures. While some view the donkey as a representation of stupidity, other cultures value it as a symbol of loyalty and position. Association is vital in placing the meaning behind this dualistic dreaming symbol.

**Doomsday:** Dreams of Armageddon or doomsday scenarios are fairly common in modern dreaming lore. They represent the end of the world as we know it. These dreams should be explored in terms of their symbolic meaning, as well as overall correlation to waking life.

**Door:** Doors in dreams act as gateways to differing times, places, landscapes, and ideas. Because they are highly symbolic, they usually connect to the varying components of our minds, spirits, or thoughts and should be explored in context of the other dreaming elements and experiences.

**Dove:** This lovely white bird is found in ancient Egyptian and Greek mythology as a symbol of peace and a sacrificial being. In Christian traditions, it is also valued as a diplomatic representation offering an olive branch at the end of the Great Flood.

**Dracula:** Originating from the fifteenth-century figure, Vlad the Impaler, the legend of Dracula is usually correlated with the undead or a creature of mystical dark powers. Because of modern film and movie lore, there is also a basic association with sexuality and gothic romanticism; however, association will define the importance of this dreaming symbol.

**Dragon:** A powerful symbol of the unknown and the mythical, the dragon is the only symbol in Chinese astrology that is not a real animal. It represents power, force, intuition, and discovery. The dragon also personifies heroic skill in medieval European folklore and fairy tales.

**Dragonfly:** Unlike the symbol of the dragon, the dragonfly is an intuitive symbol connecting to flight, speed, and awareness. In China, it represents the summer season, and to the Native Americans it is a symbol of higher knowledge, beauty, and understanding.

**Drama:** Acts of drama or elements in a dream relating to drama often connect to themes of theatrics or polarities of meaning. Depending on how drama was featured in the dream, new avenues of emotional insight or creative problem solving may be important to the dreaming message.

**Draw or Drawing:** The act of drawing or sketching in dreams relates to spatial orientation, creativity, and design. Many dreams feature pictures or images that later are revealed as important symbolic representations. Pay attention to details and metaphors in dreams featuring this theme.

**Dreaming:** Dreams within dreams are unusual and they take on the dimension of the surreal. Often dreams about dreaming relate to higher levels of spiritual exploration or pursuit. Interpretation of dreaming dreams should be probed, paying attention to detail and symbolic meaning.

**Dress:** An article of clothing closely associated with femininity, dresses are also connected to sexuality and identity. Depending on the type of dress, the color, and how it was worn, the dream may contain a variety of meanings.

**Drinking:** Dreams of drinking or quenching thirst are common and often relate to a physiological dream state or the dualistic concept of satiation and desire. Depending on the sensations or experience, the dream may take on symbolism of consumption and replenishment.

**Drowning:** Drowning in dreams is a common scenario, relating to the experience of fear and anxiety. Much like with dreams of choking or being unable to breathe, people who have a fear of water will find this dream terrifying. Explore parallels to a waking situation or concern.

**Drugs:** Drugs and alcohol in dreams are highly associative but tend to relate to the concept of loss of control or an illusionary reality. Often drugs are symbols of daily elements of conflict or other fear, and dreams with this symbol should be explored on an associative and contextual plane.

**Drunk:** *See Alcohol*

**Duck:** This water bird is known in the West as a quaint creature with a wonderful "quack" found in children's stories and folkloric resonance. In China, however, the duck is not only enjoyed as a delicacy, but also thought to be a masculine force of potency. Personal association will define a dream featuring this symbol from the natural world.

**Dump:** The dreaming landscape of a dump or a wasteland is confusing because the creation of garbage is a human act. Cluttered and in disarray, a trash yard can either be an experience of discovery or a place of doubt depending on the main concern and story line found in the dream.

**Dune:** Dunes are elusive desert formations, made of sand, pliable and changeable in the dreaming landscape. While they relate to the image of an oasis *(see Oasis),* they may also be much like a beach, a symbol of stationary resolve and guidance.

**Dusk:** The time of day when cycles begin to wane into the nocturnal side of life, dusk is found in many symbolic and spiritual traditions representing peace and renewal as well as rest and respite. Dusk is also associated with romance and wisdom because it is the period when the sun sets below the horizon.

**Dust:** Many dreams feature dust or clouds of dust that, much like mist, act as a force of interference for the dreamer. Dreams featuring dust can also relate to dirt and filth and should be explored in context to the larger dreaming story.

**Dynamite:** Explosive and powerful, dynamite is a twentieth-century symbol for that which can destruct, erupt, or cause change. If dynamite was featured, the dream should be probed in terms of emotional legacy and the larger dreaming story line.

**Eagle:** This regal and forceful bird has many representations in heraldic and also Egyptian traditions. It symbolizes power and dignity as well as integrity and truth. In America, where it is part of the national seal, it is connected with freedom and democracy.

**Ear:** The ear as part of the human anatomy relates to hearing as well as truth on a symbolic level. Many folk expressions like "an ear of corn" or "up to my ears in debt" relate to the ear playing a role in fundamental choices. Context will play a defined role in a dream of ears or hearing.

**Earth:** The earth is part of the symbol systems of four elements (water, fire, and air) and connects to humanity's quest for grounding in the natural world. Throughout the modern world, there are many cultures that represent the land as a mirror of humanity. In Australia and Hawaii, the earth is known as mother and creator. A dream of the earth can also reflect a return to simplicity. Depending on how the element was featured, context will usually play a larger role.

**Earthquake:** Even though earthquakes have been around since the beginning of evolution, the theme of being in an earthquake is a modern one of destruction and crisis. If you have experienced an earthquake, your associations will be strong and vivid. If you have not, the earthquake may be symbolic of unsettling events in your daily life.

**East:** In the east we associate the rising sun with the dawn of a new day. This image acts as a symbol for rebirth. The East can also be connected with Asia or what we know as the Far East. If you were traveling east, your dream may relate to direction, and context should be explored relating to the larger dreaming story.

**Eating:** Dreams about eating and nourishment can relate to hunger on a physiological level. The image of being fed or eating relates to satiating desires. Context and association take on a high level of importance in eating dreams.

**Eclipse:** On the lunar scale, an eclipse represents one planet overtaking or blinding another. Symbolically, to eclipse means to cloud or to obscure from view. If you dreamed of a solar or a lunar eclipse, probe your own intuitive vision and insight.

**Egg:** The egg is strongly associated with new life and the birth of spirit. In many symbol systems it also connects to unborn identity or the power of the individual. The raw unfettered form of life is a symbol of birth, newness, and raw material.

**Egypt:** Known as the birthplace of civilization, Egypt often is associated with ancient traditions and mysterious fortune. Many symbols of Egypt like the Sphinx and the pyramids have a strong mythological representation in modern culture. Indeed, Egypt gave birth to the symbol system with hieroglyphics.

**Eight:** Numerologically, eight is represented as a number of strength and power. Eight is an even number and also connected with the integration of intellect and spiritual insight.

**Electricity:** Dreams of electricity or electric light connect to associative ideas of power and force. The theme of electricity connects to energy in its raw form. Are you seeking energy? Is the force in your dream connected to your life? Examine these questions along with the property and the dream story.

**Elephant:** These wonderful and ancient beasts are highly regarded in both India and Africa where they roam in the wild. While their modern identity is equated with being endangered, they also hold a great mystical history connected with strength, healing, and intelligence.

**Elevator:** Themes of being trapped in an elevator or falling in an elevator are fairly common and connect to anxiety or lack of control. If you experienced an elevator dream, integrate emotional sensations with the dreaming story to interpret the importance of this modern symbol.

**Eleven:** Eleven is known as a master number along with 22 and 33. It symbolizes vision in its highest form. Eleven connects to prophecy, the future, and a deep level of intuitive insight.

**Embrace:** Human embrace is a powerful sensation. If you dreamed of embracing another or of being embraced, you are surely exploring your humanity and emotional connection to others.

**Embryo:** *See Egg*

**Emerald:** Because of its deep green color, the emerald is often associated with the earth and plant life. It is also symbolic of freedom and the planet Jupiter, representing wisdom and individuality.

**Employment:** Dreams of employment often relate to identity and the search for economic or work value. Themes of employment or employer changes can connect to symbols of career advancement and how it connects to life's purpose and meaning.

**Empty:** The theme of emptiness is dualistic and emotional. Dreams of finding empty objects or containers often represent problem-solving concepts. An empty room, an empty cup, or an empty pocketbook may also relate to a sense of missing elements in life.

**Erection:** Sexual dreams and erotic dreams can connect to a physiological state; however, dreaming of having an erection or seeing an erection usually connects to sexual and emotional desire. Explore the motivations of sleep for interpretation and meaning.

**Eruption:** The vista of a volcanic eruption or a geyser expresses unchained forces or natural explosion. Be it Vesuvius or Mauna Loa, an eruption can relate to emotions or your intellectual concepts. Unchannelled ideas and energies should be explored to define the meaning of this dream.

**Escape:** Dreams of escape or fleeing from something connect to the emotion of fear and the sense of being controlled. Depending on who was escaping and why, context will play a vital role in a dream featuring this theme.

**Evergreen:** As part of the forest, the evergreen plays a symbolic role as a life force in the dead of winter. In Christian traditions, a decorated evergreen reflects the light and warmth of natural life, as well as spiritual longevity.

**Exam:** Taking an exam in a dream is a common theme of anxious anticipation when the exam was unexpected. Depending on how powerful and confident the dreamer feels about the exam, the dream may relate to purpose, identity, intellect, and ability.

**Execute:** The act of execution or killing in dreams is symbolic of life cut short or taken quickly. Violence and its meaning connect to the human condition and rage. Explore the concept of violence and aggression to find a higher purpose within the contextual dreaming message.

**Exercise:** Physical activity and the associated value of health are found in many dreams. Depending on the dreamer's associations with concepts of physical power, the dream may relate to themes of happiness, strength, and fortitude or, alternately, work, endurance, and human limits.

**Eye:** Of all the human senses, the eye has a great symbolic representation of vision and insight. In justice, the eyes are covered for the ultimate truth to be seen. It is also connected with intellect and the soul. If the symbol of an eye played a featured role, examine the emotions you felt and connect them with the message of the nocturnal journey.

**Face:** The face is a part of the human anatomy associated with identity and personal beauty. The components of the lips, the eyes, and the mouth reveal themes of sensuality. Depending on the nature of the dream and the importance of the face, the dream may connect to themes of identity, self-awareness, and human understanding.

**Fair:** Large events like carnivals and fairs are found in many dreams. They often feature a variety of symbolism and players. Who was at the fair? How did it make you feel? Explore the emotional and intuitive connection in order to understand this dream.

**Fairy:** Fairies are folkloric creatures that are likened to angels with mystical abilities. They often symbolize fantasy and magic, acting as messengers or instruments of childhood joy and creative force.

**Falcon:** This hunting bird shares a similar mythological source to the eagle because of its strength and profile. In England, it is prized in heraldic traditions as well as in modern culture. Falcons are often noted as birds of incredible perception and instinct, making them an important symbol in any dream.

**Fall (season):** The season of autumn is a time of harvest and reward for the work during the year. It is celebrated in every culture as a time to take stock and renew ideas. It is also a time of creation for the coming year, a time to plant new seeds and give birth to new ideas. Context and the dreaming story are vital in understanding a dream set in the fall.

**Falling:** Dreams of falling are fairly common along with themes of climbing and running. This symbol implies control and a search for understanding of a situation or theme. Context and association will play a vital role in these dreams.

**Family:** Personal support systems and family connections frequently play a vital role in our dreams. Explore who carries a greater meaning in your dreams and how family dynamics parlay into the dreaming story.

**Fat:** The concept of being fat or thin in a dream often connects back to physical determinants and our ideas about outer appearances. Depending on who was overweight and why, the dream may relate to inner prejudice or being "weighed down" by something.

**Father:** The representation of a father relates to everything patriarchal and symbolic in the figure of guidance on a male level. In Christianity, God is known as the Holy Father. The symbol of the father usually connects back to paternal guidance and strength. Personal association will usually tell the story of a dream featuring this symbol.

**Fear:** The emotion of fear is one that can be found in many dreams. Many people dream of anxiety or peril over internal and external conflict. It is vital to explore the source of the dreaming fear in order to understand the motivations of the dreaming emotion.

**Feather:** The feather holds great symbolism in Mexican, Pacific, and Native American cultures. While it traditionally represents lightness of being, it also relates to plumage, adornment, and power. Peacock feathers are representative of vanity, whereas eagle feathers connect to pride and the human heart.

**Fence:** Fences act as symbols because of all that they enclose and also all that they exclude. Modern myth adds the concept of marriage and family with the phrase "white picket fence." Fences are symbolic of home and rustic scenes as well as boundaries and walls.

**Field:** Vast expanses of land like fields and plains relate to the unbound spirit and the connection between limitation and freedom. Often fields are connected to journeys and discovery. Association and emotional connection will tell the larger story of a dream featuring a field.

**Fig:** The fig leaf is often symbolically represented as a human vestment or clothing. The fig itself is symbolically connected to Eden and other biblical stories as a sweet and pleasing fruit. To Buddha it represented inner knowledge. Dreams of tasting or viewing figs may relate to themes of sweetness or other riches in life. Association is vital in interpreting a dream of a fig.

**Fight:** Dreams of conflict or fights usually relate to the person or object of confrontation. Depending on who was doing the fighting and what it represents, inner emotions of anger, frustration, and doubt may be at play. Context is vital for understanding.

**File:** This everyday symbol for holding documents or other information has a modern significance in dreams. Depending on what the file held or a given desire to open the file, elements of problem solving may be at work in the dreaming story.

**Film:** Film has become a modern parable for the celluloid version of our world. Much like a mirror image, a film can tell a story, be a contextual thing, or even act as entertainment. Story and form will aid in understanding a dream where a film or a movie played a role.

**Find:** The quest to find something or someone plays a vital role in the land of dreams. Trying to discover an element or a person connects to the nature of discovery and desire. Emotional and intuitive skills will play a vital role in determining the nature of the search and its connection to waking life.

**Finger:** The fingers are a part of the human body typically associated with a sense of touch. They also act as an instruction tool with the definitions of "pointer" or "index finger." Closely connected with the hand, they are symbolically part of individual identity and ability.

**Fire:** A strong and forceful symbol of energy and consumption, fire can be found in many spiritual and mythological texts. In the Bible it is connected with inspiration as well as the flames of hell. In Polynesia, it relates to the natural force of the gods and their power over humanity. Explore the primary function of the fire and how it related to the dreaming story.

**Firefly:** Fireflies often reflect the essence of childhood and the innocence of simplicity. Since they connect to symbols systems of fire and light, they can also represent divine presence and order.

**Fireman:** Firemen often act as archetypal symbols of good over evil. If you know a firefighter, your associations will be very different from someone who does not. Explore the context and placement of this heroic figure and how it relates to the larger dreaming story.

**Fireplace:** Warming and healing in form, a fireplace typically connects to heart, home, and the goodness of nourishment. Fireplaces in ancient Europe represented the eternal flame and the light of God that could not be extinguished.

**Fish:** Strongly associated with the sign of Pisces in astrology, the fish is a water dweller and can symbolize the unconscious mind or the unfound reality beneath the currents of emotion. In many oceanic societies fish are associated with love, peace, and the afterlife.

**Fishing:** The act of fishing relates to probing the depths of the water and searching for a catch. This could connect symbolically to other areas of life, career, or love. Context and association will play a vital role in interpreting this dream.

**Five:** Highly connected with the symbol of the star or the pentacle, the number five represents freedom and good fortune. It is also associated with creativity, represented in the five-petaled lotus and the lily flower.

**Flag:** A symbol of statehood and honor, there are many flags of symbolism and unique identity. If a flag was featured in your dream, it may be also highlighting something. Focus on the iconography and probe personal associations with this symbol of glory.

**Flame:** Single flames hold the symbolism of an inextinguishable fire, or the idea of eternal life. Strongly associated with reincarnation, the flame also connects to the journey between one element and another. Probe the connection between the flame and concepts of passion, ideology, and spirit.

**Flirtation:** Dreams of flirtation bring issues of desire and identity together. The act of flirting delves into concepts of need, desire, and human attention. If flirtation is a theme, the larger issue of emotional reaction may play a role. Context and association are vital in understanding dreams of flirtation and response.

**Floating:** Levitation or floating in a dream is a very surreal experience and many people wonder about the significance of this event. Floating relates to weightlessness or to the act of meditation and being free from burden. Explore this concept and focus on the central story of sleep in order to interpret a dream featuring a floating anomaly.

**Flood:** Floods are a unique dreaming theme because they relate to mass destruction but can often reveal enlightening events because of the pliable factor of the presence of water. Floods symbolize the floodgates of thought or the wave of a force over humanity. Probe intuitive and emotional connections with this dream.

**Flower:** Flowers, with their vibrancy and fragile nature, often symbolize youth and beauty. They are also representative of the innocence of life and creation. Flowers or fields of flowers can relate to love and romance or to the perfume and ecstasy of nature.

**Flying:** Flying dreams are wonderful, and many people awaken feeling free and unencumbered. Nineteenth-century English lore believed that dreams of flying portended love. Certainly the sensation of flying can connect to any heightened emotion and the freedom of being able to explore worlds beyond the waking dimension.

**Fog:** The presence of fog in dreams can act like a surreal and literal translation of confusion and doubt. Fog is the blockade between light or illumination and darkness. In Nordic myth it is known as the land between heaven and the sky, holding value much like the clouds.

**Follow:** The act of following or pursuing in dreams is often related to themes of control, fear, discovery, desire, or resolve. The need to locate a person or a thing can also relate to concepts of spatial orientation or problem solving. Association, emotion, and story line will define the dream of following or being followed.

**Food:** Food symbolizes nourishment, satiation, and sometimes adventure. If your dream featured food and you were hungry, the dream may have a physiological root. Emotion and desire should be explored in order to place a food dream in a proper context. Focus on what food was featured and why.

**Foot:** Feet and footprints are highly symbolic in many spiritual traditions because they relate to freedom and movement. It is said that walking in Buddha's footprints will bring enlightenment, and in Christianity feet are valued as a point of humility. In Hawaii, footprints of the gods are said to lead the way to ancient ritual sites.

**Foreign:** Dreams that feature foreign countries or people usually connect to definite components of a story taking place. The symbolic reference relates to themes of unfamiliar territory or the unknown. Depending on the experience in a given place or with a specific person, the dream can take on a variety of meanings relating to context.

**Forest:** Forests are often symbolic of an undiscovered country or a part of the mind. They differ from individual trees in dreams because a forest is typically part of a valuable natural landscape or journey, often connecting to spirituality and inner wisdom.

**Fort:** Fortresses or forts represent protective structures or places to be safe from any outside forces. They can have a mystical quality and can represent a strong point of view. Context and waking parallels must be examined to explore a dream featuring a fortress.

**Fountain:** Fountains are springs of water that illuminate, decorate, and create romance. They act much like a modern version of a geyser, and they represent a meeting place or a never-ending infinite force.

**Four:** The number four is a strong and vital number often connected with discipline, order, and balance. It is associated with the cross because of its four points as well as the four seasons and other worldly elements.

**Fox:** While the fox is noted as part of the hunt, it is also a symbol of intellect and beauty. In Persian traditions it is linked with fire, and in Asia it is connected with eroticism. Modern views often convey sexual expression, such as "too foxy for me."

**Frame:** Highly symbolic because they put pictures or art in context, frames often emphasize placement in dreams. They can represent individual identity, creativity, or artistic force and should be valued within their intuitive context.

**Free:** Dreams of freedom or escaping from a given set of circumstances can be very powerful and usually connect back to letting go of old ideas or emotions. Dreams of freedom can be healing in nature and should be cherished as a rite of passage in your dreaming pursuits.

**Friend:** Dreams relating to friendship usually incorporate basic themes of human understanding. Dreams representing the nature of a specific friendship should be explored from an intuitive perspective, integrating the symbolic nature of the dream.

**Frog:** While these land- and water-loving creatures have a negative connotation in folklore, the frog represents wisdom in many symbol systems and is adored as a healing being by many cultures. Association plays a strong role in this dream interpretation.

**Frozen:** Frozen things or landscapes often represent things that are immovable or fixed. Depending on the nature of the dream, the dreamer may be seeking out new ways of problem solving or working with issues that have previously been unalterable in your world.

**Fruit:** Symbols of the sweet part of the natural world, fruit is connected to the sensual aspect of life and the season of spring. In dreams, fruit can represent many emotions including bliss and joy. The tasting of fruit may relate to themes of nourishment, discovery, sweetness, bitterness, happiness, or peace.

**Funeral:** Dreams of funerals and death can relate to transition or a spiritual representation of the afterlife. If you experience a funeral in your dream, it is important to understand that it may mean that you are really exploring changes in your waking world. Work on embracing the dream as a metaphor for the value of life and of relationships.

**Furniture:** Furniture is much like rooms of a house in that they often connect the dots in a dreaming story. Symbolically, furniture may represent an intellectual or emotional level of thinking. Context and intuitive construct should be used in exploring a dream featuring furniture and its arrangement.

**Gallery:** Galleries of art or other displays are viewing arenas. They often feature significant or relevant events and objects. Explore the sensation found in the landscape and work on integrating context and theme.

**Gambling:** Dreams of gambling often connect back to the concept of life and the games we play. They also reveal our perceptions of luck and the mystery of the unknown. Dice markers and other symbols can bring numbers and significant events in dreams.

**Game:** Tactical maneuvers and the acts of sport are related to games of every sort. From chess to football, games in dreams relate to our sense of ability and our purpose in life's efforts. Dreams of watching games may relate to problem solving or emotional experience within a given framework. Explore the nature of the game to decipher the dreaming meaning.

**Gangster:** The gangster image is a twentieth-century metaphor for power and corruption. Many people dream of gangsters wielding machine guns or perhaps luring them into a world of crime. This archetypal image is an everyday symbol for the crime world and its general contextual landscape.

**Garage:** Garages and other large vacant buildings like warehouses often act as storehouses for the dreaming collective. If you have a personal association with garages or mechanics and cars, the dream will have a greatly different meaning than that of an empty garage.

Probe the landscape and your intuitive sensations along with the dreaming story.

**Garden:** This natural landscape has a rich history of positive construction in myth and religion. Of course, the Garden of Eden is an old biblical story of love and redemption. In Buddhism and Taoism, the garden represents a path of enlightenment or nirvana. Because of their green and floral content, gardens also carry a great symbolism of peace, harmony, self-reflection, and understanding.

**Garlic:** An ancient plant mythologically connected to lightning, garlic was once symbolic of higher learning. In modern association it has been connected with good health and general well-being. Because many people have a strong opinion on this bulbous plant, garlic in dreams can be a positive or negative experience depending on association.

**Garnet:** This deep red stone has a great history and is known as the Greek wedding stone. Red garnet is an energizer that is mythologically believed to work with the circulatory and generative sexual systems. It stimulates life force or *chi*. Green garnet is known as a purifier. Its greatest usage comes in combination with red garnet to create proper physical polarization, i.e., balancing of yin and yang. Black garnet works with grounding and balancing the mental, emotional, and physical bodies.

**Gate:** Gates carry a strong spiritual and symbolic meaning because they represent an entrance to a given destination. In Christianity, there are the gates to heaven and hell. In Buddhist symbolism, there is a gate into the afterlife. Dreams featuring a gate may relate to individual path, a new way of thinking, or a new perspective relating to the dream story and context.

**Genie:** The mythical and phantasmagorical figure of a genie is often connected to the magic of transformation and creation. In modern fable, genies are portrayed as well-wishing Buddhas, able to grant secret desires.

**Ghost:** The concept of spirit life or "hauntings" brought ghosts into folklore in the early fifth century. Apparitions exist within every mythological culture, and the view of a ghost in a dream usually has a personal association. Fear is typically associated with seeing a ghost. If the ghost represented a vision of a loved one departed, the dreamer may be integrating their soulful and spiritual placement.

**Giant:** A figure from fable and folklore, the appearance of a giant in a dream can represent many things relating to size and ability. Depending on the dreaming story, the giant may be an archetype for self or anything that looms over the dreamer's mind. Emotions will play an integral part in interpreting a dream of a giant or anything related to change in human size and shape.

**Gift:** Gift giving in dreams often carries a dualistic meaning. Giving or receiving unexpected presents can bring a pleasant sense of bounty or, alternately, a feeling of unworthiness. Probe the context and landscape of the dream along with emotions and instinctual ideas about the gifts being offered or taken.

**Giraffe:** Tall and elegant, demure and yet powerful, the giraffe has a unique place in the animal kingdom and in dreaming lore. Because of its ability to see a great distance, giraffes can often represent perspective or the untamed heart of docility. Association is essential in interpreting a dream featuring a giraffe.

**Girl:** Dreams of unknown people tend to represent their gender group. If you dreamed of a young girl, the role she plays in the dream will probably tell the larger story. As a quality of femininity and youth, innocence may also be important in understanding the dream.

**Girlfriend:** Typically, dreams of spouses, lovers, and friends connect back to basic questions or emotional issues of the dreamer. If you dreamed of a girlfriend, probe the nature of the story line and context in order to unravel the larger message and purpose of the dream.

**Glass:** Fragile, delicate, and transparent, glass is often associated with water or the paradoxical nature of life. Dreams of broken glass can relate to disillusionment or lost desires. Glass in its beauty and perfection can represent that which is unchangeable and impenetrable. Explore the intuitive dynamic of dreams featuring glass in the landscape.

**Glasses:** Eye glasses are representative of vision or insight. They often are featured in dreams with a great degree of insight. Explore how the glasses connect with the overall intuitive message of the dream and ask yourself how your life's questions relate to the dreaming construct.

**Glue:** Dreams that feature things held together with adhesives are related to the concept of integration or placing two different ideas together. The larger message of the dream may relate to human understanding or connection on a material plane.

**Goat:** In varying mythological traditions, the goat appears, offering many forms of symbolism. A figure of durability and tenacity, the goat is associated with the sign of Capricorn. These creatures are also known as scavengers and are often associated with landscapes of the plains and mountains.

**God:** Many people dream of God and feel that they grow closer to their spiritual and faithful pursuits in the vista of seeing their Deity. The ability to connect on a higher plane is highly soulful and personal, making a dream featuring God a divine journey. Explore your life's path and your spiritual and religious definitions if you find yourself facing God in the land of dreams.

**Goddess:** Much like a dream of God, concepts of the Goddess relate to female energy and, often, the idea of mother earth. In varying mythological traditions, there are many Goddess stories and icons. Depending on the nature and context of the Goddess vision, the dream will likely tell a story of divine power and universal force.

**Gold:** This precious metal is often associated with wealth, success, and power. In biblical stories there is the story of the Golden Calf. The color of gold is also treasured by the Aztecs as a representation of the Sun God. Modern understanding of the metal and color contextually places gold with monetary value and a standard of precious measure.

**Goose:** In ancient cultures the goose was associated with femininity and home life. Much like the swan, this long-necked bird has a great deal of grace and beauty. Fairy tales like Mother Goose bring a welcome and pleasing image to mind, and the story of the goose that laid the golden egg illustrates the power of motherhood.

**Gorilla:** This huge ape is known in modern views as a powerful buffoon or a comical representation of humankind. In reality, gorillas are powerful and intelligent animals, and much revered in Africa and Australia. Context and association should be explored in order to define a dream of this complex and misunderstood beast.

**Government:** Powerful and bureaucratic, government or governing as a symbol often relates to judicious choices or, in some examples, "red tape." Context and ideology relating to government and its place will define the dream.

**Grail:** Grails and chalices carry a great symbolism with medieval legends and the story of the Holy Grail. As a cup of Christ, the grail holds a significance of eternal life and salvation. A goblet for many things from wine to water, it is also known in Celtic traditions as a spiritual holder of truth.

**Grandparent:** Relatives and family members often appear in dreams acting as a background of heritage and familial understanding. If you dream of your grandparent or grandparents, your ideas, emotions, and representative emotions about your family will play a pivotal role in understanding the dream.

**Granite:** This hard and sturdy stone is found in many ancient structures and represents permanence and durability. Granite has a water-soluble property, making it shine, and it can also symbolize industry, invention, and the idea.

**Grapes:** Grapes serve a symbolic function of the fruits of labor or bounty and reward during the time of harvest. Because they are used to make wine, they are symbolically associated with drink, spirituality, and well-being. If your dream featured grapes, explore the context and story line of the dream for greater understanding.

**Grass:** Often connected with vitality and health, the image of grass is a vision of growth and natural creation. Traditionally grass also relates to unity and wholeness because of the concept of a single blade and its relation to the whole. If your dream featured grass, context and association will play a vital role in the sensations and messages of the overall dreaming story.

**Graveyard:** Featured in horror movies and other popular myths, a graveyard is often a frightening and eerie symbol of death. Graveyards are burial grounds and connect to our definitions of life and afterlife. Probe spiritual perspectives on soul and the meaning of death in your world.

**Gray:** Like the expressions "gray matter" and "gray area," this color has become a modern representation of ambiguity and vague dimension. In dreams, a gray landscape might feel frightening or calming, depending on the dreamer's emotional response and the dream's larger message.

**Green:** The color green carries a symbolism of honor and vitality, regality and luster. Because it is connected to nature, it also is associated in many myths with growth and regeneration. The emerald is thought of as a powerful gem of mystery. Culturally, the color green is strongly associated with Ireland and American money.

**Groom:** Wedding themes are fairly common, and dreams featuring brides or grooms are ceremonial in nature and theme. Often the image of the groom may represent a masculine association or a symbol of romance on a general level. Context is vital in understanding this dreaming theme.

**Guilt:** The feeling of guilt is extremely powerful and can often overtake the dreamer. If the dream yielded an overall sensation of guilt, probe the daily parallels to this emotion. Why did you feel guilt? Did the dream open your eyes to new ideas on how you feel? Connect the dreaming story to daily events in order to understand the legacy of the dreaming emotion.

**Gun:** Guns and other weapons of destruction or defense are found in dreams of anxiety. Depending on the nature and use of the gun, it may be a symbolic threat or a tool for hunting or sport. Personal association is the key to understanding a dream featuring guns and pistols.

**Guru:** Much like a priest or a rabbi, a guru is a figure of teaching and wisdom. If your dream featured a guru, probe the nature of your associations with this Eastern model of spirituality and faith. Explore what the dream itself is teaching you.

**Hair:** The biblical figure of Samson offers us a window into the mythology of hair as a life-giving representation or a symbol of pride. The story of Rapunzel also represents the idea that hair is closely associated with identity. Many people dream of hair being cut off or growing in uncommon places or unexpected ways. The intuitive sensation and identifying message will reveal the central meaning of a hair-related dream.

**Hall or Hallway:** Many dreams feature hallways or passageways acting as a bridge between one dreaming component and another. The feeling of being led to a given destination can also be present. Hallways can also represent the intuitive connection between the mind and the spirit.

**Hammer:** A tool for the mason and blacksmith, the hammer carries a long-standing symbolism in ancient and modern mythology alike. Early European cultures equated it with power, industriousness, and good fortune. The former Soviet empire used it as a symbol of the worker and a proletarian view of cooperation.

**Hand:** This part of the body is often associated with humanity, brotherhood and sisterhood, or servility and purpose. In Islamic tradition, the five fingers represent a claim of faith. In Christianity, the hand of God is connected to Jesus and the crucifixion. In palmistry, the hand takes on the role of divination. Judge a dream featuring a hand in terms of the role it played and the function it served in the larger dreaming story.

**Handicapped:** Dreams of handicapped individuals will relate to individual experience; however, a dream of a disabled person can often reflect the imperfect nature of the physical body. Depending on the emotional reaction, the dream should be explored with personal association in mind.

**Hanging:** Abstract dreams featuring hanging objects or other surreal events often relate to perception and new dimensions of view. Depending on what was hanging and how the dreaming story played a role in their presence, the dream should be explored from an associative perspective.

**Harbor:** Known as a safe resting place for ships and vessels, the harbor is a symbol for spiritual rest and refuge. Harbors appear in dreams in a variety of ways. If your harbor brought you emotional reprieve, you may be on a new journey of self-awareness and enlightenment.

**Harp:** The harp with its intricate and beautiful design and rich melodic sounds has a symbolism connected to human passage into the afterlife. In Celtic traditions, Daghda, the god of plenty, used it to beckon the forthcoming seasons. The harp is also associated with heaven and is depicted as an instrument that angels play. If your dream featured harp music, examine the sounds it made and the way the overall dreaming picture made you feel.

**Hat:** Hats, headdresses, and other headgear take on many varying forms, typically representing social order or cultural definition. A top hat, for example, may represent wealth or magic, whereas a helmet or headdress may represent an archetypal warrior. If a hat was featured, explore the context and story coupled with the type of hat and its use.

**Haunted:** Dreams featuring haunted rooms or houses often connect with the dreamer's basic and general fears and anxieties. Emotions and intuitive concepts relating to the larger dreaming story are vital for understanding.

**Head:** Known as the center of awareness as well as the brain and the mind, the head is the part of the body that historically symbolizes truth or individual ideology. Explore perceptions and ideas relating to concepts of the mind or of individual identity.

**Healer:** A dream featuring a healer or someone who possesses the ability to cure often acts as a symbolic representation of the larger dreaming quest. If the healer played a part in curing the sick or the injured, the dream may connect back to individual ideas of faith and human curative powers of restoration.

**Healing:** Many dreams feature a theme of healing, emotionally, physically, or spiritually. Healing dreams are usually positive and deeply profound in nature and in theme. The essential aspect of interpreting the dream can be found in the potential that resides for future avenues of repair.

**Heart:** The human heart is a symbol for life and the epicenter of human physiology. Symbolically it represents passion, love, spirit, soul, and all emotions. It is included in all religions and mythologies and has profound representation in legends, cultural traditions, and fairy tales. If your dream featured the symbol of a heart, explore the sensations and value of this important universal symbol.

**Heart Attack:** Many people have dreams that feature a heart attack or stroke or other life-threatening events. These dreams portray a given set of circumstances that connect to our ideas about life, death, and the purpose of humanity. Depending on who was having the heart attack, the dream can take on varying meanings. Explore the nature of your connection to the heart attack itself along with its victim.

**Heat:** Dreams of extreme heat or cold relate to the polarity of human emotions and ideas. They can often weigh down or burden the dreamer and offer a true sensation of the given element. While some find it a comfort, others find it a sign of pressure. Context and intuitive legacy will define a dream of extreme heat.

**Heaven:** In every language and culture there is some concept of heaven. While Christians call it heaven, Hindus call it Nirvana. In tribal cultures it is commonly known as "the upper world." Depending on our works and deeds in life, we have the ability for our souls to achieve eternal peace. In dreams, this theme parallels to the dreamer's reference point and spiritual traditions.

**Heights:** Views from higher ground or high places are usually indicative of a new point of view or a vantage point. These dreams can represent newfound wisdom or fear, depending on how the dreamer views heights. Probe the context and nature of the dreaming story along with the sensations of sleep.

**Helicopter:** A modern symbol of flight and sometimes war, the helicopter is found in dreams featuring movement and transportation from one point of the dream into another. Many people find that dreaming of a helicopter changes the dream point of view, enabling them to look down on the world below.

**Hell:** Unlike heaven, the landscape of hell is found in specific myths and religions, and it represents the underworld, damnation, or the dark side of life. It is a mirror for heaven in that all bad deeds are placed as a burden on the individual to be handled in the afterlife. The emotional concept of hell is that of torment, anxiety, and original sin. Association and conceptual reasoning must be used when examining a dream of hell.

**Hen:** Often equated with the idea of motherhood, the hen is similar to the rooster in that it is the adult counterpart to the chicken. In romantic and biblical traditions, it is a symbol of patience and love. In Africa, the hen represents divine guidance and is valued as an animal of wisdom. Modern phrases like "henpecked" also give it a definite feminine quality in symbol and myth.

**Herb:** Because of the modern fascination with herbs and their curative powers, they have taken center stage in popular culture. Herbs have always had a place in mythology and symbolism connecting to medicine and the study of natural healing.

**Hermit:** The figure of the hermit is represented in myth and folklore with tales like Rip Van Winkle. The archetypal symbol of the hermit is often connected to an ascetic or monastic existence. The concept of wisdom gained from isolation also plays a part in this symbolic representation of emotional, intellectual, and spiritual retreat.

**Hexagram:** The six-pointed star is a symbol that carries a great significance in many cultures. It is usually known as the Star of David *(see Star of David),* but it also carries the significance of the four elements in Freemasonry. In biblical references it represents Yahweh or the four-letter name for God.

**High-rise:** *See Skyscraper*

**High School:** Dreams of high school are quite common in dream study. Often a dreamer will be sent back in time to explore problem solving or deal with a component of the past. High school or middle school represents themes of learning and development. These dreams may connect to lessons being learned or relearned in your waking reality.

**Highway:** Highways are everyday symbols of the open road, or on a conceptual plane, a path of infinite possibility. If your dream featured a highway, the contextual aspect of travel probably played a part in the greater dreaming story. This highly important symbol of change, evolution, and the human journey may act as a backdrop for the larger dreaming picture.

**Hiking:** Hiking and climbing dreams can relate to ascent and human challenge. While some hiking dreams offer a study of the surroundings or a dreaming landscape of nature, others relate to a path of exploration or a journey of unique proposition. Context will define this dreaming aspect.

**Hill:** Hills are natural symbols of obstacles or challenges in the natural world. Much like the expression "the hills and valleys of life," these rolling green components can offer the dreamer a chance at a new point of view or personal paths to intuitive exploration.

**Hippopotamus:** This unusually proportioned wild animal gets its name from the Greek meaning "river horse." For Egyptians, the hippopotamus was a symbol of the regenerative forces of nature, but the huge animal was also a dangerous creature even in the rivers of the afterlife. Symbolically they are associated with protection and power. They are featured in the Bible as part of the early evolution of the animal kingdom. Personal association is vital in interpreting a dream of a hippo.

**Honey:** Symbolically, honey represents sweetness on an archetypal plane. In mythology and religion, it takes on a greater significance in varying cultures. Much like bread, it is valued as a staple of life and is representative of human compassion. In Judaism, it is a symbol of delivery. In China, it represents sexual pleasure. Modern culture uses the word "honey" as a term of affection.

**Home:** Since homes and residences are highly personal, they take on an associative role in dreaming. Dreams of homes or of previous homes usually reflect the mind or mental framework of the dreamer. They can also connect to spirituality, individual history, and emotional association.

**Homeless:** Dreams featuring displaced or homeless persons can relate to many emotions depending on the dreamer's viewpoint and interactions. Often dreams of homeless people reflect the heart of the human condition and a dualistic fear and search for greater understanding of life's tragedies.

**Hook:** The hook is an interesting symbol, relating of course to hooking a fish or catching something. Folkloric stories like "Peter Pan" give the hook a sinister quality. In Hawaii, however, the fishhook has a deep spiritual symbolism of power and fortitude as well as intuitive ability.

**Horse:** The horse symbol goes back to prehistoric periods, and many cave paintings of these animals can be found in Australia and the Middle East. Symbolically and mythologically, they represent varying traditions of strength, speed, vitality, and also a messenger of nobility.

**Horse (flying/winged):** *See Pegasus*

**Hospital:** Known for their clinical and sometimes austere environment, hospitals in dreams typically connect to the sick and the medical world. Many people dream of hospitals in order to explore their ideas of humanity and the concept of mortality. Association and emotional impressions should be explored for interpretation.

**Hostage:** Hostage dreams are fairly common and relate to lack of control or having one's life overtaken by circumstances beyond normal control. Context and story line will aid in the quest for emotional parallels to the waking world.

**Hotel:** Known as an impermanent residence or a place of travel, hotels carry a connection similar to that of unknown homes or buildings. Hotels can reflect a variety of meanings and landscapes. Explore the overall picture and nature of the hotel. Often hotels with many rooms are symbolic of the many options found in life.

**Hourglass:** This symbol of time and the fleeting motion of its passage also has a dual meaning in its shape. The phrase "an hourglass figure" conjures an image of femininity. Because of this shape, it is also strongly associated with the sign of infinity and may relate back to a quest for connection with time and history.

**House:** Houses, differently from homes, often reflect components of a dreaming story or a place for the dream to take shape. They can represent the emotional or intellectual mind, an associative experience, or even another persona. Context and intuitive reasoning must be used when interpreting dreams featuring houses or a house as the backdrop.

**Hugging:** The experience of being held, of embracing another human being, cannot be underestimated in the dreaming story. It often provides a healing or emotional sensation. If you dream of hugging or being hugged, your dream may reflect a nightly spiritual nourishment and a new resolve for greater human compassion.

**Hunting:** Many dreams featuring hunting or being hunted depend on the associations of the dreamer. Dreams of being pursued often relate to themes of anxiety or fear. Hunting in dreams can relate to a quest for power or the concept of hunting as sport. Personal ideology and association will play a key role in interpreting a dream of hunting.

**Hurricane:** Natural disasters like tidal waves and hurricanes act as larger than life forces in dreams, often sweeping the dreamer into an unfamiliar landscape. The central theme of control is usually part of a dream featuring a catastrophic event. Dreams of hurricanes can also reflect emotional or psychological turmoil. Mythologically, natural disasters symbolize the natural world rearing its head over the indiscretions of humanity.

**Husband:** Much like boyfriend or girlfriend dreams, a dream featuring a spouse usually connects back to the personal association of the dreamer. If you dreamed of an unknown husband, associative emotions and ideas should be used in probing the larger dreaming message.

**Hut:** A smaller and more exotic version of a house, a hut represents shelter, containment, and home. It can represent the inner workings of the mind or the birthplace of individual pursuits. Depending on the role it played in the dreaming story, a hut may take on different meanings.

**Ice:** Since ice is associated with the cold, it can be found in many Nordic mythological stories. Often it represents that which is fixed, immovable, or frozen. Explore your connection to frozen elements and work on integrating the imagery with the emotional message.

**Idol:** Idols are usually spiritual or cultural symbols in dreams. Whether you dream of a personal idol or a material idol, you may be seeking out new ways of defining your identity. Idols represent the connection between humankind and the material realm.

**Illness:** Illness in dreams connects to the sensations of being weak and vulnerable. Often people have anxiety-connected dreams when they are in the throes of physical affliction. Work on understanding how the dreaming symbols parallel waking life.

**Indian:** From India or from Native American culture, the Indian is a representation of a profound spiritual tradition in human form. Personal association is vital in interpreting a dream of an Indian. Work on connecting the story of the dream with this archetypal figure.

**Injury:** Injuries in dreams, much like illnesses, often reveal feelings of being fragile and unable to control physical well-being. The raw, unencumbered self takes hold of the dreaming story and asks the dreamer to face aspects of vulnerability and the human condition.

**Insect:** Many insects like dragonflies have profound mythological meanings. However, the common impression of insects can also reflect fear or irritation. This dreaming symbol may relate to themes of frustration, anxiety, or other emotions depending on the dreamer's associations and ideas of the insect and how it was featured in the dream.

**Invasion:** Dreams of alien or foreign invasions relate to themes of material boundaries and control. The core message may relate to a sense of fear, resistance, or violation. The dream should be explored on an associative level, exploring the nature of the invasion and what it symbolically represented.

**Iron:** This element is known as the most enduring and strongest in all of human history. In ancient cultures it was thought to be a healing property. Today, we view it as a thing of fortitude with expressions like "made of iron." Depending on how it was placed in the dream, themes of strength and force may be at play.

**Island:** Islands are protected places or shelters from the modern world. Symbolically, they can connect to any emotional, intellectual, or spiritual theme. If the island is a refuge, themes of healing may be relevant. If the island is desolate, the dream may connect to issues of stress or loss. Context plays an important role in an island dream.

**Ivy:** Ivy is a beautiful and yet sometimes poisoning vine. It has symbolic importance in Greek mythology in the form of the crown and ivy wreath representing ecstasy and power. It also connects to higher thoughts and the idea of eternal life.

**Jacket:** As an article of clothing, the jacket can define or complete a form of attire. Depending on the nature of the dream, a jacket may connect parts of the dreaming story. However, it usually acts as a symbol of attire or outward appearances on the whole.

**Jade:** In the East, jade has always been held as a precious stone of imperial quality. It connects to symbol systems of water and the ocean because of its green and opalescent tones. In some cultures it is also connected to beauty and the realm of the senses.

**Jail:** Dreams of being incarcerated or put in jail are common in theme and can relate to stress or daily anxiety. If the prison was a powerful symbol, ask yourself what confines and restricts you. Context is essential in interpreting a dream of being in jail.

**Jaw:** The jaw is a component of the mouth relating to the spoken word. The dream may relate to communicating with others. Many people also report dreams of teeth and jaws during the psychophysiological state of grinding teeth or clenching the jaw during sleep.

**Jealousy:** Jealousy is a powerful emotion, and in dreams the sensation can relate to being envious of others or perhaps of a cultural aspect of life. Depending on who is jealous and where energies are being directed, the dream may relate to waking experiences with jealousy and self-love.

**Jellyfish:** This oceanic creature is transparent, illusive, and sometimes carries a lethal sting. Depending on one's associations with this sea creature, fear or joy may be present in the dream. Association is vital in unraveling the mystery of this illusive symbol.

**Jesus:** Jesus was the human manifestation of humility, sacrifice, and compassion. The source of Christianity, He represents a divine light, the higher self, and a soulful journey of healing and resolve.

**Jewel or Jewelry:** Associated with adornment and beauty, jewels and jewelry also carry a spiritual tradition symbolizing truth, health, and wisdom. Many jewels are said to carry varying properties. Jewelry such as rings and bracelets can represent emotional unity or relationships and partnership.

**Job:** Work and career themes often connect to identity. Depending on the nature of the job or task undertaken, the dream can have a variety of emotional symbols. Context and intuitive reasoning should be used when interpreting a dream about a job.

**Journey:** Journeys are a symbol for the human spiritual path. Journeys in dreams may represent a new path or a step toward realization. Journey dreams much like vision quests are positive signals of change and self-discovery.

**Joy:** Bounty and happiness relate to dreams where joy is the primary emotion. Connect the dots between the sensation of elation and the dreaming story. Is the nocturnal joy teaching you to find bliss in your daily life? Association and emotion will tell the larger story of the dream.

**Judge:** Balance, justice, and analytical thinking are revealed in the symbol of a judge. Judges also represent the higher self or human awareness, a moral code or conduct. Probe the issue of who is being judged and why.

**Jump or Jumping:** Many dreams feature actions and motions like jumping, climbing, and running. The act of jumping can offer a unique form of transportation from one place to another. It is also related to the symbol system of flying, bringing the dreamer to new vistas and, at times, elated emotions and sensations.

**Jupiter:** The Greek god Jupiter was the lord of the heavens and carried the ability to strike down the unjust with lightning. The planet Jupiter connects to the element of communication and humanity. The stones amethyst and emerald are also associated with this ruling planet of masculine astrological connection.

**Key:** Keys have a great symbolic power, as they are the connection between the locked and unlocked components of ourselves and others. Many saints wear keys around their necks as symbols of keeping faith. In dreams, keys may represent unfound realizations and discoveries.

**Kidnap:** Dreams of being kidnapped or taken from a safe environment reflect a loss of familiarity or a search for greater control. The emotional construct of a kidnapping dream will usually tell the underlying story.

**Killing:** Dreams of killing or being killed often relate to self-discovery or humanity. Death is known as transition on a symbolic level.

Depending on the scope of the dream and who was being killed, emotional sensations will likely define this dreaming symbol.

**King:** A heraldic emblem for sovereignty and influence, the king represents patriarchal association and regal power. In mythological traditions, kings were believed to have spiritual powers and, within their ceremonial circle, wisdom for all.

**Kiss or Kissing:** Kissing relates to all things passionate or romantic. Many people dream of kissing strangers or individuals they have no desire to kiss in waking reality. The intensity of emotions will likely define the intuitive connections of sleep.

**Kitchen:** This room is part of the domestic side of the home and relates to the creation of food and nourishment. If your dream took place in a kitchen, explore your own ideas about the domestic side of life. Context will define this dreaming landscape.

**Knee:** As part of the leg, the knee is a joint which acts as an important component to walking or physical movement. Personal association and context will take on an important role in a dream where a specific body part is featured.

**Knife:** Knives as weapons have a rich history and tradition in armed cultures and mythology. From the samurai in Japan to the esho of Africa, a knife is a defensive weapon and known as a symbol of force and honor.

**Knight:** Nobility and power are found in the symbol of a knight. The old phrase, "a knight in shining armor," brings images of safety and power. Throughout history, knights in any culture were known as warriors and people of honor, defending the realm that they occupied.

**Knot:** Knots carry an important symbolism in Celtic traditions, representing the energy of humanity and unity or division. The symbol of infinity is often represented in a knot. In Tibet the mystic knot symbolizes focus and longevity in spiritual life.

**Lab:** Dreams that feature laboratories or other clinical labs are often associated with the concept of experimentation or science. Depending on the context, the dreamer may be journeying into new ideas of compartmentalization. Association and the dreaming story will provide the greater message of the dream.

**Labyrinth:** Originally associated with the cross, this maze or curved formation is a symbol of the universe. Because of its design, it also represents the concept of the human journey or a spiritual path to the center of oneness.

**Ladder:** Ladders connect to the concept of ascension and possibility. The symbol of the ladder has a strong tradition in Christianity as the connective path between heaven and earth. In Jacob's dream, angels were viewed as climbing a ladder toward God. Ladders are also representative of learning or attainment of success, thus the phrase "working my way up the ladder." Dreams featuring this highly spiritual and important symbol should be explored in theme, content, and intuitive message.

**Lake:** Like any enclosed body of water, lakes often relate to a limited symbolic area. The dreamer may be crossing the lake, swimming in the lake, or trying to reach shore. Water symbols have strong associations to emotion and spirituality, but depending on the context and placement of the lake in the dream, there may be many ways to explore the dreaming meaning.

**Lamb:** While the symbol of the sacrificial lamb from Christian texts is often associated with this young sheep, the lamb is also associated with the basic qualities of goodness and innocence. The lamb is found in many heraldic and Christian shields and crests representing a higher power of morality. In folkloric tales and songs like "Mary Had a Little Lamb," the image of softness and sweetness is revealed. Context and association must be used in exploring a dream featuring this symbol from the animal kingdom.

**Lapis:** This deep blue stone, often with inclusions of white calcite and iron pyrite, is symbolically associated with creativity and universal compassion. Often found in the jewelry of ancient cultures, it was known to be a powerful spiritual component and represented vision and psychic ability.

**Laughing:** Many dreams feature the act of laughter and the emotions that accompany this healthy and jubilant act. Laughter in dreams also relates to the release of energy and the renewal of spirit, much as it does in our waking world.

**Laundry:** Many dreams feature laundry being strewn about a room or the act of cleaning clothing. Dreams of laundry carry the obvious association of cleansing, but they also may relate to identity and transition of material concepts. Explore the nature of the symbol or the action attached to it to understand a dream with the theme of laundry.

**Laurel:** The laurel wreath is most often associated with the Greek god Apollo and the adornment of power. However, the laurel leaf is also found in a few other ancient symbol systems representing peace and victory.

**Lawyer:** The figure of a lawyer is a modern archetype of the law and its material representation. Depending on the dreamer's view of lawyers, the dream may take on any number of meanings. The chief associations with this symbol are balance, legality, conduct, and discipline.

**Lead:** The property of lead is symbolically linked to writing or the early form of the pencil. However, much like iron, it is also mythologically connected to strength and purpose. Modern views on lead have brought the association of lead paint and lead poisoning. Personal association and context will determine the nature and meaning of the dream.

**Leg:** A vital part of the human anatomy, the leg is connected to movement, action, and the ability to walk. Dreams of being injured or unable to use a leg may relate symbolically to the dreamer's waking actions. Context, placement, and the dreaming story line must be explored in order to define the importance of the symbol.

**Lei:** This necklace vine or flower wreath, worn around the neck or on the head, is the Hawaiian symbol of good will and adornment. It represents the spirit of aloha and the basic goodness of the Hawaiian people.

**Lever:** Pulling levers and pushing buttons are common dreaming metaphors for a changing portion of a dreaming dynamic. If your dream featured a lever or any other form of active connection, explore the underlying message of the dream and its connection to your waking world.

**Levitate:** Levitation, an ancient form of self-actualization, is often experienced in dreams and relates to feelings of bliss, happiness, and weightlessness. Because of the spiritual connection, levitating in dreams can also represent a new journey of soul and divine order.

**Library:** Much like the environment of a bookstore, a library is a backdrop of learning or higher truth. Dreams featuring libraries may take the dreamer into decision-making scenarios or other significant acts of reading or education. Personal association as well as context must be probed in order to understand a dream featuring a library as backdrop.

**Light:** This universal symbol of illumination and divine force can be found in dreams in a vast array of forms and contexts. The dualistic theme of light and darkness is found in every religious, mythological, folkloric, and spiritual system. Light is always a positive and blissful theme and symbol and can connect to many other associations like truth, spirit, philosophy, and the concept of the idea itself.

**Lighthouse:** A beacon in the darkness, the lighthouse is a nineteenth-century symbol of salvation or truth. A nautical element in many writings and seafaring beliefs, lighthouses are often found in dreams connecting to land. Much like the symbol of the anchor, they can lead or lure the dreamer back to shore.

**Lightning:** This ancient symbol of destruction and natural power can be found in Greek and Polynesian myth alike. Connected to the concept of awakening, lightning is also associated with vitality and electricity.

**Lily:** This lovely and fragrant flower has origins in Judeo-Christian traditions relating to death and rebirth of the soul. The color of the white lily also is often associated with purity and innocence. In Catholic traditions, the lily represents varying saints and is a tribute to their faith and work in life. Personal association to this exquisite flower will play a role in interpreting the dream.

**Lion:** This wonderful wild cat is found in many symbol systems from heraldic traditions to African folklore. In Thailand, the lion is known as the incarnation of the Hindu god Vishnu, representing divine protection against evil. Like the eagle, it is also commonly connected to strength, wisdom, and omniscience. Often used as a representation of imperialism, the lion is also referred to as the "king of beasts." In the astrological symbol system it is connected to the planet of the sun and the sign of Leo.

**Little:** Changes in size often occur in dreams and reflect transition or transformation. The surreal world of dreams can create anything from a giant paperclip to a tiny elephant. Look at the dreaming symbols as they connect to the larger story and explore the element of transformation in your daily life.

**Living Room:** Parts of houses and homes are known to represent the various components of our minds or even our way of thinking. Living rooms as backdrops are connected to comfortable areas or gathering places. Context and association are essential when integrating this dreaming background with the larger dreaming message.

**Lizard:** These small reptiles are often found to have diverse connotations in many cultural or symbol traditions. However, in ancient Roman traditions, the lizard was a symbol of safety and protection. They carry a great importance in Polynesian traditions, their chirp being known as the echo of truth in Bali. While the creature has a great dichotomy in meaning, many people fear lizards and therefore should interpret a dream of a lizard according to individual association and belief.

**Lobby:** Lobbies are often found in dreams as gathering places or as a material representation of a symbolic entryway. Dreams with this background should be explored in terms of the lobby's placement and relevance to the larger dreaming theme and story.

**Lock:** Along with keys, locks hold the significance of being used to open or enter a given domain or space. In dreams, they often play an important role when the dreamer addresses problem-solving issues of unlocking a door or being locked in or out of a given place. An important symbol to be probed in terms of metaphor, with the use of intuitive reasoning.

**Locker:** Lockers are often connected with school or learning and the representation of identity at a given point in time. Many people dream of being back in high school or at a gym and being unable to open a locker or finding something unusual inside. Probe the nature of the locker's importance along with its metaphoric message in order to interpret the dream.

**Lost:** Feelings of being lost or of losing certain material possessions is a common dreaming theme. The sensation or emotion of loss usually connects back to an important element in the dreamer's emotional outlook or intuitive placement. The experience of loss in a dream should be explored in terms of its placement and the symbolic representations associated with its message.

**Lottery:** Lotteries represent modern-day themes of winning or unusual luck. These dreams typically connect to the dreamer's material aspirations or ideas. The concept of the lottery is a numerical roulette of chance and expectation.

**Lotus:** The lotus flower is a highly spiritual symbol in Hindu and Buddhist traditions. It can be found in many art and architectural forms throughout Asia. It relates to enlightenment, and the opening lotus is a symbol for awakening, sensual pleasure, or nirvana.

**Love:** The emotion of love is probably the most powerful of all the dreaming sensations. Along with anger, hate, and fear, it leads the dreamer into strong and vital themes of his or her personal history, ideology, and spirit. Dreams featuring the emotion or message of love should be explored on every level including theme, story, and intuitive reasoning and personal association.

**Love Affair:** Much like dreams of love and romance, experiences of having a new or unique love affair connect to the dreamer's inner journey of human understanding or sexual connection. There may be elements of need, desire, or passion that are being explored in this highly associative dreaming theme.

**Luggage:** The appearance of luggage in dreams often relates to the themes of both travel and identity. Many people dream of losing or misplacing luggage, and these dreams connect to anxiety or perhaps the dreamer's view of self. Context and placement in the dream will usually tell the larger story.

**Lust:** Lust in dreams can represent an emotion or sensation of sexual desire, as well as the concept of greed. Many people have dreams featuring themes of lust and their emotional needs. These dreams must be explored in relation to theme and personal context.

**Machine:** Dreams featuring machinery or other modern symbols of action and reaction can act in many ways depending on placement and importance in the nocturnal landscape. The concept of a machine usually connects to creation, manufacture, or usefulness. Probe the context and orientation of the machine and its connection to the dreaming story.

**Magazine:** Magazines, newspapers, and other reading materials can either act as associative symbols or carriers of messages in dreams. Many people dream of reading papers or magazines as part of a larger dreaming story or message. Explore the entire dreaming context in order to determine the importance of the symbol and its meaning.

**Magic:** The symbol of magic and magicians connects to mythological roots or the modern concept of entertainment. Concepts of illusion, phantasms, and miraculous happenings may be at play. The tradition of magic and alchemy is one that usually represents a positive sign of transformation.

**Mail:** Delivery, news, and correspondence are all themes associated with mail and letters. Many dreams have a significant meaning featuring letters or opening mail. Often the message is of importance to the larger dreaming story. Probe the context and symbolism for greater understanding.

**Make-up:** Make-up is often equated with feminine precepts, but it also has a ritualistic connection relating to theater as well as tribal and cultural themes. Dreams featuring make-up or a change in appearance should be explored in relation to the wearer and the intuitive association of the archetype in the overall dreaming story.

**Man:** A masculine element in any dream plays a direct role with the dreamer's impressions and placement in his or her world. Association with patriarchal power and fatherly protection also relates to individual identity and personal association.

**Mandala:** This Buddhist and Hindu symbol of meditation is similar to the labyrinth and yet its primary meaning is that of imagination, manifestation, spiritual patience, and focus. If you dreamed of a mandala, you may be integrating these themes into your waking world. Explore the relevance of this Zen-like symbol of personal prophecy.

**Mansion:** Large and impressive versions of homes, mansions connect to concepts of status, wealth, and dominion. Mansions are also equated with romantic European domains and are featured in gothic stories and medieval mythology. Like a modern version of the castle, their connotation is entirely personal to the associations of the dreamer.

**Map:** As guides, routes, or directive materials, maps can have a great significance in the land of dreams because they often connect the dreamer to surroundings or a new environment. Like clues to a puzzle, maps are very symbolic and should be interpreted by relating to the entire dreaming story and theme.

**Maple:** The national symbol of Canada, the maple tree has ancient connections to honor as well as the natural world. A tree that produces sap and intricately detailed leaves, it is also associated with creativity. The maple symbol should be explored on an associative and intuitive level in terms of dream meaning.

**Marble:** This ancient stone is often associated with regality, wealth, and privilege. Because it is very soft and easily breakable, it is also connected to concepts of value and fragility.

**Marriage:** The cultural and spiritual tradition of marriage is found in every society, and the basic concept is that of eternal union or the universal connection of man and woman on a higher plane. Many people dream of marriage, be it their own or that of others. In dreams, this theme can relate to love and romance or other quests of human connection. Personal parallels and concepts must be explored when interpreting this important and yet diverse symbol, act, and theme.

**Mars:** Originally the Greek god of war, Mars is also a planet. Astrologically it is connected to the sign of Aries and, in modern concept, known to be a hot dry planet producing red dust. Science fiction has given it a unique and odd significance among popular lore, but personal perceptions of this unusual planet should be probed if it is featured in the dreaming landscape.

**Mask:** Masks have a rich and diverse history in mythology and symbolism. In fact, the mask is a symbol of theatre, presence, disguise, and also character. In dreams, they can convey many different meanings. Masks are also known as expressions of spiritual power or imperial status for the wearer in some ancient cultural and spiritual traditions from places such as China, India, Mexico, and Central Europe.

**Maze:** A general symbol or representation of the act of problem solving, mazes are often found in dreams, offering a puzzle for the dreamer to unravel. Parallels to daily life must be explored in order to interpret the presence of a maze as landscape or article in dreams.

**Meat:** Meat often appears in dreams as a representation of food and can have varying connotations. In some dreams meat can be raw and offensive. Other dreams feature this symbol as a welcoming and hearty meal. Context and personal association will aid in placing the relevance of this symbol.

**Medal:** Dreams of winning prizes or medals often relate to glorification or the power of human accomplishments and endeavors. Emotional and intuitive reasoning should be used when interpreting a dream of winning or presenting a medal.

**Medicine:** Medicine is closely associated with science, healing, and human physiology in modern thought. In Native American traditions, medicine and its study are connected to a higher spiritual power and shamanism. In Cheyenne and Plains Indian traditions, the medicine wheel symbolizes the various lunar cycles. Taking medicine in dreams can have positive or negative connotations depending on the dreamer and his or her personal associations.

**Medusa:** This ancient character from Greek mythology, Medusa was a woman whose actions changed her into a snake-haired vixen. Her gaze could turn a man to stone. This myth is often associated with negative connotations of fear and sexual shame; however, the placement of this figure in a dreaming story is vital in order to interpret its meaning.

**Melting:** Many dreams feature themes of morphing or melting objects, people, and places. The surrealistic act of melting often symbolizes transformation or transition. If the action of melting played a role in the dream, explore the theme and relationship of each element in order to integrate the dreaming theme with the message.

**Mercury:** The Greek god of industry, Mercury is most commonly known as the winged messenger or the spirit of the traveler. The planet Mercury is connected with the astrological signs of Gemini and Virgo and symbolic of mental activity, shrewdness, eloquence, and meticulousness.

**Mermaid:** While the obvious association to fishes and sea creatures are found in the symbol of the mermaid, the original legend comes from Oceanic folklore. Mermaids were written about as early as 1740, and they were believed to have the mystical powers of the ocean combined with the spirit force of femininity and beauty.

**Metal:** Depending on which type of metal was featured, the dream can take on any number of symbolic representations. The basic associations of the element are that of strength, endurance, and force. Context and placement, along with the specific type of metal, will define the dreaming symbol.

**Military:** Often representative of order, defense, and also discipline, military aspects or the presence of the military can relate to war or strategic action. Association and emotional relevance will be important for interpreting this symbol depending on the context of its placement in the dream.

**Milk:** While milk is white and often equated with purity, wholesomeness, health, and nourishment, it is also one of the oldest drinks in human civilization, coming from cows, goats, and other animals. The idea of a nurturing force comes from mother's milk, and in Hindu, Jewish, and Christian religions, delivery from evil was referred to as entering the "land of milk and honey."

**Minister:** Much like any holy person, the minister is the Christian representation of propriety, sanctity, and fatherly guidance. Depending on which religion the dreamer embraces, the figure of a minister in a dream can have many meanings. Association is vital in interpreting the importance and relevance of this symbol.

**Miracle:** According to the Catholic faith, a miracle is an impossible act or occurrence made possible by the divine order of God. Miracles in dreams are highly personal and almost always relate to the dreamer's deepest desires or conceptual ideas. Probe the context, symbolism, and purpose of this highly important dreaming symbol.

**Mirror:** Mirrors are elusive and reflective objects which carry a vital importance in dreams and dreaming. Often they symbolize a need for exploration on a spiritual or material plane. They can also reflect the true self or the concept of illusion.

**Mist:** Much like fog, mist is a veiled and opaque natural force, which can symbolize a thin barrier or blockade in a dream. Dreams featuring a misty landscape may also be connected to water or other emotional themes. Probe the placement and also the intuitive sensation when defining a dream featuring this symbol.

**Mistletoe:** Typically associated with Victorian England, this flowering plant with red berries was treasured as a Christmas symbol of love, romance, and good fortune. In Celtic and Germanic traditions it was believed to be sacred and often used in rituals in search of immortality.

**Mob:** The modern view of the "mob" or organized crime is found in movies and films; yet the formation of an actual mob of people is an image often found in dreams. This uniform representation of a collective force can play a role in story or dreaming design. Probe the context and the overall sensation for understanding and new awareness.

**Monastery:** A holy refuge or place where monastic life is led is a backdrop relating to seclusion, meditation, and simplicity. Monasteries are found in almost every country around the globe, and if your dream featured this landscape, it is vital to examine the spiritual connotations and connections to the overall dreaming story and message.

**Money:** Universally, money represents finance, commerce, wealth, and resources. Of course, the dreamer's ideas and daily concession to money will play a vital role in the dreaming scene. Money in dreams can also relate to industry, success, energy, and value.

**Monk:** Often relating to the image of authority and piety, monks are much like any religious archetypal figure, and their role in the dream should be explored in relationship to the dreamer's concepts of faith and religion.

**Monkey:** While monkeys traditionally relate to humankind and human behavior, they hold a sacred place in Hindu mythology relating to sexuality and the inner soul of desire. Since they are often comical and mischievous, many view them as clownlike. In Chinese astrology, the year of the monkey is one of joy and creative endeavors.

**Monster:** Monsters and creatures that lack a concrete human definition are found in dreams and typically frighten the dreamer. Some monsters that relate to folkloric tales, like "Beauty and the Beast," can have positive connotations depending on the insights of the dreamer. Explore the underlying meaning of the monster and how it connects to the dreaming message.

**Monument:** Monuments or structures in dreams that relate to a higher level of symbolism are fairly common. They typically are part of a dreaming landscape and may be leading the dreamer to a higher realization or a new path in the dreaming story. Probe the context and specific symbolism of the given monument for a greater understanding of the dream.

**Moon:** The most spiritual and widely used planetary symbol next to the sun, the moon's mythology connects to many themes in different cultures, usually relating to femininity and also wisdom, guidance, protection, and afterlife. If your dream featured a moon, explore the shape, the various phases of the lunar cycle, and your own connection to this planet of principle and travel.

**Mother:** A human symbol of protection and nurturing, many people have dreams featuring their mother or an archetypal symbol of this social force of female strength. In Oceanic and Native American traditions, the earth is known as the "Great Mother," and in Christianity, the Virgin Mary is known as the Mother of God and, therefore, humankind.

**Motorcycle:** Much like all modes of transportation, motorcycles are often featured in dreams as a means of getting from one place to another. Motorcycles are equated in modern myth and folklore with the pioneering adventure, the open road, or the maverick spirit.

**Mountain:** Because mountains rise high above the visual human plane, they are often connected to spiritual enlightenment or attainment in mythological and religious systems. They can be found in dreams acting as symbols of attainment or climbing to new heights of awareness. Dreams of standing on mountaintops or experiencing new vistas from or near mountains are all important and highly positive dreaming images—associative, symbolic, and spiritual.

**Mouse:** Mice have often been equated with fear and evil in dreams because they so closely resemble rats. Yet, these tiny creatures have a great history in many symbol systems relating to intellect, thrift, and observation. In ancient Egypt, the mouse was a symbol of the human soul. Because this symbol is so highly paradoxical, association and mythological concepts should be combined when interpreting a dream featuring the mouse.

**Mouth:** An instrument of speech as well as the funnel of nourishment, the human mouth is a part of the body that is also equated with sensuality. In dreams, the use of the mouth or its importance in the dreamer's intuitive mind should be explored.

**Movie:** *See Film*

**Movie Star:** *See Celebrity*

**Moving:** Many people dream of moving objects, things, or residences. The act of moving relates to movement on a general level and can represent a new formation of ideas, emotions, or even questions about the dreamer's identity. Context and story will define this dreaming theme.

**Mud:** While mud is commonly connected to dirt and filth, it is also valued as a cleansing and healing property in Pacific and Asian cultures. Personal association and conceptual ideas about this wet form of earth should be used when interpreting the dream.

**Mummy:** A human symbol originating in an ancient Egyptian ritual of mummification, the mummy was believed to offer the deceased a window to immortality. In modern lore and horror themes, mummies have become known as creatures of darkness or the living dead.

**Murder:** Dreams of murder and death are usually a transitional representation of a waking concern in the dreamer's mind or life. Many people dream of seeing murder or murdering others. The emotional background of fear, anger, shame, and vulnerability all come into play. Context and association are vital in interpreting a dream featuring the theme or action of murder.

**Muscle:** Muscles are a dualistic and yet highly important part of the human physical anatomy. Often associated with strength and power, they can also refer to weakness or inability to maintain control in dreams. Depending on how muscles were featured, the intuitive message and metaphor will tell the larger story.

**Music:** As Shakespeare commented, "Music be the food of love." Although it can have varying meaning in dreams, it is often a positive element for the dreamer. Dreams that feature musical tones or interludes connect to creativity and a higher level of thought. Context and association will define musical dreams.

**Nail:** Because of its association with crucifixion, the nail has many variants in its symbolism. In mythological traditions, it represents the purposeful spirit or a material representation of unification. In modern views, nails are connected to sturdiness or ruggedness and durability. Depending on how the nail was used and featured in the dream, context will likely define this unusual and ancient symbol.

**Naked:** The theme of being naked or nudity in dreams is fairly common and can represent vulnerability or the raw and fragile self. Often the dreamer finds him- or herself nude or partially clothed in unfamiliar or unusual surroundings and settings. Identity, vulnerability, emotion, and truth are all possible meanings for a dream of the naked self.

**Native:** Dreams that feature native individuals of an unknown origin are often associated with the dreamer's concepts of cultural dimensions and their value. This archetypal human symbol for origin and inherited human design must be interpreted by using context and the larger dreaming story and message.

**Native American:** An archetypal symbol of Native American culture in a dream may often relate to spiritual concepts or connections to Native American traditions. Depending on how the individual or Native American theme played a role in the dreaming landscape and story, the sleeping sight may take on an important cultural or visionary meaning.

**Nausea:** Many people experience the sensation of nausea in a dream correlating to a given emotion. Feelings like rage, desire, anger, and anxiety can all accompany a dream of nausea. Probe the central message of sleep in order to interpret this dreaming construct.

**Nazi:** This twentieth-century symbol for evil is found in many dreams because it so acutely portrays a modern illustration of mass hysteria, hatred, and ignorance. Nazi themes typically relate to brutality, war, anger, and fear.

**Neck:** The part of the body most commonly equated with femininity, the neck is also symbolic of connectivity and the vitality of the human spine. Because it connects the head to the body, it is often found in dreams relating to strangulation or being unable to breathe. The emotional and intuitive sensations must be explored when interpreting a dream featuring this symbol.

**Necklace:** Associated with jewelry and adornment, the necklace has an important place in cultural as well as spiritual traditions. In imperial traditions, necklaces were worn to signify order and position. In religious orders, monks and nuns also wear specific necklaces representing their humility and loyalty to God. Modern views connect the necklace to femininity. Personal association and context will define a dream featuring this symbol.

**Needle:** Needles often carry dualistic meanings because they have the ability to thread or connect two elements together, and yet they are sharp and can also pierce or prick. Threading a needle is a symbol for problem solving or some form of association. Probe the use, context, and intuitive connection to the needle in the dream.

**Neighbor:** Neighbors are often featured in dreams as representations of collective humanity or a sense of community. If a specific neighbor was featured, association will play an important role. If not, the concept of neighborly acts and ideas will be part of the dreaming story and message.

**Neighborhood:** As a landscape of houses and homes, the neighborhood is a symbol of that which is familiar. Much like the symbol of an individual neighbor, these dreaming backdrops usually relate to the dreamer on a personal level, often featuring neighborhoods from the past and present.

**Nest:** Associated with the concept of nesting or the creating of a domicile, the image of a nest in dreams can relate to birds or even a symbolic representation of home. Context and placement in the dreaming story will reveal the importance and relevance of the symbol.

**Net:** Connected to the sea, fishing, and fishermen, nets can also represent a gathering force or a method of capturing spiritual enlightenment. The ancient Hawaiians believed that the net was a thing in which to catch souls, and the god of Maui caught the sun in order to steal its fire. Explore the symbol of the net and how it is featured in the dream in order to probe the inner meaning of the story and theme.

**Night:** Dark and elusive, the theme of nighttime can have a dualistic meaning in that it may represent mystery and illusion or confusion and inability to see the truth. Mythologically, it represents the vast womb of the soul; and in Roman Catholic tradition, evening services are often held to represent a moment of reawakening and vigil.

**Nightclub:** An environment or landscape of music, dance, and entertainment, nightclubs and bars are often connected to the dreamer's associations of revelry and debauchery. However, personal connection is always vital in exploring a dream with this backdrop.

**Nightgown:** Bedclothes of any sort, pajamas, long johns, or nightgowns, are often associated with sleep and restfulness. Some people feel vulnerable or naïve in their nightclothes, and dreams featuring these articles of attire are usually personal and highly associative in nature and in theme.

**Nine:** One of the more highly symbolic numbers in numerology and number systems, nine is a derivative of the trinity and also representative of higher insight and unique awareness. It also plays a key role in many symbols systems, such as the nine orders of angels in Catholicism and the nine springs in Chinese mythology.

**Noah:** The biblical figure of guidance and a shepherd of God, Noah is also connected to the Great Flood as well as all animal kingdoms. Context, story line, and intuitive associations will reveal the larger dreaming message of this highly spiritual symbol.

**North:** Also equated with the North Star, this direction has been associated with wisdom and a path of higher learning or spiritual education. Because northern regions of the earth are cold, there can also be environmental associations depending on the dreaming story and theme.

**North Pole:** Cold, frozen, and expansive, the North Pole is connected to the folkloric tale of Santa Claus and his reindeer. It is also featured in Nordic myths as a symbol of the divine center of the natural world.

**Nose:** Associated with the sense of smell, the nose is also closely associated with identity and intuitive study. Phrases like "he has a nose for it" and "turn your nose up at it" explore themes of social integrity as well as human instinct.

**Nuclear:** The theme of nuclear destruction is common in many dreams connecting to the twentieth-century view of annihilation and death. Dreams of this nature should always be interpreted and explored relating to the emotional sensation and the underlying message of the story line.

**Nude:** *See Naked*

**Numbers:** The concept that numerical values relate to spiritual concepts goes back thousands of years. Numerology is the esoteric connection between a given value and its representation. Birthdays, lucky numbers, and other numerical symbols can all be associated with various truths in dreams. *(See also individual numbers.)*

**Nun:** Spirituality, religion, faith, and humility all relate to the symbol of the nun. Because nuns represent the feminine order of Catholic or orthodox traditions, they can also symbolize divine motherhood, sisterhood, and goodness.

**Nurse:** An archetypal symbol of care, nurturing, and healing, nurses are featured in many dreams that connect to personal journeys or some form of transformation. However, the symbol will also refer back to the dreamer's relationship to this profession of health, wellness, and comfort.

**Nut:** Much like seeds, nuts are part of the natural world and are often equated with growth and an earthly representation. Depending on the dreamer's association to nuts or what type of nut was revealed in the dream, varying interpretations may follow. Probe the context and connection to this food and natural symbol for the dreaming meaning.

**Oak:** The mighty oak tree has a strong symbolic and mythological root from Greek traditions as well as Northern European culture. It is connected with strength and durability and revered as the image of natural survival and design.

**Oasis:** Much like the concept of a refuge, an oasis is strongly connected with the idea of a valley in a desert land. In a dream, it can relate to a component of life undiscovered or a journey of self. Probe the context and associations of sleep.

**Obelisk:** The unusual form of an obelisk, a tall and four-sided pillar, had special significance in ancient Egypt, representing the sun and its entry point to the world below. While a symbol of fertility in India, obelisks can be found all over the world architecturally, in Paris, New York, and Rome, for instance.

**Ocean:** The ocean is a highly symbolic element that spans the world we know today. For many, it connects to healing and the mysterious emotional sense within the human spirit. Association is essential in interpreting a dream featuring the ocean.

**Octopus:** This eight-armed creature of the sea has many myths connected to it, at one point strongly associated with Medusa and her many arms. Octopi are loving and peaceful creatures but because of their forceful grip and poisonous ink, they have come to be feared by many. In Mediterranean mythology their symbol is connected with the unfolding universe. Personal association is vital in exploring a dream of this sea mollusk.

**Odor:** *See Smell*

**Office:** The modern landscape of an office appears in many dreams, providing a workaday world environment of order and precise appearance. Depending on how the office played into the dream, the story line will have definite relevance. Probe how the dreaming landscape connects to daily life.

**Oil:** Much like its valuable counterpart of gold, oil is known by many as a sign of riches and wealth. As an element, oil can represent the crude and slippery work of a mechanic. If the oil was natural, like olive oil, or simply an unknown oil, probe the slick and uncontrollable elements in the dream and how they connect to the larger story.

**Old:** Dreams featuring old things or older people usually probe the aging process and how we view the passage of time in our lives. The emotional reaction, the object, or the featured player may be less important than the intuitive impressions of sleep.

**Olive Tree:** In Islam, both the olive and the fig tree were prized as holy manifestations of the natural world. Strongly associated with peace, the olive branch is found in Greek mythology connected to Athena as well as the god of the sea, Poseidon.

**Omen:** The mythological concept of an omen is usually that of warning or foreboding of a future event. Yet, omens of sleep can take any form. Explore the message and focus on proactive and contextual interpretations.

**One:** The number one is a masterful number known as the digit of unity, a representation of spirit and soul in the word *oneness*. It is also connected with winning, wholeness, power, and excellence, with phrases like "number one."

**Onion:** Often equated with the ability to make one cry and its strong odor, the onion is also valued along with garlic for its medicinal properties. Onions are found in many early Greek texts as a food of wisdom and higher learning.

**Open:** Openings or the ability to open an object can connect to being receptive to new ideas or changes in the dreaming landscape. Probe the parallels to waking life and place the active discovery in its proper context.

**Opera:** Operas, grand in scale and production, are a feast for the eyes and ears. If an opera was featured, personal association will play a large role in interpretive definitions. Musically, operatic themes are traditionally told through story lines of drama and passion.

**Operation:** Dreams that contain an operation, be it medical or otherwise, are usually connected to a process of examination or an execution of a task. Probe the context and emotional connection to the dream in order to unravel an operative dreaming construct.

**Oracle:** This ancient symbol of mysticism and prophecy can take on many forms. There are stone oracles, paper oracles, and also oracles made from precious metal. If you discovered an oracle in your dream, it is vital to explore the message and journey into the heart of potential future wisdom.

**Orange:** The modern-day connection to the orange is that of health and a source of vitamin C. Oranges are often symbolized by sunshine and happiness, but personal association should be used when interpreting a dream of this sweet and juicy fruit.

**Orb:** Known as the pinnacle of the staff, the orb represents unity of all things in its form and symbolism. Spherical in shape, it can be found in many heraldic traditions and is often mounted with a cross, bringing a further spiritual representation of life and afterlife.

**Orchid:** This highly sensual flower is known in the vast Pacific regions as the diamond of the natural world. Its perfume is so unique and intoxicating that it is often used in the celebration of love and romance and in wedding ceremonies.

**Orgasm:** Sexual experiences in dreams are often accompanied by an orgasm, which is commonly referred to as a "wet dream." The experience of an orgasm in sleep or the element of arousal will play a defining role in the dreaming process and definition.

**Orphan:** Dreams featuring an orphan, be it a baby bird or child, typically connect back to the need to rescue or a protective nature. Dreams of being orphaned are fearful in construct, as we explore our mortality and the connection to the parental force in our lives.

**Ostrich:** This large, land-roving bird is known for its plumage as well as its large eggs. In heraldic traditions it is connected to the idea of strength and speed and noted for its regal qualities.

**Owl:** A highly spiritual symbol, the owl is traditionally associated with wisdom. In Native American and Aztec traditions, it is connected to death or the transition from one form of life into another, thus revealing a new perspective and view.

**Ox:** One of the twelve symbols of the Chinese zodiac, the ox is known for its durability and methodical qualities. Many legends feature oxen as representations of servility and purposeful works.

**Oyster:** Along with its hidden gem, the pearl, the oyster is prized throughout the world as a symbol of delicacy and rarity. In Asia it is valued as a fertility-giving food and in Imperial Russia it was cherished as an aristocratic food likened to caviar.

**Pack or Packing:** Related to organizational skills and compartmentalizing, packing in dreams usually relates to a larger dreaming metaphor. While it can symbolize travel, it may also connect to themes of home life, identity, and continuity.

**Package:** Packages are often related to surprise or themes of the unknown in dreams. While the act of opening a package can have an anticipatory quality, a container or package can also be featured in problem-solving scenarios.

**Pain:** Dreams that feature pain and agony for the dreamer or for others can relate to a number of emotional themes such as fear, shame, anger, and pride. Physical pain or emotional pain in dreams should be explored relating to real-time experiences as well as the overall dreaming story and message.

**Painting:** A creative act much like drawing, painting involves color scheme and freedom of movement. Whether painting a wall or a canvas, painting in dreams typically connects to creative vistas and new ways of thinking.

**Palace:** Similar to mansions, palaces take on a more mythical quality in dreams because they are featured in imperial traditions as well as fairy tales and folklore. Depending on how the palace was placed in the dream along with intuitive and associative reactions, the dream may take on any number of meanings relating to wealth, position, fortune, or domestic bliss.

**Palm Tree:** Featured in many Christian and Catholic traditions, such as Palm Sunday, the palm tree is an ancient symbol of rebirth, spiritual ascension, and regeneration. In modern thought, many see it as a symbol of holiday and relaxation relating to tropical destinations and days in the sun.

**Pan (cooking):** As tools for cooking and heating food, pots and pans are often found in dreams and can relate to reflective themes or everyday objects as part of a greater dreaming story. Context and association will define a dream with this symbol.

**Pan (Greek god):** The Greek myth of the shepherd goat is widely interpreted in literature. The original story of Pan revealed him to be a figure of natural power, representing an all-knowing force of nature. Closely associated with the reed, which he plays, the figure of Pan can also be associated with childhood and youth in stories such as "Peter Pan."

**Pandora's Box:** The Greek myth of Pandora's box translates into modern thought as a daunting symbol of temptation and demise. The story of Pandora tells the tale of opening the box which brought wrath, plague, and negativity to humanity. Dreams featuring this powerful symbol should be explored using context, association, and intuitive reasoning.

**Panther:** Known for its predatory insight and vision, the panther is a symbol of purity and honesty in ancient Greek and Roman myths. In heraldic traditions, the panther is closely associated with the dragon and represents power and regal nature. Panthers featured in dreams are highly dualistic and should be explored using these symbol systems along with associative experience.

**Panties:** Undergarments and lingerie usually relate to that which is unseen as well as sexuality and identity. The context of how the specific article of clothing was featured in the dream will likely reveal its greater symbolism and meaning.

**Pants:** An article of clothing traditionally associated with masculinity, pants are also functional and sturdy items worn by both sexes. In dreams, context and association will define their meaning and importance.

**Parachute:** A modern article designed for air-to-earth landing, parachutes are often found in dreams as a symbol for rescue, resolve, and openness, as well as escape or danger. Depending on how the parachute worked or functioned in the larger dreaming story, the dream may have a number of varying meanings.

**Parade:** Parades are found in dreams connecting to a collective concept of ceremony, pomp, reward, or celebration. Parades in dreams can also act as a connective link between one dreaming landscape and another. The intuitive and emotional reaction to the parade experience will provide the symbolic link to its dreaming meaning.

**Paradise:** Akin to the Garden of Eden in Christian symbolism, the concept of paradise is found in every culture and spiritual ideology. It is found in such images as islands, Nirvana, or Heaven. Paradise in dreams is usually a positive and blissful experience relating to vision, insight, and higher awareness.

**Paralysis:** Dreams of paralysis, or being unable to move, speak, or comprehend, are very common and usually connect to a level of stress or anxiety. While these dreams have waking connection, the emotional and intuitive experience should be used when exploring their meaning.

**Paranoia:** Many dreams offer a landscape of fear and misunderstanding. The sense of paranoia can be overwhelming in dreams, and the larger dreaming story should be explored along with its symbolic meaning and interpretation.

**Parrot:** A modern-day symbol of mimicry and the bridge between man and animal, the parrot also has roots in many Oceanic cultures as a symbol of wisdom and knowledge.

**Party:** Filled with activity, people, and decoration, parties in dreams can have a dualistic meaning depending on the dreamer's impressions and experiences. This backdrop of human celebration should be explored using context and association with the featured players and the overall story line.

**Passport:** A modern symbol for entry or the ability to cross a given border, a passport featured in a dream may play a pivotal role in the dreaming story or experience. Context and identification will likely

♦

define the larger dreaming message.

**Pastry:** *See Dessert*

**Path:** Highly symbolic relating to journey, personal progress, and individual insight, a path in a dream may lead to any number of landscapes, symbols, or realizations. Paths should be explored in terms of their connection to waking life and the higher intuitive message.

**Patio:** *See Porch*

**Pattern:** Shapes, geometric concepts, and patterns in dreams are highly evolved symbolic representations and must be explored in terms of their metaphoric meaning and their connection to the dreamer's waking life. If a pattern was featured and acted as a symbol of intricacy or design, probe the personal association and context.

**Peacock:** This beautiful and multicolored bird has ancient origins in Persia and India and was originally a symbol of the sun. In Christian traditions, it became a symbol for resurrection and spiritual rebirth. Modern folklore has connected it to vanity and pomposity.

**Peak:** Summits, peaks, and other high levels of natural elevation often represent vistas or perspective in dreams. Often the dreamer may strive to reach a given height, thus bringing the theme of ascension and accomplishment into the dreaming picture. Context is essential when interpreting a dream with this symbol.

**Pear:** Because pear trees live a long time, they are often associated with ancient traditions and are found in many mythological systems. In the twelfth century the pear was known as a feminine sexual symbol. Also found in the Garden of Eden, the pear is known as the mother of Eve.

**Pearl:** Along with shells, pearls are known as natural gems in symbolic traditions. In Oceanic cultures they are a symbol of rebirth or spiritual awakening. In ancient Greece, the pearl was the symbol for Aphrodite. Because of their spherical shape, they are also connected to lunar symbol systems. Because of their luminescence and white color, they are also connected to innocence, virginity, and purity.

**Pebbles:** Pebbles are often found in dreams featuring watery divides or brooks and streams. Because they are closely connected to minerals and other raw natural elements, pebbles commonly symbolize the simplicity of nature as well as treasure and tenacity.

**Pedestal:** Because a pedestal is an object which elevates that which is placed upon it, it is commonly found in dreams symbolizing higher position, perspective, regality, and authority. Dreams featuring a pedestal should be explored in terms of context, use, and placement.

**Pegasus:** Originating in ancient Greek myth, the winged horse called Pegasus was known to have superior powers of speed and poetic justice. In fairy tales and folklore, Pegasus later became a symbol of the ocean and the sentient power of the sea.

**Pelican:** The pelican has a strong place in symbolic traditions because of its ability to fish with its long neck and beak. Often equated with feminine mystique or the concept of intuition, the pelican also carries a strong association to purity because of its ivory color.

**Penis:** The male sexual organ can have many symbolic meanings in dreams. Its basic representation is that of potency and power, but if featured in a sexual nature, it is more likely to relate to the players and larger dreaming story line.

**Pentacle:** The five-pointed star can be found in many medieval and alchemical traditions as a symbol of power, ritual, and oath. However, it is also found in Christian and ancient Egyptian texts as a symbol of the heavens.

**Performing:** Dreams of performing, i.e., singing, dancing, speaking, playing, or acting in public, are common and connect to self-awareness and individual identity. Depending on the dreaming action and story line, the dream may connect to waking issues of human understanding, pride, vanity, value, creativity, or perception.

**Perfume:** A sense of smell in dreams is fairly uncommon, and perfumes in dreams can act as an intoxicating symbol of sweetness and seduction. If there is a personal association to the given scent, a symbolic message may be present, and intuitive reasoning should be used for greater discovery.

**Period (menstruation):** Many women dream of having their period in dreams and the experience can carry any number of meanings associated with femininity, identity, shame, guilt, or embarrassment, depending on the context and the dreaming story line.

**Pet:** Because owning a pet is a personal and associative experience, pets are often featured in dreams relating to individual history and the concept of parenting. Context and association will usually define a dream featuring a pet or the sensation of owning a beloved creature.

**Pharaoh:** The Egyptian equivalent to king or emperor, the Pharaoh carried the powers of the gods and had the ability to transcend mortal life. Dreams featuring this symbol may take on a mystical quality, and spiritual ideology should be considered when exploring the larger dreaming message.

**Phoenix:** This mythological bird with a horn is found in Chinese, heraldic, and Egyptian traditions and is closely associated with the sun. Because it had the ability to rise from fire, it is symbolic of rebirth, individual spirit, and genesis.

**Photograph:** The twentieth-century vision of humanity is often found in photographs, and the image of a photograph in a dream often carries personal or associative meanings. Depending on what the photograph represented or the emotional connection, the dream must be explored in context and with the overall story.

**Photographer:** Unlike the photograph itself, photographers in dreams often take on the role of associative symbols representing vanity, glamour, or ego. Because of their modern connection to the term "paparazzi" they are also representative of power and relentlessness.

**Picnic:** This tranquil and natural setting for a meal or other gathering is often found in dreams symbolizing innocence, happiness, and basic contentment. The dreaming story, along with the featured players, will likely relate the larger message and meaning.

**Picture:** Pictures, paintings, and portraits often contain some form of symbolic representation in the dreaming landscape. Depending on what was depicted and the emotional significance, the dream may have connections to personal history or individual path.

**Pig:** While pigs are known in modern thought to be sloppy and gluttonous creatures, they are actually highly intelligent and carry a strong mythological symbolism as creatures of good luck in early Chinese and Germanic cultures.

**Pigeon:** Often thought of as city dwellers, these creatures carry the same symbol tradition as the dove *(see Dove)*, and their placement in the dream should be explored using their associative connections as well as story placement.

**Pill:** A modern symbol of curative power, the pill has a dualistic meaning. Pills can represent both dependence and destruction or healing and resolution. Context, association, and personal identification should be used in interpreting a dream featuring this symbol.

**Pillar:** A modern idiom for purposefulness with phrases like "a pillar of strength" and "a pillar of society," the pillar has its roots in ancient Greece as a building component of temples. They are also symbolic of the connection between humanity and the heavens or the afterlife.

**Pillow:** As a component of sleep, pillows can often be found in dreams representing the act of dreaming itself. They are also often likened to clouds because of their soft and billowy nature. Context will define this dreaming theme.

**Pilot:** An archetypal symbol for the pioneer spirit, dreams of pilots or piloting can be associative as well as symbolic. Depending on the sensation of flying or the figure of the pilot, this symbol may represent new awareness, insight, or travel.

**Pine Cone:** An ancient Greek symbol of masculinity and virility, the pine cone has a place in the natural world and is also associated with modern Christmas or seasonal holidays.

**Pink:** A color connected in modern folklore to femininity, pink is also the color combination of white and red, representing individuality, passion, and purity. It is often used on St. Valentine's Day, and association will likely define the importance of this color in a dream.

**Pirate:** A swashbuckling figure from novels, the pirate has taken on a modern-day meaning of fun and adventure. In their original form, they were thieves and cutthroats, and personal association and ideology will play a role in defining this dreaming archetype.

**Plague:** The theme of a plague in dreams is similar to that of the doomsday scenario *(see Doomsday)* where mass destruction from disease is imminent. However, unlike the concept of Armageddon, a plague is something beyond human control and relates to symbolism of illness, poor health, and physical limitations.

**Planets:** Differing from the stars, planets are usually featured in dreams relating to mythical journeys or universal themes of exploration and ideology. They can have a mystical relationship to the dreamer or offer a perspective to earth. The specific planet or the intuitive association with it should be probed for meaning and understanding.

**Plant:** A form of natural life, plants in dreams can often have a very important significance. They are symbolic of the parallels between humanity and nature, as well as having the ability to grow.

**Platform:** *See Pedestal*

**Play or Playing:** The act of playing, either freely or on a given instrument, is usually one of joy and happiness in dreams, connecting to the dreamer's current perceptions of leisure and relaxation or creativity and purpose.

**Plow:** An ancient symbol for industry and farming, the plow often represents action and growth in dreams. Dreams of plowing a field or using a plow connect to nature and industriousness.

**Plum:** Known as a symbol of youth and innocence in Asia, this purple fruit is also associated with hope, sexuality, and passion. Use intuitive reasoning as well as symbolic importance when interpreting a dream featuring this symbol.

**Poetry:** The reading or writing of poetry has a paradoxical construct because it is creative in action and in thought. Unlike any other art form, poetry is strongly connected to myth and symbolism as well as romance and passion.

**Poison:** As a symbol of toxicity and death, poison is a common element in dreams. Dreams of drinking or eating poisonous foods relate to the dreamer's ideas of fear, internal conflict, and death and should be probed in relationship to waking realities.

**Police:** As an archetypal symbol of authority, law, and order, a police officer in a dream can either be frightening or comforting depending on the dreaming story as well as personal associations to this time-honored occupation.

**Politician:** Often connected with concepts of defense, position, diplomacy, and strategy, the archetypal symbol of a politician in a dream relates to the dreamer's views on position and culture. Explore context and intuitive placement when interpreting this highly associative and yet powerful symbol.

**Pomegranate:** This Mediterranean fruit which is red in color and distinct in taste was originally cherished by the Greeks as a fruit for the gods and, if eaten, offered fertility and medicinal powers.

**Poor:** Dreams relating to money or themes of wealth and poverty often connect to the dreamer's identity or concept of self-worth. These dreams must be interpreted relating to personal history as well as association to money and its purpose in life.

**Porch:** The modern-day bridge between human life and nature, porches, patios, conservatories, and lanais are all related to the connectivity of two worlds. This symbol will take on an associative or symbolic meaning depending on how the landscape factored into the overall dreaming story.

**Pornography:** Obviously connected to human sexuality, pornography is often featured in dreams as a comparative portal into behaviors of seduction or erotic fantasy. Depending on how it played a role in the dream, it may relate to the dreamer's waking life or a general motif of another meaning.

**Portal:** Portals are often connected to the concept of time or the idea of leaving one world and entering another. Found in many science fiction texts, portals are surreal images in dreams because they do not exist in the linear world. Context and placement will play a role in defining this dreaming symbol.

**Pottery:** Much like glass, pottery is an earthen version of that which is breakable, delicate, and also represents a concrete household item of general use. Context, association, and the placement of the symbol of pottery will define its importance in the dream.

**Prayer or Praying:** A powerful symbol for internal will and spiritual desire, prayer in dreams, much like in waking life, connects the dreamer to his or her higher self. The feelings and associations of the dream can often be overwhelming and should be explored in relation to the entire dreaming paradigm.

**Pregnancy:** Pregnancy dreams are more common for women. The emotional legacy of a pregnancy-related dream might be that of joy or fear, depending on the waking parallels, to the dreamer's ideas and associations with being pregnant. The basic symbolism of pregnancy is that of birth or transition.

**Present:** *See Gift*

**President:** The political figurehead of democracy, the president is an archetypal symbol of government and power. Dreams featuring a presidential figure should be explored in relation to the dreaming story and the role played by this powerful symbol.

**Priest:** The figure of fatherhood and holiness and the Catholic faith, priests in dreams, much like ministers and monks, offer a symbol of God or spiritual concepts. Depending on the dreamer's connections and impressions of his or her faith, the dream may carry a strong spiritual message or meaning.

**Prince:** The male imperial symbol of an heir to the thrown, princes are often featured in fairy tales and folkloric traditions as rescuers and figures of dashing desire. Context and association will likely define a dream carrying this symbol of individual regal strength.

**Princess:** The female counterpart to the prince, the archetypal symbol of the princess is symbolic of beauty, generosity, and regal position. Depending on how the princess was featured in the dreaming story, the dream may connect to concepts of femininity or other aspects of individuality and identity.

**Prison:** *See Jail*

**Procession:** *See Parade*

**Prostitute:** An archetypal symbol of selling one's body for money, the act of prostitution is as old as time. Dreams featuring this symbol should be probed in terms of the emotional sensations and intuitive experience and how it was integrated into the larger dreaming message.

**Psychic:** Dreams featuring the presence of a psychic or the sensation of being psychic are important because their overall message can be one of awakening or self-discovery. Depending on how this symbolic concept of vision is integrated into the dream, there may be a number of higher meanings.

**Pub:** Bars and pubs are landscapes of drink, relaxation, and general debauchery. The way that this backdrop was integrated in the larger dreaming story will define the greater purpose of the dream.

**Puddle:** Many people dream of stepping in puddles or jumping over puddles, and these symbols often act as connective elements in the greater dreaming story. Alone, they can represent clouded thought or doubt.

**Purple:** A hue that rests between blue and red, the color purple or violet is symbolically connected to intuition, creativity, spirituality, and metaphysics. Dreams featuring this color should be explored on a symbolic as well as associative level.

**Purse:** A compartment for holding objects of femininity or identity, a purse can be a highly symbolic and personal element in a dream. Depending on how it played a role in the larger dreaming story, its presence may relate to issues of self-awareness, financial issues, or individual path.

**Pursuit:** Many people dream of pursuing a given person or object or, alternately, being pursued. These dreams can carry an experience of challenge or fear, depending on the story line. Context and association will be vital when interpreting this dreaming theme and meaning.

**Pyramid:** The pyramid in its glory symbolized a life-giving force to the ancient Egyptians. It is an evocative three-dimensional symbol and it represents the world's core. Its apex symbolizes the highest point of spiritual attainment. The body of the great pyramid represents one's unfinished business or ascent into enlightenment.

**Queen:** The regal status of a queen is the symbol of elements that are divine and also human. Dreams featuring a queen may be connected to feminine symbols of power and position as well as individual identity.

**Quest:** Quests are highly spiritual symbols in dreams because they ask us to use our inner sense of purpose to pursue a higher goal. In Native American lore, the vision quest takes the searcher on a journey of self-discovery and intuitive awareness.

**Quicksand:** Quicksand in dreams is often found as a symbol for the eroding and timeless aspect of human existence. Many people fear quicksand because of its myth of suffocation although they have never seen it in their lives. Quicksand can conceptually relate to dreaming themes of anxiety, doubt, and fear.

**Rabbi:** Much like any religious figurehead, the rabbi is the Jewish symbol of teacher, spiritual advisor, and holy person. Featured in a dream, the rabbi can bring wisdom or merely a type of spiritual presence. Integrate the dreaming story with the overall intuitive message.

**Rabbit:** Traditionally the rabbit conjures up furry images of curious creatures and in Chinese calendars is a symbol of intelligence and keen insight. Because they are included in many children's tales, their associative connection often relates to childhood and innocence. Personal connections and ideas about the hare or the rabbit are essential if this creature played a role in the dream.

**Race:** Dreams of running in or viewing a race relates to the concept of time as well as the dualistic idea of winning and losing. Depending on the nature of the race and the emotional sensation connected to it, the dream many have varying forms of story line and meaning.

**Radio:** Radios, television sets, and other modern symbols of communication like cellular phones are often featured in dreams. They can be entertainment or a specific dreaming voice or message. Since radios are often associated with music, the feelings connected to the object and its sound will play a large role in interpreting the dream.

**Rage:** *See Anger*

**Railroad:** Railroads represent a linear track of travel and connect to any sort of journey that the dream may be pursuing or viewing. Much like a road or a highway, a railroad station or train track can symbolize a path yet to be taken. Context, story line, and associative images will define the dream.

**Rain:** The powerful symbol of rain is found in many mythological traditions. It can represent cleansing of the spirit as well as rebirth or the bringing of new life. In Hawaiian and other Polynesian societies, rain can be brought on by a dance and is closely connected with God. In China, it represents the feminine principle of Yin. No matter how you view rain, it offers a change of landscape in the dreaming motif and should be valued in the context of the entire dreaming picture.

**Rainbow:** The wonderful hues of the rainbow usually carry seven colors. In Christian traditions, these represent the seven gifts of the Holy Spirit or sacraments, doctrine, office, polity, prayer, and power. In the natural world the rainbow is the giver of life and happiness, being highly important in Hawaiian and Oceanic traditions. In Africa, it is heralded with the sky and the energy flowing between heaven and earth.

**Ram:** Known as the astrological symbol of Aries, the ram has a place in biblical symbolism as the leader of the mountain animal kingdom and a figure of masculinity. Its associations are that of energy, purpose, and resolve.

**Rape:** Dreams of rape and violation are common in relationship to fear and anxiety. Dreams of this nature are terrifying and often awake the dreamer from sleep. The larger symbol of violence and the degradation of life plays a defining role.

**Rapids:** Fast and forceful, the image of watery rapids conjures up the speed and power of water. Many people equate the rapids with the daunting force of nature or the swift movement of change. Much like a tidal wave, they represent natural direction and power.

**Rash:** Dreams featuring an annoying itch or a rash can symbolically have great value because they may be identifying an irritating situation or problem from waking life. If your dream featured a rash, probe the emotional and intuitive sensations you felt and explore how the feelings relate to daily events and human connections.

**Rat:** Another symbol from the Chinese calendar, the rat is known as industrious and cunning as well as being a symbol of higher learning in India. In the West, the rat has taken on negative connotations with diseases, being the bringer of the bubonic plaque in Europe. Rats are also negatively depicted in fairy tales and folklore. Modern expressions like "rat race" liken it to the symbol of the insect world in its mass force.

**Raven:** This black, crowlike bird has been equated with death because of modern writings from Edgar Allen Poe and also folkloric representations. However, it traditionally and mythologically represents wisdom and philosophy as well as transition. In Greek traditions and the Old Testament, it is represented as a bird which misplaces secrets or valuable information.

**Ravine:** Much like a ditch or a recess, the ravine often represents an area to be crossed. It can also be a valley of water or another representation of the recesses of our minds or emotions. Probe the dreaming landscape in correlation to waking life and events in order to interpret the dream and its meaning.

**Razor:** Sharp, thin, and also used as a weapon, this simple tool for shaving takes on a modern symbolic meaning with terms like "razor's edge" and "razor thin." The interpretive connection is that of anything on the cutting edge or events that are tenuous. The use and placement of the razor in the dreaming story will define the overall intuitive meaning of the dream.

**Reading:** The act of reading in a dream typically connects back to the nature of what is being read. Often words, phrases, and entire sentences appear in dreams in order to enlighten the dreamer to an event or individual truth.

**Recipe:** Recipes are akin to puzzles or maps in their symbolism because they provide the dreamer with a set of instructions. Sometimes a recipe can appear, but the dreamer cannot make it out. Emotion and context will provide a better picture of the dream direction.

**Red:** The color red has great presence in all symbol and mythological traditions. Equated with love, passion, blood, anger, and fire, it carries an association of energy and vitality. Biblically it represents the blood of Christ, and in Buddhism it is a sign of creativity. Since most of the associations with the color red are positive, a dream featuring this primary hue will likely have some degree of positive purpose and may challenge the dreamer in many ways.

**Reef:** Reefs are interesting structures, much like natural mazes, that house marine and aquatic life. They can represent a myriad of images and in dreams be seen as giant fish tanks. Since reefs are also barriers to the open sea, they represent a protective quality and function in the watery world.

**Refrigerator:** Designed to hold food and to keep things fresh, refrigerators in dreams can act as a place for safekeeping or perhaps hidden discovery. The symbol of food and nourishment is also important, but context and the dreaming story will define a dream that features this modern daily appliance.

**Relatives:** Relatives in a group or in singular appearance play a role of heritage and familiarity in dreams. Sometimes they can act as part of a dreaming story line, and at other times they can bring messages. Depending on the nature of your relationship with each individual, your dream may take on any number of associative meanings.

**Repair:** The act of repairing an object or even a relationship takes on a unique role in dreams. Often repairing something refers to a waking event or emotions. Sometimes the dreamer cannot complete the repair. Other dreams feature watching something being repaired. Whatever the case, dreams of repair are important and should be explored for their content as well as their message.

**Restaurant:** This backdrop of eating and service represents nourishment or entertainment. Many dreams feature a restaurant as backdrop, but associations usually take on a specific role in the overall dreaming message.

**Reunion:** Dreams that feature the theme of reunion, be it a high school or class reunion or simply a gathering of familiar and old friends, are associated with the past. The emotional sensations of sleep will usually bring on the larger message. The goal in interpreting a reunion dream is to integrate the past with the present in emotion and intuitive reasoning.

**Rhinoceros:** This amazing and rare creature is known today as an endangered species. In Africa it is valued for its ability to overpower its prey. In Asia, its tusk is considered to have healing powers. Symbolically, it can connect to rarity, uniqueness, and also power, but association will probably tell the larger story.

**Rice:** This modern-day symbol of marriage is also a staple of diet and has strong mythological and spiritual connotations. In China it is much like bread, known as a symbol of nourishment, humanity, and giving. In Southeast Asia the "Rice Mother" is an ancient goddess representing life. In Buddhist traditions it is known as part of the order of humility and compassion. A single grain of rice, much like a grain of sand, is symbolic of the connection between the individual and the whole.

**Riches:** Dreams of newfound wealth or riches can connect to the dreamer's desire for material change or the search for monetary resolution. Many people dream of winning the lottery or finding a buried box of treasure. The deeper intuitive story will aid in understanding dreams of newly found riches.

**Ring:** A symbol of unity and eternity, the ring is also connected to the symbol of the circle, a sign of infinity. Rings are connected to love and the act of commitment or marriage, but they also symbolize status and position, as in the case of the Pope's ring. Medieval views on rings were that they held possible blessings and their power might bring fortune or demise to the wearer. Rings play highly symbolic and purposeful roles in dreams, and their appearance should be interpreted using association context and intuitive understanding.

**Riot:** Many dreams featuring mass hysteria or large crowds symbolize collective pursuits or human reaction. The actions of the crowd and tone of the dream will provide a greater avenue of understanding.

**River:** Rivers are often equated with the basin of civilization or the transient nature of the universe. They also represent spirituality, flow, and unity with nature. Because there are many rivers throughout the world that carry great symbolism, like the Ganges, the Thames, and the Seine, they become central to iconography. They are also found in forests and natural landscapes bringing the concept of path and navigation. Crossing a river is also a theme of overcoming an emotional obstacle.

**Road:** Synonymous with path or choice of destination, roads are often featured in dreams as a connective aspect or a part of the dreamer's journey. They are symbolic much like a highway or a trail in that they offer the dreamer a given set of intuitive choices. Roads are strong images and should be interpreted along with the entire dreaming story line and emotional sensation.

**Roadblock:** Roadblocks are symbolic of blockades, walls, or other concrete elements that prevent the dreamer from moving forward. Featured in dreams, they can represent any number of things and connect entirely to parallels to the dreamer's intuitive journey, as well as to his or her waking connections.

**Robbery:** Dreams of being robbed or having things stolen are fairly common in the dreaming world. An unknown assailant may appear and snatch a symbolic item, or parts of the dreamer's home may be missing. If you dream of a robbery, probe the meaning of the lost or missing items or your feelings about material value, betrayal, and trust.

**Robe:** *See Cape*

**Rock:** Mythologically known as a symbol of stability and permanence, rocks can appear in dreams in many forms. Throughout the world there are many important spiritual rock formations like Stonehenge, Ayers Rock, and the Rock of Gibraltar, all connecting to the power of the unknown and the force of durability. Rocks are also used in masonry and in the creation of tombstones, thus representing the permanence of the human soul and the eternal afterlife.

**Rocket:** This twentieth-century craft has become associated with space travel, adventure, and exploration to worlds beyond our own. Rockets also have a connection to childhood, as many toys are crafted in this form. Themes of discovery and exploration may be at play.

**Rodeo:** This western motif for a circus is a grand event, featuring roping, riding, and other skills. If you have never attended a rodeo, your perceptions will be quite different from someone who has. Its main associations are horses and cowboys, but context and personal history will provide the basic connection of this dreaming image.

**Roller Coaster:** Many people have dreams featuring roller coasters because these modern-day amusement structures symbolize speed and disparity of height. Phrases like "a roller coaster of emotions" also permeate dreaming perceptions. Because these rides can be terrifying as well as thrilling and exciting, the dream story and overall feeling will bring the nocturnal message to light.

**Roof:** Often connected to shelter and the cover of a domicile, a roof acts as a symbol of protection. In modern thinking the expression "keeping a roof over my head" gives it a meaning of earning a living or being able to provide for oneself. It can also represent a view from an elevated viewpoint.

**Rooster:** Known for its loud and alarming cry, the rooster has a long history of mythology and symbolism. It is part of the Chinese calendar, representing fire, tenacity, and pride. Much like the lion, it is also known in European traditions as a regal or powerful emblem of masculinity. Since its crow is the awakening sound on a farm, it has a common-day connection to time, as an animal version of the alarm clock.

**Roots:** A natural world example of an anchor, roots are associated with plants, trees, and other life. Modern phrases like "It's in my roots" convey the meaning and representation of heritage, lineage, and family history.

**Rope:** Ropes are intuitively symbolic in many different ways. They are durable and often relate to connectivity, but they are also representative of things that can be tied, the creation of knots, or a link to another place and time. Depending on the nature of how the rope is featured in the dream, it may aid the dreamer in placing one component of a dream with another. If the rope is used to tie or untie, the dream may connect to problem solving.

**Rosary:** This Catholic symbol of worship is strongly connected with prayer and also a tangible method of connecting faith and the act of resolve. Dreams featuring this highly spiritual symbol may connect to different approaches to religion or spiritual offering depending on the views and faith of the dreamer.

**Rose:** Originally associated with the Greek god Adonis, roses have a vast history in myth and symbolism, as well as spiritual connotation. Typically, the rose connects to blood or the human extension of natural love. It is also represented in crucifixes and heraldic symbols of arms representing power and compassion. This lovely and fragrant flower has a place in common thought as a symbol of passion, romance, and everlasting love.

**Ruby:** Much like its counterpart the garnet, this deep red stone is often equated with passion and brilliance. It is also associated with the planet Mars. Interestingly, in early pagan traditions, rubies were believed to ward off bad dreams.

**Rug:** This basic household object often acts as part of the dreaming landscape. Some dreams feature rugs that are being pulled out from under individuals while other dreams have rugs placed in new surroundings. Much like a lawn, the rug is a natural foundation or grounded awareness.

**Runes:** The origin of runes is unknown. It is believed that these small stone tablets were created by Celtic or Germanic peoples, yet they are crafted similarly to ancient modes of hieroglyphics. Used for divination, they have also had a place in early forms of writing in Nordic countries. Contrary to modern interpretations of evil use, which originated in Nazi Germany, these small tablets are a mystic representation of communication and the early skills of human understanding.

**Running:** The theme of running to or from places and people is very common in the dreaming world. The obvious parallel is movement and the transition from one place in time to another. Running can also connect to many emotions of fear and anxiety or exhilaration and freedom. Context, identity, and association will define a dream featuring running and the runner.

**Sadness:** Dreams featuring an overwhelming sense of sadness can relate to any number of concepts and emotions including loss, rejection, and isolation. These dreaming themes should be explored in terms of featured players and the overall contextual message.

**Sailor:** This archetypal symbol of adventure and travel also connects to the symbol systems of the ocean. Sailors have a modern connotation of being salty old souls, and their presence in dreams should be explored in relationship to the greater dreaming story.

**Sale:** Dreams featuring a sale or a bargain shopping experience relate to themes of deal making or finding undiscovered treasure. Depending on the emotional sensations, the dream may represent finance, personal discovery, or reward.

**Salt:** This ancient symbol can be found throughout biblical and mythological traditions, typically representing indispensability as well as provision. In India, salt became a core component of Gandhi's movement to overtake the British Empire. Salt is also commonly seen as a mystical element as people throw it over their shoulder before a meal.

**Samurai:** This ancient Japanese position of warrior class is often seen as among the most intelligent and ferocious in traditions of defense and war. Often associated with their sword, samurais are archetypal representations of the warrior force and Zen concept of the power of one.

**Sand:** Found in desert and island regions, sand is often connected to themes of infinity and minutia. Comparative expressions such as "like a grain of sand" illustrate a metaphor of size and importance. However, association will likely define this natural element, as sand is also symbolic of escape, relaxation, and renewal.

**Santa Claus:** This archetypal symbol of the Christmas season is often known as "Father Christmas" and connects to themes of fatherly love, compassionate giving, and also general holiday cheer. Known for his red suit and white beard, Santa Claus carries a symbolic relevance to childhood as well as goodness and joy.

**Sapphire:** Because of its deep blue color, sapphires have traditionally been connected to the ocean and the sky in many symbol systems. Also considered a healing stone in India, the sapphire is commonly known for its preciousness and its value. In ancient Christian and Celtic traditions it was symbolically linked to truth.

**Saturn:** Originating in Greek myth, Saturn was the father of Jupiter and is often associated with communication, expression, and also the process of aging. The planet Saturn is connected to the sign of Capricorn in astrological traditions and is representative of individuality, tenacity, and universal being. Because of the rings that surround it, many are fascinated with this planet and personal association as well as context should be used for interpretation.

**Scales:** Symbolically representative of justice, the scales are also connected to the astrological sign of Libra and themes of balance and human knowledge. Found in Tibetan, Persian, and Hindu traditions, the scales are representative of afterlife and the measures of karma within consequence and action.

**Scar:** Experiencing or seeing scars in dreams may represent themes of healing, rejuvenation, and regeneration. Depending on the emotional reaction and dreaming design, there may also be elements of remorse and reaction at play.

**Scarab:** This ancient Egyptian beetle is a symbol of the rising and setting sun and the basic concept of "being." Often fashioned from semiprecious and precious stones, this symbol is highly valued in Egyptian tradition and carries a Christian representation of the resurrection.

**Scepter:** Usually associated with a regal position such as emperor, king, or queen, the scepter has a mythological history for yielding power and force in the human domain. Its biblical representations indicate humility, and in Mayan culture scepters were used to bring rain. Context will be vital in placing the relevance and intuitive value of this highly important cultural symbol.

**School:** Dreams of being in an academic or school environment are highly associative depending on personal history and individual approach to learning. Many people have dreams about returning to school in order to complete a mission or to close a chapter of life. Contact and the larger dreaming story will likely define a dream with this backdrop.

**Scientist:** This archetypal figure of exploration and intellectual pursuit can have a dualistic meaning depending on the dreamer's personal association. Science itself is a symbol of discovery and research, and context should be valued in understanding the nature of this figurehead in a dream.

**Scissors:** Much like other sharp objects, scissors are often featured in dreams as weapons or instruments of threat, as well as their normal use for cutting. Often dreams of using scissors relate to problem solving or spatial connection, and so the overall dreaming story should be interpreted for understanding and meaning.

**Scorpion:** Known for its lethal sting, the scorpion is a desert creature that has mythological and spiritual roots in Greece, Egypt, Persia, and China. While typically associated with its poison or venom, the scorpion is also representative of tenacity, illumination, healing, and resurrection.

**Sea:** *See Ocean*

**Seal:** Often connected with the seven seals in the Revelation, seals were an ancient Greek method of documentation. They carry a mystical association of basic symbolic tradition and should be explored in terms of their relationship to the intuitive message of the dream.

**Seal (animal):** These peace-loving land and sea animals are known throughout the Arctic and Pacific as animals of peace and beauty. The Hawaiian monk seal is known for its rarity and friendly demeanor.

**Searching:** The theme of searching is commonly found in dreams and can connect to a waking parallel. Depending on the events in the dreamer's life, there may be elements of discovery, renewal, perspective, and healing.

**Secret:** Dreams featuring some form of secrecy connect back to basic themes of trust, illusion, mystery, and value. Depending on the importance of the secret and the characters involved in the dreaming story, there may be a higher level of self-awareness involved in the dreaming message.

**Security:** Dreams that carry the sensation of security are usually very positive. They often connect to themes of love, romance, and human understanding and should be explored in context and using tools of association.

**Seed:** Seeds are important symbols because they relate to birth, renewal, growth, ideas, and advancement. Often a seed in a dream can act as a symbol for a waking event and should be explored in context and with intuitive reasoning.

**Seven:** One of the more important numbers in numerical symbolism, seven is often valued as a lucky number and can be found throughout biblical and other ancient texts representing holiness, divinity, virtue, sin, and even masculinity. Because of its dualistic and varied traditional meaning, it should be interpreted on an intuitive level in a dream.

**Sewing:** The act of sewing is a creative endeavor and, yet, highly purposeful and utilitarian in nature. Many dreams featuring the act of sewing can relate to problem solving and should be probed using intuitive reasoning and overall dreaming story line.

**Sex:** While sex is a common dreaming subject, the players in a sexual dream often carry more relevance than the actual acts that occur. Depending on the emotional experience and how the dream connects to waking realities, the message may be one of delight, discovery, healing, and resolve or, alternately, shame, disillusion, anxiety, and fear.

**Shadow:** The symbolic concept of the shadow is that of the human soul, as well as the casting of light upon darkness and vice versa. Shadows can represent mystery, eclipse, loss, illumination, experience, and salvation. Shadowlike figures are common dreaming experiences, and the intuitive connection will usually tell the larger dreaming message or purpose.

**Shaman:** The Native American healer or equivalent of teacher or priest is a powerful symbol in a dream. This archetypal figure represents leadership and vision, and the dream may relate to a journey or path. Context and placement as well as intuitive reasoning should be explored.

**Shark:** These ancient creatures are known for their predatory nature and ferocious bite. However, the shark is also a highly intuitive creature that is valued symbolically in Asia as an image of intelligence and insight. Modern lore has made many people fear the shark, so personal association will be important for interpretation.

**Sheep:** Found in biblical texts, sheep are known for their ability to follow and are often associated with the countryside and the symbol of the shepherd. As a domestic creature, the sheep, much like the lamb, is connected to themes of sacrifice, helplessness, and stupidity.

**Shell:** Symbolically representative of nature's gemstone, shells in dreams can represent discovery, rewards, bliss, and also hidden treasure. Many shells, like the conch, have a greater mythological history; however, the shell itself is a symbol of the ocean and her magical offerings.

**Shield:** An ancient form of protection in battle, the shield can represent many things in a dream, depending on how it was used. Often associated on a folkloric level with battle and the dragon symbol, the shield should be valued in terms of overall meaning and what it was used to defend against.

**Ship:** While ships are known in common language as vessels for transport over the water, they are also symbolically connected to the afterlife and the dimension of the human soul. Found in early Celtic and Norse mythology, they represent the voyage into the unknown and the eternal afterlife. Placement and purpose should be explored in the dreaming landscape.

**Shipwreck:** Dreams of shipwrecks or conflict at sea are fairly common and act as a symbol for conflict and struggle. Depending on the nature of the wreck or the intuitive connection to the event, the dream may have a higher intuitive message and should be explored in context and association *(see Water and Ocean)*.

**Shirt:** This article of clothing, closely associated with the upper body, is often found in dreams relating to identity and sexuality. The experience of "losing one's shirt" is a symbol for loss of status or money, and this image should be explored on a contextual and associative level for greater meaning.

**Shock:** The act of feeling stunned or being in shock is a common dreaming theme relating to larger issues of fear as well as change. Often the dreamer feels that events are beyond his or her control. Explore the overall story line and dreaming sensation for waking parallels.

**Shoes:** Shoes are very closely connected to individuality and identity and because they are so personal and associative, they should be explored on an intuitive level in the dreaming story. Often found in fairy tales and folklore like "Cinderella" relating to feminine identity and romance, slippers may carry the meaning of awakening or insight.

**Shooting:** Dreams that feature the act of shooting are a modern idiom for hunting, death, or destruction. Depending on the dreamer's association with guns *(see Gun)* on a basic level, the contextual placement of the act will reveal its symbolism and importance.

**Shopping:** While shopping is a commonplace activity in the modern world, its meaning in dreams can be one of choice, selection, and desire. Association, along with intuitive reasoning and dreaming sensation, will define its importance and daily relevance.

**Shorts:** *See Pants*

**Shovel:** Dreams of digging or the use of a shovel are often symbolic of unburying or burying things. Depending on how the shovel was used, the dream may relate to higher levels of awareness or concepts of self, and association is vital for interpretation.

**Shower:** The act of cleansing in the dreaming landscape can be a powerful experience. Showers are common in dreams and while they may relate to a more sexual story line, their presence can also connect to themes of healing, repair, and renewal depending on the overall dreaming message and context.

**Shrine:** Often connected to themes of elevation and worship, shrines can be found in every religious order. Shrines are representative of many things depending on the dreamer's personal spirituality and ideology. The way the shrine was featured along with its overall intuitive meaning will likely provide the greater meaning of the dream.

**Shrink:** The act of shrinking or magically growing in dreams is part of the surreal landscape relating to transformation and the process of integration. Many dreams carry this symbol for change. Probe the ideology and greater interpretative value for meaning.

**Sick:** Dreams featuring the sensation of being sick or the experience of sickness on a general level relates to human frailty and concepts of life. Depending on how this element played a role in the larger dreaming story, there may be a larger message of healing and resolution.

**Sickle:** An ancient Babylonian tool for harvesting food, the sickle has come to be associated in the twentieth century with communism. It is also found in Greek lore representing fertility and abundance.

**Sidewalk:** A linear, modern version of the pathway or walkway, sidewalks in dreams often represent intuitive journeys because they carry the dreamer along a given route. Context and emotional association should be explored in order to understand the importance and waking parallels of this dreaming landscape.

**Silver:** An important metal in many symbol systems, silver is commonly known as a noble metal, often worn by the ruling class in ancient cultures. It is most often associated with the moon within European as well as Mexican tradition, and its use can reflect the act of devotion. Personal connection and spiritual ideology will form the interpretation of this dreaming symbol.

**Singing:** While singing in dreams tends to be a joyous and harmonious experience, the basic act is one of release, communication, and freedom. Depending on the emotional sensation, the dream may carry any number of values and messages.

**Sinking:** Many dreams feature the experience of sinking, be it in water or another surreal landscape. The sensation is usually one of fear and anxiety; however, the symbol is that of lack of control and should be probed on an associative and intuitive level.

**Sister:** Familial connections are important in dreams because they feature human connection and, depending on the true nature of the relationship, a clear and emotional message. Sisters are archetypal representations of sisterhood and power and symbolically represent the feminine unity.

**Six:** Found originally in the Old Testament, the number six has a history relating to the hexagram and the Star of David *(see Star of David)*. Traditionally, the number six represents mercy and creation. In China, it is symbolic of the six human emotions.

**Skating:** Skating, much like the act of dancing or flying, incorporates themes of freedom and expression. Skating can also carry themes of lack of control, depending on the dreaming experience, and context and story line will likely define the greater dreaming message.

**Skeleton:** Symbolic of death and the afterlife in Mexican tradition, the skeleton is also representative of biology, evolution, and science. Depending on the reaction to the skeletal form, the dream may relate to the dreamer's concepts of these themes or other aspects of mortality.

**Skiing:** While skiing is a sport that many people enjoy and find to be an exhilarating experience, the act or theme of skiing in dreams connects to concepts of descent, speed, and vantage point. Association, context, and placement will determine the importance of this theme.

**Skin:** Much like the teeth, skin in dreams usually connects to themes of anxiety such as the experience of a rash or having blemished skin. Overall feeling, context, and association will determine the dreaming theme and message.

**Skirt:** This article of clothing, often associated with femininity, is connected to gender and identity. In dreams, context and association will define the meaning and importance.

**Skunk:** Often most noted for its ability to create a foul-smelling odor, the skunk is an oddity in dreams because many people have a distinct association with this creature and yet have never actually encountered one. Association and impression will determine the importance of this symbol.

**Sky:** Vast and overpowering, the sky can take on any number of roles in a dream depending on the view and the impression. As one of the four elements, the sky has ancient mythological roots linking it to heaven and the vast expanse of the human soul.

**Skyscraper:** Modern landscapes of skyscrapers and high-rises are representative of humankind's progress or the overwhelming, towering energy of a large city. Personal association will play a vital role in interpreting the dream, depending on how the dreamer views this backdrop in his or her life.

**Sleeping:** Much like dreams within a dream, the act of sleeping in a dream is often reflective of basic awareness of the act itself. If another person was sleeping, there could be an insightful dream experience. Association, context, and emotional reaction will dictate the importance of this symbol.

**Slipper:** *See Shoes*

**Smell:** A sense of scent or odor in a dream is unusual but not uncommon. The feeling that one is being drawn toward something that smells distinctly can relate to the basic exploration of human instincts and ideas.

**Smiling:** Smiles in dreams act much as they do in waking life. They can have an infectious quality for good or calm and often provide a positive experience. They can also relate to themes of pride, perspective, and individuality.

**Smoke:** Smoke as an element in the dreaming landscape can connect to themes of fire, cloudiness, or haze. Smoke can represent the inability to see clearly or other aspects of danger and fear. Placement and context will reflect the importance of this symbol.

**Smoking:** A highly associative symbol, the act of smoking in a dream or of viewing others smoking usually connects back to the dreamer's ideology. Intuitive reasoning should be explored in this dreaming theme.

**Smothering:** *See Suffocate*

**Smuggling:** The act of smuggling involves hiding something on an illegal or illegitimate level. Dreams of smuggling can relate to themes of identity, morality, or other cultural and societal themes and should be explored in terms of context in the larger dreaming story.

**Snail:** This sea and land mollusk has great resonance in folkloric traditions, representing wisdom and thrift as well as methodical principles of self-reliance. It was known in biblical tradition to represent harmony because of its shell.

**Snake:** This symbolic reptile appears in both religious and mythological symbols systems. In the East the snake is known as a peace-loving creature, and in the West, mainly in biblical traditions, the snake was representative of the underworld, evil, or the devil. Personal association and the overall dreaming experience will dictate the meaning of this dualistic symbol.

**Snow:** Because it is simultaneously calming and cold, snow has a dualistic representation. The snowflake is symbolic of individuality, but snow itself can relate to transformation and change depending on its placement in the dreaming landscape.

**Soldier:** This archetypal figurehead represents war, defense, and action. Often soldiers in the dreaming landscape can relate to parallels of conflict and resolution. Associative and intuitive experiences should be explored.

**Sorrow:** *See Sadness*

**Soul:** Dreams featuring the concept or sensation of soul are highly intuitive and often reflect themes of life and afterlife. These dreams should be probed in terms of waking parallels and other karmic pursuits.

**South:** Southern themes are often symbolic of warmth and rest with common modern expressions like "going south for the winter." The Southern Hemisphere contains many cultures that mythologically embrace the sun *(see Sun)*, and this direction should be explored in context as well as overall dreaming relevance.

**Spark:** Representative of passion and light, sparks are connected to the symbolism of fire and its accompanying meanings. Sparks in dreams may relate to fear or discovery, and depending on the experience, the emotional association should be explored.

**Space:** The vast expanse of the universe is a common dreaming theme. Space is often a symbol for the unknown, exploration, and discovery. Depending on the dreaming impressions, the dreamer could be journeying on a new quest of self or individual identity; however, context and placement will likely define symbolic importance.

**Spacecraft:** A vehicle for exploring space, this vessel has a surreal quality in dreams because most people have never actually been on a spacecraft. Individual ideology relating to travel and discovery will determine the importance of this symbol.

**Speaking:** *See Talking*

**Spear:** Found in Oceanic and other tribal cultures, the spear is often associated with fierceness and speed. Akin to the knife in weaponry, it can act as a symbol for defense, attack, and war in the dreaming landscape.

**Speeding:** The act of speeding in dreams is fairly common and can occur in planes, cars, or any other vehicle that can take the dreamer into a framework of action. The sensation can be one of fear or exhilaration depending on the larger dreaming story and sequence.

**Sphere:** As a geometric form, the sphere relates to circular symbols of unity, infinity, and the universe. Depending on how the sphere is featured and the associative message, the dream may relate to greater concepts of unity and connection.

**Sphinx:** This creature from ancient myth, which is half man, half lion, is associated symbolically with invincibility and regality. Found in Greek and Egyptian traditions, the sphinx can carry varied associations and should be explored intuitively.

**Spider:** While the spider is found in many cultural and world symbol systems, it typically carries a negative association of cunning and trepidation. In medieval European culture it was respected as an omen of good fortune. Context and individual interpretation should be explored relating to this dualistic symbol.

**Sports:** Sports or games of any sort relate to themes of joy, happiness, athleticism, freedom, and purpose. Depending on what game was played and the outcome, the dream may carry other meanings relating to individual path.

**Spring:** A season of rebirth, spring carries many associations of renewal and regeneration. As plants begin to blossom, so does the human spirit, and this landscape should be explored symbolically and intuitively in dreams.

**Spy:** Dreams relating to espionage or themes of spying on others can relate to concepts of invisibility or omniscient voice. Depending on the overall sensation along with the dreaming story, there may be a voyeuristic message or theme.

**Square:** This geometric shape originated from the cross and represents balance and union on a symbolic level. In Chinese traditions it is representative of magic. Associative reasoning should be used for greater understanding.

**Squirrel:** Known in early Christian symbolism as an animal of distrust, the squirrel enjoys a more palatable connection in modern soci-

# SEEKING INFORMATION ON

**holistic health, spirituality, dreams, intuition or ancient civilizations?**
Call 1-800-723-1112, visit our Web site, or mail in this postage-paid card for a FREE catalog of books and membership information.

Name: _____

Address: _____

City: _____

State/Province: _____

Postal/Zip Code: _____ Country: _____

Association for Research and Enlightenment, Inc.
215 67th Street
Virginia Beach, VA 23451-2061

**For faster service, call 1-800-723-1112.**
www.edgarcayce.org

PBIN

ety, often representing softness or swiftness.

**Stab or Stabbing:** Dreams of stabbing something or being stabbed relates to a theme of invasion. Depending on the weapon or the emotional experience, the dream may relate to concepts of struggle, frustration, or resolution.

**Stadium:** *See Arena*

**Stage:** A backdrop for any type of act or action, the stage is a basic symbol for human life. While dreams featuring a stage may be theatrical, they may also carry a greater day-to-day message and must be explored for theme and intuitive message.

**Stairs:** Akin to ladders, stairs are important in dreams because they relate to the theme of ascension and often take the dreamer into new dimensions of thought or action. Probe the intuitive message along with the dreaming story for meaning.

**Stamp:** This basic element for sending and receiving mail has general significance and symbolism in the dreaming world as a mode of sending a message or the act of communication.

**Star:** Stars are highly symbolic elements that symbolically connect to themes of astronomy, spirituality, or human exploration. Stars are often found in dreams because they are only visible at night. Context and placement will determine their importance in the dreaming story.

**Star of David:** The six-sided Star of David is symbolically connected with themes of resurrection. This wonderful Hebrew symbol connects to many themes of rebirth, goodness, compassion, and light and should be probed relating to all of these themes.

**Statue:** A fixed image of an individual or artist's representation of an abstract idea, statues are highly symbolic because they relate to a greater vision from the dreamer's mind. Depending on the type of statue and the emotional connection to it, the dream may carry a higher significance or intuitive purpose.

**Steak:** Dreams of meat or other dietary connections are highly associative. While steak is known in the modern world as a "power meal," its importance in the dream will be defined by personal connection and symbolism.

**Stealing:** Dreams featuring acts of theft or stealing are connected to material possession, ownership, loss, gain, and identity. Depending on who was stealing and what was taken, the dream may carry personal significance in terms of individuality, ideology, and issues of problem solving.

**Steam:** *See Mist*

**Steppingstone:** Steppingstones are often symbolic of transition and can be found in dreams representing the dreamer's journey or individual path. The symbol of the steppingstone should be explored in terms of direction and the overall dreaming story.

**Stone:** While stones carry the quality of indestructibility and permanence, they also carry many individual symbolic representations. If the dream featured a landscape of stone, the overall backdrop is one of durability and purpose.

**Stork:** While this bird carries a modern folkloric interpretation as the deliverer of babies, it is also found in the Old Testament connected to the return of spring and the resurrection of Christ.

**Storm:** Many dreams feature storms which act as symbols for some form of conflict or division in the dreamer's waking world. These dreams are highly intuitive and should be valued using context association and basic symbolism.

**Stove:** An instrument for heating and cooking, a stove can often act as a catalyst for fire or other dreaming events relating to domesticity or food. Probe the placement and overall dreaming message for interpretation.

**Stranger:** Dreams that feature anonymous individuals or strangers are highly symbolic. They often involve greater themes like love relationships or individual pursuit and should be interpreted within the dreaming perspective.

**Strangle:** Dreams of strangulation often relate to strong sensations of fear, anxiety, or suffocation. The act of strangulation might represent a form of frustration or a sense of being controlled by people or circumstances. Explore the intuitive message along with the emotional legacy.

**Straw:** Found in many folkloric and biblical stories, straw is an earthly element known for its ability to warm and feed. It also is associated with weakness, with expressions like "the straw that broke the camel's back," and should be explored on an associative and intuitive plane.

**Strawberry:** Strawberries have associations of sweetness and often innocence. Being fruits of the earth, they can also relate to sensuality and human exploration. Depending on the experience and context, these wonderful red berries can often act as a positive symbol of growth and happiness *(see also Berries).*

**Stream:** Creeks, brooks, and streams carry the basic symbolic association of water *(see Water)* and yet also are associated with rivers *(see River),* the flow of movement, and the metaphor of the journey. Explore the placement of the symbol along with individual associations for the dreaming meaning.

**Street:** Connected to linear architectural themes of movement and humanity, street scenes often act as backdrops for elements and actions in dreams. Depending on what occurred on a given street and the associations with it, the dream make take on a greater intuitive meaning.

**String:** Much like thread *(see Thread),* string carries associations with time or industry. Also connected to childhood themes, string can act as a measuring tool in dreams and should be explored in context.

**Stroke:** The act of having a stroke in a dream is a common symbol for loss of control, loss of life, or any other life-altering or -threatening theme *(see also Heart Attack).* Depending on the associative and intuitive sensation, the dream may relate to change, anxiety, or disillusion.

**Submarine:** An underwater vehicle for exploration as well as warfare, the submarine occupies a unique place in modern ideology, relating to the wonders of the sea. Association and story line will define the significance of this dreaming backdrop.

**Subway:** This modern method of travel is found around the world in many cultural and city centers. Dreams carrying this symbol may relate to change, transition, new horizons, or other experiences of movement and should be interpreted within the context of the entire dreaming story.

**Suffocate:** Themes of smothering or suffocation are frightening and can relate to concepts of lack of control or misplaced focus and will. Explore the intuitive message along with the emotional experience for greater meaning and understanding.

**Sugar:** Sweet and often tempting, sugar can be representative of things that are forbidden or abundant depending on the dreamer's impressions and associations. Theme, story, and context should be used when interpreting this symbol.

**Suicide:** Dreams of suicide are uncommon, but they relate to death, transition from one life into another, or the unique theme of self-annihilation. Depending on the dreamer's association with this symbol, the dream may also take on greater messages of healing and rebirth.

**Suit:** Associated with the archetypal symbol of the businessman or woman, a suit is an article commonly associated with propriety and impersonal conduct. Association and context should be explored in relation to the larger dreaming scheme.

**Suitcase:** An object for transporting or carrying individual items, the suitcase is a symbol relating to identity, persona, individuality, and travel. Depending on how the suitcase was featured and how it connected to other aspects of the dream, it may carry a vital representation relating to the dreamer's individual life journey.

**Summer:** This season of fruitfulness and abundance is often associated with the sensation of happiness, contentment, peace, and bliss in the dreaming world. A personal association and intuitive relevance will define the importance of this dreaming landscape.

**Summit:** *See Peak*

**Sun:** While the sun was worshipped by the ancient Egyptian, Celtic, and Aztec cultures as their deity, it is also representative of healing, wisdom, divinity, and the metal gold. The sun is also connected to circular themes in geometry *(see Circle)*. Context and placement should be explored along with the use of intuitive reasoning.

**Sunglasses:** Commonly connected with themes of anonymity and disguise, sunglasses can also relate to concepts of sight, vision, and lack of clarity. In dreams, they connect uniquely to the wearer. The overall intuitive experience of the dreaming story will likely define the importance of this modern-day symbol.

**Sunrise:** *See Dawn*

**Sunset:** *See Dusk*

**Surfing:** This unique sport was practiced in Hawaii as early as the fifteenth century. Because surfing carries a modern connotation of freedom on the open water, it also can relate to themes of experience, challenge, discovery, and adventure in the dreaming landscape.

**Surgery:** Since surgery can be a terrifying experience, its presence in dreams often relates to themes of anxiety, stress, purpose, self-discovery, and resolve. Depending on the dreamer's individual history, the dreaming symbol may be one of a higher spiritual order, and context should be used for interpretation.

**Surrender:** Dreams that feature the act of surrender or release are often freeing experiences. The act of surrender can feel paralyzing, and yet the dreamer often feels freedom. Therefore, larger parallels and metaphors must be explored.

**Swamp:** Dreams that feature a swampy or marshy area or enclosure relate to confusion, murkiness, or cloudiness. Because this symbol in a dream will likely be associative, it is important to explore placement and context.

**Swelling:** Many dreams carry surrealistic themes of morphing and shifting or swelling and shrinking. These dreams carry a transitional theme of change and discovery and should be explored on a symbolic level.

**Swimming:** The act of swimming is one of intuitive athleticism and sentient movement. Often swimming in dreams is connected to themes of escapism, power, and intuitive reasoning. Because swimming is an action in the water, other emotional or mythological themes may be at play. However, association and personal experience with swimming will likely be the larger determinant.

**Swimming Pool:** Pools of water relate to the basic symbolism of water *(see Water),* as well as carrying additional themes of action and potential. Because of their ability to reflect light as well as their finite spatial orientation, swimming pools are featured in dreams for varying meanings and should be explored in relation to the overall dreaming story.

**Sword:** This ancient symbol of defense takes on a quasi-mystical proportion in world myth because of its power for balance and resolve. Swords often represented mobility, fierceness, position, and class. In the Arthurian legend of the sword and the stone, the weapon became an instrument of divine order. Context, association, and placement will define the meaning of this highly significant symbol.

**Table:** A central household piece of furniture, tables are commonly known as gathering places or domestic and family symbols. In dreams, tables can play a role of bringing together various players in a dreaming story, as well as being a sturdy applied symbol for human connection.

**Talking:** Dreams that feature talking or omniscient voices are often reflective of a greater message. Depending on what was said or heard, the primary message of the dream may be revealed within one sentence. Context, association, and intuitive reasoning should be used when interpreting a dream carrying this type of communication.

**Tan:** This color carries very little symbolic association but is often connected in imagery to desert landscapes and other vistas from the natural world. The color tan in dreams often has a calming effect and can also relate to the act of tanning or beach settings.

**Tank:** Dreams featuring tanks—fish tanks, water tanks, or air tanks—are generally representative of containment. Depending on how the tank played a role in the dreaming landscape, the larger theme may be one of breaking free of an old world in favor of new insights and vistas. Dreams relating to military tanks as weapons should be explored in relationship to the symbol of the military *(see Military)* or themes of defense.

**Tarot:** This ancient Egyptian and Italian symbol system is often connected with intuitive arts and exploration. Featured in dreams, it reflects the power of symbolism and should be explored within the context of the larger dreaming story.

**Tattoo:** Tattoos are interesting symbols in dreams because they traditionally reflect bodily adornment but can also carry an association of shame and branding. Depending on whether the dreamer has a tattoo and his or her personal ideology about tattoos, there may be a variety of impressions or reactions.

**Tavern:** *See Bar or Pub*

**Tea:** An Eastern symbol of meditative thought, tea is known all over the world as not only a valuable commodity but also a drink of rest and relaxation. The drinking of it carries a ritualistic cultural association in Japan as well as in Great Britain.

**Teacher or Teaching:** Dreams featuring the archetypal image of a teacher or the act of teaching are highly symbolic of life's journey and the concepts of learning, awareness, communication, and understanding. Intuitive reasoning should be explored relating to who was teaching, what was being taught, and the overall message of the dream.

**Teeth:** Many people dream of teeth falling out, crumbling, or other themes of disrepair. This common dreaming theme usually connects to some aspect of stress or anxiety in the dreamer's waking life.

**Telephone:** A twentieth-century mode of communication, the telephone can act as an alarm in dreams with the sounds of ringing and the dreamer's need to answer the call. An instrument of communication in the dreaming landscape, the larger themes of who was calling or the overall emotional sensation should be probed.

**Telescope:** Similar to the camera, the telescope gives the ability to see at great distance or into other worlds. This symbol could represent a transition of perception, new concepts of ideology, or perhaps a wiser point of view.

**Television:** A twentieth-century form of entertainment and communication, the television is often known as an instrument for contextual change in dreams. Televisions in dreams can reveal meaning or relate to the dreamer's personal associations depending on placement and importance in the landscape and story line.

**Temple:** Found in many ancient cultures from the Aztecs to the Romans, these holy structures were used for worship and ritual as well as serving the purpose of a cultural meeting ground. Their structures usually contain columns and internal space of sacred connection. Found in dreams, these symbols are highly resonant and should be valued on the highest intuitive level.

**Ten:** One of the most powerful numbers in numerical symbols systems, ten is also representative of the number one, being a derivative, and reflects completion, wholeness, and personal power. Modern terms, like he or she is a "ten," reflect the idea of being a winner or of having individual strength.

**Tent:** Rustic structures of shelter, tents are usually likened to a nature retreat or an impermanent home. Because tents are transient, the association will likely be personal. Context and the emotional sensation of the dream will integrate the landscape with the dreaming story.

**Terror:** Dreams featuring themes of fear and terror can be paralyzing, often causing the dreamer to awaken in a cold sweat. Depending on the dreaming story and the symbolic resonance, the dream may relate to any number of waking issues and should be explored on an associative plane.

**Test:** Dreams of tests or challenges can relate to problem solving in the dreamer's waking life *(see Exam)*. Depending on how the challenge was met, the dream may carry diverse and important symbolic meaning, but should also be probed in terms of emotional legacy and resolve.

**Theater:** A backdrop of creativity, drama, magic, and also general theatrics, theaters can be powerful dream symbols, relating to illusion, creation, conceptual ideas, and intuitive reasoning. Dreams with this landscape should be explored in terms of context as well as the overall dreaming message.

**Theft:** *See Stealing*

**Thirty-three:** One of three master numbers in the study of numerology *(see Eleven and Twenty-two)*, thirty-three is the symbol of success and the ultimate attainment of a goal. It also represents spiritual enlightenment and the awakening of the higher self.

**Thistle:** An ancient Celtic symbol, still carried as the national emblem of Scotland, the thistle is known for its spiky qualities. Known as a medieval curative plant, it is traditionally symbolic of the natural power of illness and negativity.

**Thorn:** Often connected to the rose, the thorn is a bittersweet symbol of passion and pain. Found in the Bible as a briar, it also represents suffering and compassion as it was worn by Christ at the crucifixion.

**Thread:** A material instrument for sewing, thread is akin to string because of its relationship to measurement and time. Depending on how it was featured and the dreaming story, it may relate to linear concepts or acts of connection.

**Three:** Representative of creativity and higher awareness, the number three also has a spiritual connection to the Holy Trinity as well as the geometric symbol system in the form of the triangle. It can represent diversity, ideological connection, and symmetry.

**Throne:** A symbol of higher position, the throne can be found in every culture and hierarchy throughout history. Connected to the figurehead of king, queen, chief, or emperor, a throne featured in the dream may relate to elevated views of self or others, as well as human expectation and tradition.

**Thunder:** Known and experienced in many ancient cultures as God's expression of anger, thunder can be a powerful dreaming symbol for conflict and confusion. In Oceanic and Nordic traditions, thunder is connected to the natural world and its protective individual soul.

**Tiara:** Similar to the crown, the tiara is a feminine headdress often worn by princesses and other figureheads in higher cultural systems. While the tiara can be found in the Old Testament as a crown of God, it is also connected to folkloric images of romance and beauty and should be explored on an individual and associative plane.

**Ticket:** This symbol of entrance and admission represents the basic concept of crossing from one place to another. Tickets are common dream symbols because they universally relate to movement, travel, and placement, as well as to entry and traverse.

**Tiger:** A powerful symbol of ferocity and predatory tenacity, the tiger is found in many cultural and mythological systems, including Chinese, Greek, and African traditions. It represents force, power, vitality, energy, passion, and also femininity.

**Time:** A higher symbol of nonlinear force, time is an important element in dreams because it connects to the concept of higher awareness and intuitive reasoning, as well as individual journey and path. Explore this dreaming symbol in parallel to waking realities and individual history.

**Tire:** These common objects of auto machinery are often found in dreams because of their rubbery nature and also their role in transportation. Dreams that feature a tire melting or breaking tell the dreamer to explore the larger dreaming journey.

**Toad:** Often associated with ancient alchemy and European traditions of magic, the toad also carries a representation of enlightenment in China as well as parts of the Pacific. This dualistic symbol is also found in fairy tales representing ugliness and should be explored in relation to the larger dreaming construct.

**Toilet:** Because this household component is an item of necessity, many dreams feature toilets overflowing or as part of a dreaming story relating to waste, shame, or embarrassment. These dreams are highly associative and can connect to waking stress or anxiety. Context will likely define a dream carrying this symbol.

**Tomahawk:** The Native American version of a hatchet, the tomahawk can be found in specific cultures and represents force, spiritual power, balance, hunting ability, and also defense.

**Tomato:** Because of their unique shape and their rich red color, tomatoes are often symbolic of abundance, nourishment, and, like the orange, of the summer season, where they are known to ripen in the sun.

**Tombstone:** A stone representation of death or the final resting place for the human soul, tombstones are usually fixtures in dreams and may represent the passage from one life into another or the basic idea of death. Context and placement will define the importance of this dreaming symbol.

**Tongue:** Carrying the obvious connection to speech, the tongue has a place in ancient Egyptian lore relating to lying and also appears in the Christian concept of "speaking in tongues." Dreams featuring the tongue are highly associative and should be explored relating to the overall experience and context.

**Tool:** Dreams that feature tools are often relating to concepts of work, creation, or problem solving. Since tools are material representations of purposeful and constructive acts, they may carry a positive association; however, their use is what will define their meaning in the dreaming landscape.

**Torch:** This ancient form of light is found in the Bible, as well as in Oceanic and Greek mythology, representing light and the eternal force of God. In modern thought, we connect the torch to Hawaiian and Tahitian cultures, as well as to the spirit of sport and the lighting of the Olympic torch.

**Tornado:** These storms or funnel clouds are often found in dreams and relate to themes of natural disaster and chaos. Tornadoes can take on otherworldly proportions in dreams and often cause the dreamer to explore their purpose in the dreaming story. Context, association, and placement will reveal the importance of this symbol.

**Totem:** Symbolic of ancestral spiritual force and tradition, the totem pole can be found in Native American and Nordic cultures and often has a mystical representation in the dreaming scene. Depending on personal association, it may connect to a spiritual quest or an individual journey of identity and placement.

**Tower:** Originating with the biblical tower of Babel, this vertical structure is also found in medieval history as a symbol of power. Similar to a fortress, the tower is also connected to folkloric traditions in stories like "Rapunzel" and should be explored in terms of placement and intuitive importance in the dreaming landscape.

**Toy:** Connected to childhood and playfulness, toys can have a great deal of symbolic importance, depending on personal history and association. Dreams featuring toys should be probed relating to their placement and the role they play in the larger dreaming message.

**Traffic:** Typically related to themes of industrialism, congestion, frustration, and movement, traffic can play a determinative role in the dreaming landscape. Often traffic acts as a barrier to a destination in the dreaming story.

**Train:** As a mode of transportation, trains often take on a romantic place in dreams, as they are a less modern form of travel and also allow for scenic views and vistas of surroundings. Dreams of trains connect to goal and destination and will likely be defined by all the components in the overall dreaming story.

**Travel:** The theme of travel in dreams cannot be understated, as it is common and also relevant to the greater dreaming message. Dreams featuring arrival, departure, and basic modes of travel usually connect the dreamer to a personal journey and will be understood in terms of context, outcome, and dreaming design.

**Treasure:** Dreams that feature the search for or the discovery of treasure connect to the basic themes of bounty, reward, wealth, mystery, discovery, investigation, and problem solving. Because hidden or sunken treasure is found in many folkloric stories, there may be a mystical element to the dream, and intuitive reasoning should be used when exploring this dreaming symbol.

**Tree:** Because trees are a natural symbol of the earth whose branches extend upwards, trees often take on a human role in symbolic interpretation. The tree represents knowledge, as found in Eden, and also the act of regeneration or reincarnation in Buddhist tradition.

**Tree as a Woman:** Connected to the Greek myth of Diana, the symbol of a tree as woman or a tree turning into a woman also symbolizes Mother Earth and the force of intuitive power.

**Trial:** Dreams of being on trial or in court are often perplexing and anxiety oriented. These dreams relate to themes of judgment, objectivity, subjectivity, and also prosecution. Context and the larger dreaming story will likely determine the meaning of the dream.

**Triangle:** One of the most fundamental geometrical symbols, the triangle is also associated with the Holy Trinity as well as the pyramid. Its apex represents the heavens and its base, the earth. Depending on how this symbol was placed, there may be greater symbolic connections to the number three or other dreaming aspects.

**Tripping:** Dreams which feature the act of stumbling or tripping over objects can connect to hesitancy or the concept of not being able to reach a given goal or destination. Focus on larger themes of association and emotional legacy for interpretation.

**Tropical:** Tropical landscapes in dreams can be soothing and surreal as the dreamer experiences tranquillity in the natural world. Depending on personal associations with this backdrop, there may be greater journeys of bliss or self-discovery involved.

**Trousers:** *See Pants*

**Truck:** *See Car*

**Trumpet:** Found in the Revelation, the trumpet carries biblical connotations and is often depicted as the musical sound of the heavens in summoning the angels. Personal association and context is vital in understanding the importance of this dreaming symbol.

**Trust:** The element of trust in a dream is as emotionally vital as it is in waking reality. Dreams of gaining or losing trust all deal with the concepts of reliability, loyalty, and truth. Personal and emotional connections along with the featured players will determine this dream meaning.

**Tunnel:** Tunnels, much like portals *(see Portal)* and other narrow passages, relate to the symbol of time and act as a connective element in a greater dreaming journey. Often the experience is one of confinement and can be anxiety oriented, but the larger dreaming scope and journey should be valued for interpretation.

**Turquoise:** This blue stone is known as the "skystone" in Native American tradition because of its connection to the water and the sky. It is associated with the planet Jupiter and was believed to bring the spiritual element into the physical realm in ancient Turkish culture. Today, it is valued for assisting in expression and meditation.

**Turtle:** Because these sea creatures live for a very long time, they are found in many ancient traditions representing wisdom, empathy, and also intuitive ability. In India, turtles are believed to be the second reincarnation of Vishnu. Because of their hard shell, they are believed to carry infinite strength, and drawings of turtles are found throughout Australia and Oceanic cultures from prehistoric periods.

**Tuxedo:** This male article of dress often connects to the ultimate in opulence or gentlemanly refinement. Tuxedoes featured in dreams can carry connotations of wealth or romanticism and should be valued in the context of the overall dreaming story.

**Twenty-two:** One of the three master numbers in numerology *(see Eleven and Thirty-three),* the number twenty-two is symbolic of balance, control, restraint, and also leadership. Dreams featuring this number may relate to mastering a skill, art, or other spiritual goal.

**Twin:** The concept of having a twin is one of cloning or the duality of one. The sign of the twins is also that of Gemini in astrological symbolism. Depending on whether the dreamer has an experience of being a twin or not, the dream may connect to identity, individuality, and mirrored insight.

**Two:** A highly symbolic number representing union, joining, balance, and also cooperation, two is a significant number in dreams because it also relates to the biblical formation of the animals on Noah's ark. Context, association, and symbolic interpretation will be vital in deciphering this dreaming symbol.

**UFO:** Flying objects and other space vehicles are part of modern mythology and they relate to our desire to reach beyond the world we know. Viewing a UFO in a dream connects to individual views on space travel and universal themes and pursuits.

**Umbrella:** This simple daily item of protection from the rain often acts as a profound symbol in dreams. The umbrella can act as any type of shielding or protection from events or acts beyond the dreamer's control.

**Underground:** Dreams of subterranean caverns or spaces often reflect the subconscious mind or anything hidden from human senses. It is vital to explore a dream of underground aspects with emotional association as well as its context and placement in the dreaming story.

**Undress:** The act of removing clothing relates to relinquishing restrictions and is found in many dreams of undress. If you are viewing others undress, the dream may relate to sexuality. If you were undressing, the dream could connect back to your identity and your raw and unencumbered self.

**Unicorn:** This mythic animal from ancient folklore is known to be a symbol of magical enchantment and good luck. With its spirelike horn and its horselike body, it also represents the ability to achieve the impossible. Other associations from Christianity and early Greek traditions are that of power and an iron will.

**Uniform:** Clothing of an identifying nature plays a symbolic role in sleep because it represents the wearer as well as the association of the uniform. Whether it is a chef's uniform or a soldier's uniform, the translation to the dreamer is usually quite significant and can tell a larger story of identity and parallel ideas.

**Universe:** The universe is a symbol for many things from the universal spirit and soul to the human mind. It often relates to infinite potential and the unknown. Exploration also can play a role in dreams featuring a universal landscape. Probe the meaning and parameters of the dreaming search and intuitively connect to its message.

**University:** Places of higher learning are typically representative of the journey of our mind and of intellectual pursuits. Of course, association plays a unique role depending on the dreamer's educational background. Probe the context and delivery of the dream for understanding and evaluation.

**Untie:** Dreams which feature untying knots or other things relate to problem-solving abilities and often are symbolic of a waking truth. Ask yourself what you are looking to untie in your daily reality.

**Upside Down:** The dreaming world often delivers unique and surreal examples of concrete truth. When objects or landscapes appear upside down in a dream, the element of polarity must be explored. Point of view usually relates the larger dreaming truth.

**Urinate:** The act of urinating or viewing urination in dreams relates to the concept of release and the physiological limitations of the human body. Many people dream of defecation and other bodily functions. Context, design, and emotional interpretation will tell the larger story.

**Urn:** Much like any decorative vase or vessel, the urn is often a symbol of that which holds something. Since it is associated with death and cremation, it is also representative of knowledge and the afterlife.

**Vagina:** The female sexual organ can have many associations and meanings in a dream. Its basic representation is that of openness and female sexuality, but if featured in a sexual nature, it is more likely to relate to the players and larger dreaming story line.

**Valley:** The image of a valley is a deep and profound symbol for our own spiritual truth because it represents differing points in life. It can symbolize a peaceful time or a valley of despair. The vista of seeing or being in a valley is also a positive sign of healing and resolution.

**Vampire:** Known as the prince of darkness, the vampire is a mythological offspring of the bat, a blood-sucking creature that roams in the night. Behind the myth of the vampire rests our perceptions of afterlife, humanity, and sexuality. Context and association will play a role in a dream of this otherworldly creature.

**Vase:** This traditional vessel for holding flowers often connects to the concept of mental or emotional structure. When a vase is broken, a dreamer takes note of the event as important. What does the vase represent? How did it make you feel? Probe the context of the dream for understanding on the act and purpose of containment.

**Vegetable:** Much like their sweet counterpart of fruit, vegetables are a food and connect to nourishment and satiation. They also are associated with good health because of the vitamins they hold, as well as their vibrant coloring.

**Vehicle:** Cars, boats, trains, buses, and other vehicles connect back to the central concept of movement or traveling. Often they carry us from one idea to another in the dreaming landscape. It is vital to use context and association when interpreting a dream of any vehicle and its use.

**Veil:** Veils have a symbolic meaning in clothing as well as language. Nuns and other religious orders wear veils as a symbol of humility and sacrifice. The concept of the veil also represents illusion and fantasy. In Islamic traditions they are a representation of concealment and propriety. If a veil was featured in your dream, probe what it concealed and ask yourself about the intuitive sensations of the dreaming story.

**Velvet:** This plush fabric is connected to sensuality, smoothness, and regality. In the modern mythology of thinking, expressions like "a velvet tongue" relate to smooth-talking people. Velvet is also known to carry feminine associations, and the sense of touch may play a vital role in dreams of velvet.

**Venus:** Known as the planet of love, Venus has a special place in mythology as well as the solar system. As a planet of feminine energy, it was originally connected with spring and also the goddess of love. If the planet of Venus played a role in your dream, association is vital in connecting the myth of love and beauty to personal views and understanding.

**Veteran:** War soldiers or veterans are archetypal symbols for battles won and lost. If your dream featured a war hero or veteran, or even a warrior, ask yourself what conflicts they represent and how they correlate to your waking world.

**Video:** Much like movies and films, videotapes in dreams often act as a story within a story. Dreams featuring video games or visual stories may also represent specific dreaming motifs or ideas. Explore the feelings and individual messages of sleep for the answers.

**Violet:** This flower and also color has dualistic meaning in both forms. The color violet is a hue that is connected with sacrifice and spiritual rebirth. The flower also relates to spiritual symbolism because of early Roman and Greek myths. Tiny in size and fragrant in their scent, violets are often connected with mourning or weeping and with expressions like "a shrinking violet."

**Volcano:** Volcanoes are highly forceful symbols of nature's revolt and unleashed power. In Hawaiian lore and in Asia, mythological traditions connect them with specific gods and goddesses like Pele. It is said that when a volcano erupts, the gods are angry with the people of the earth. Personal association and context must be used to explore a dream with this magnificent symbol of nature's wrath.

**Vomit:** Many people experience the act of vomiting or illness in a dream. Be it a personal sensation or that of watching others, the act of vomiting is one of expulsion and relates to ridding the body of toxicity. Context and emotional deluge will tell the larger dreaming story.

**Vulture:** Birds of prey are often symbolic of the hunter, and the vulture is known for its ruthlessness and cunning. This bird has a great degree of respect in many cultures and is also associated with desert and barren lands.

**Waiter or Waitress:** Being waited on relates to being catered to. Dreams featuring food relate to nourishment. If a waiter or waitress has a featured part in your dream, ask yourself about what they are delivering to you and why.

**Walking:** Walking is an experience of movement and it often connects to transition. Dreams of waking can carry a mixed mélange of images and representation. Focus on the landscape and the journey as opposed to the destination.

**Wall:** Walls and bridges and other elements which divide and separate can connect parts of a greater dreaming story. If a wall plays a vital part in your dream, explore what divides your world and also probe your own personal boundaries.

**Wallet:** Much like a purse, a wallet or billfold is a place to keep valuables and money, and it connects heavily to the owner's identity. If the wallet was empty, there may be themes of financial concern. If the wallet featured a surprise, the dreamer may be searching for a new definition of life and his or her persona. Context and association will define a dream featuring a wallet or other personal effects.

**Walnut:** This robust and hard nut has many symbolic connections. In the Pacific, it is likened to a shell and connected to the inner and outer representations of body and soul. In some European cultures it is connected to fertility. Because of its hard exterior many people connect it to questions and problems, thus the phrase "a hard nut to crack." Association will play a vital role in this dream experience.

**War:** Dreams of war and mass destruction are a common modern dreaming theme and landscape. Many people have "doomsday" dreams where they probe the value of their own humanity and purpose in life. If you experienced this dream, ask yourself how you felt. What was the dream really saying to you on a symbolic level? Context and intuitive messages will tell the larger story.

**Warrior:** The image and face of the warrior is different depending on the culture and theme of the dream. If you dreamed of seeing or being a warrior, explore how this archetypal symbol connects to daily combat and your life's stumbling blocks. Value the peaceful ways of the fighter.

**Wart:** In nineteenth-century English folklore, warts represented emotions of shame. Warts are symbolically connected to vanity, identity, and beauty. They also have a presence relating to the symbol of the witch. Depending on how the wart played a role in the dream, it may represent self-image and individual persona.

**Wasp:** This tiny black creature with a volatile sting can relate to a hidden fear. The wasp often represents an irritant or a minor threat to the dreamer. Explore your own experiences with the wasp and focus on the contextual design of the dream for understanding.

**Watch:** Time is always a major archetypal theme in the world of dreams. If you are fixated on a watch or timepiece, you may be concerned with the passage of time in your daily reality. Place this dream in a waking context and work with your dream from this vista.

**Water:** One of the four elements of the universe, water can be metaphoric or symbolic depending on the nature of the dream. Jung believed that facing the sea is an indication of the dreamer's desire to confront issues in his or her life. Many cultural and religious traditions use water to represent the odyssey of forgiveness, renewal, and healing.

**Wave:** In mythology and cultural folklore, the wave symbolizes natural forces and transitional ideas. The god Poseidon was believed to have cosmic powers to shake the earth with waves of destruction. In Hawaii, "The Wave" is a Zen-like force, harnessed by the God Kanaloa, ruler of the sea and protector of the fisherman. In Japan, the wave represents great change and creativity.

**Weapon:** Forms of defense connect back to any type of combat mechanism, external or internal. Depending on the weapon featured in the dream, you may be symbolically battling a person, feeling, or component of your life. Focus on the symbolism and context of the dreaming story in order to define the weapon's purpose.

**Web:** Spider's webs or other webs in dreams often act as a background symbol for a specific landscape. With the World Wide Web, many dreams relate to exploration and discovery. Probe the meaning of the web. Did you feel ensnared? What did the web offer you? Context and association are the cornerstones to understanding this dream.

**Wedding:** Throughout the world there are many different traditions relating to the idea of human union and marriage. Dreams of weddings usually connect back to association and the context of the dream. Where did the wedding occur? Was it a positive experience? Explore the ceremony and your emotional connection to matrimony in order to define this dream.

**Wedding Cake:** Wedding cakes are highly symbolic in many cultural traditions. They represent the feast or connection of family union. The wedding cake also relates to food and the sensual pleasures of sweetness.

**Weed:** Known for its destructive abilities on a lawn and its unattractive name, the weed is symbolically connected with rottenness and negativity. Dreams of weeds could parallel erosion or doubt. Context and association will play a vital role in interpretation.

**Weeping:** *See Crying*

**Well:** The deep and cylindrical image of a well represents a place of purpose and reserve. If your well has run dry, you may be seeking out new ways to replenish it. If the well was full, it could connect to a bounty of ideas. Wells are symbolic of source, humanity, and higher knowledge. To drink from a well is to be in unison with your spirit.

**Werewolf:** This man/wolf combination is a mythological and folkloric symbol of humanity's untamed beast. The Greek legend of Licao (hunting dog) told the story of the king of Arcadia who killed his youngest son and prepared a meal with his flesh, instantly turning the king into a wolf. In modern horror films the wolf takes on a compassionate identity as the flawed beast within each of us. Personal association must be used in interpreting a werewolf dream.

**West:** Connected to the setting sun and the great conquest of the New World, the west is often a simple symbol for direction. If the dreamer is traveling west or senses that something is to be found in a westward direction, the location of the dreamer will define association, context, and the role of this dreaming symbol.

**Whale:** In cultural mythology and spiritual texts, this large sea mammal plays a defined role in stories of redemption and power. The tales of "Jonah and the Whale" along with *Moby Dick* relate to our own redemption. Whales are often connected with being endangered, and in Norse mythology they connect to human might and the hero or the conqueror.

**Wheel:** The invention of the wheel is viewed by many as the dawn of thought, the intellectual birth canal to our own modern way of life. Symbolically, wheels can represent apprenticeship. In the Old Testament and the I Ching, they are the manifestation of change and the movement of spiritual life.

**White:** The color white has many spiritual and sacred connotations relating to purity, virginity, and sanctity. In Tibet, white is held to be the color of enlightenment and many climbers wear a scarf of white to protect them on their ascent.

**Wife:** Dreams of partners and loved ones have a strong contextual message. Symbolically a wife is the counterpart to her husband, a representation of motherhood and feminine force.

**Wind:** The force of a wind symbolically connects back to the element of air and the concept of human thought. Dreams of gale winds or forceful gusts that sweep things away relate to a lack of control of the relationship between the dreamer and their surroundings. In many spiritual traditions, the wind takes on a mysterious role as the conduit between humans and God, translating into words like *spirit* and *breath*. Emotional sensation will tell the larger story in dreams of wind. Probe the placement and purpose of the wind in order to connect the dots in the dreaming story.

**Windmill:** In Holland, the windmill dots the landscape and often is associated with industry and productivity. Windmills harness the energy of the wind in order to create energy, and they are symbolically connected with the parallel between the mind and thought.

**Window:** Windows are highly metaphoric in dreams because they relate to the avenues of our spirits and our intellectual views. Symbolically they can be found in every religion, offering the image of devotion and framework. What did you see out the dream window?

How did you feel? Placement and vista will tell the story of window dreams and their rich point of view.

**Wine:** Wine has long been associated with the blood of Christ in biblical traditions, and it often represents a medicinal property or a spiritual drink. If wine was featured in your dream, it may relate to your own ideas about spirit or healing. Probe the context and landscape of the dream for understanding.

**Wing:** Wings of any type—be they those of a bird, a dragonfly, an angel, or a dove—relate to freedom of movement and spirit. Elevation of being and ascension toward the heavens give them a profound place in dreaming symbology. Focus on how they acted as a guide and propeller to another dimension of thought and emotion.

**Winter:** One of the four seasons, winter is a time of renewal and rest. Farmers prepare for the coming year and seasonal festivities take place. It also relates to the cold and barren natural landscape and the regeneration or gestation period of life.

**Witch:** In myth and folklore, witches are known for their mystical and magical powers and their ability to cast spells. They are also mythologically related to Satan or the dark side of life. In medieval Europe and elsewhere, they came to be known as the persecuted spirit of womanhood.

**Wizard:** The wizard, much like the symbol of the witch and also the warlock, is associated with medieval mysticism and magic. If you dreamed of a wizard, you may be exploring the unexplainable and your own definitions of creation, wisdom, and knowledge.

**Wolf:** Often connected with the wild and untamed beast, the wolf has great symbolism in many mythological and folkloric tales. The wolf is associated with the wild side of life, the moon, and also the predator. In Native American traditions, the wolf acts as a messenger from the spirit world, much like an angel. Depending on the nature of your dream, the wolf could connect to an internal battle of will and fear.

**Woman:** The feminine force and power of the woman is often associated with mystery and beauty. The idea of "Mother Earth" is also a strong feminine persona. If the power of womanhood played a feature role in your dream, focus on feminine identity and personal association.

**Work or Working:** Work often relates to industry and task completion in dreams. Depending on how work plays a role in everyday life, the dream will have a strongly contextual relationship to identity and resolution.

**Worm:** These tiny creatures of the earth are typically connected with fearful concepts in dreams because of their creepy and elusive nature. If you were afraid of the worm, work on identifying the symbolic cause of the emotional sensation. Mythologically, worms are known as symbols of regeneration.

**Wound:** Wounds and other injuries in dreams relate to parts of our lives that are in need of healing or repair. Depending on the location of the wound and the emotional context, the dream may take on a variety of meanings. Focus on the underlying message and your intuitive ideas.

**Wreath:** Wreaths or garlands are traditionally associated with the circle of union or a crown of significance. They are used during Christmas, as well as for funerals or other religious ceremonies. They symbolically connect humankind to the spirit of divine order. In ancient Greece, they symbolized victory and power. In Hawaii, the Haku Lei is worn as a symbol of divine honor.

**Wreck:** Viewing a wreck or an accident relates to control and how you perceive the world around you. Emotions expressed and how you felt during the dream are important in analyzing and interpreting a wreck or accident of any sort.

**Writing:** The power of the written word is very strong and its visual imagery in dreams connects to self-expression and individual pursuits. Dreams of words or sentences usually spell out their meaning. A dream of writing reveals an intuitive brand of expression or a greater message.

**X-Ray:** An X-ray can reveal the hidden details in anything. Depending on what was being X-rayed, the dissection of the truth is being pondered. Ask yourself how the context of the dream fits in with the action.

**Yard:** In the context of a home life, the yard relates to nature and a sacred space of living. How does the yard relate to the dream? How is it placed in terms of your dreaming emotions? The power of relation-ship will tell the story of this dream.

**Yell:** To yell or scream in a loud voice can often reflect the dreamer's need to purge him- or herself of a message. Work on understanding what the emotions connect to, as opposed to only hearing the words.

**Yellow:** The saffron color represents humility in the Buddhist and Tibetan traditions. Revered in the East as a sacred color, yellow is often a vibrant and life-giving force. Work on understanding how the color connects to the rest of the dream, as well as your own feelings about this sunny hue.

**Yeti:** The legend of the Yeti originates in the Himalayan Mountains, where the Yeti is said to roam. The meaning of the word Yeti in Ti-betan is "magical creature." The Yeti is said to control the most formi-dable peaks to guard against humankind, acting as the mountain's powerful protector.

**Yin/Yang:** This dualistic Chinese symbol of dark and light, positive and negative, represents balance and unity. It is found in ancient Chi-nese representations and symbolizes a universal theme of understand-ing and awareness.

**Young:** Youth is commonly connected with vitality. Depending on how youth plays into the dream, you may be exploring the ramifica-tions of age or aging. Probe your associations with the young and how they connect to your waking world.

**Zodiac:** The symbol system of the zodiac was first formed in Babylonian civilization. This twelve-month system, based upon the stars and their connection to humankind, indicates a journey into a new way of looking at the future. The passage of time is the main meaning of this dreaming symbol.

**Zombie:** The zombie has its mythological roots in Egyptology. Yet, it is modern myth that usually defines this dreaming character repre-senting lifelessness. Examine the connection between life and human-ity.

**Zoo:** While many people associate the zoo with childhood ideology, the presence of a zoo in a dream can also represent a connection between the animal kingdom and the human world. Dreams about zoos or animal parks are highly associative and should be explored in relationship to the dreamer's personal history.

# Bibliography

Allen, Tony, 1999, *An Unseen World, The Oceanian Legacy,* London, Duncan Baird Publishers.

Aserinsky, E., and Kleitman N., 1953, *Regularly Occurring Periods of Eye Motility and Concomitant Phenomena During Sleep,* Science, 118.

Biedermann, Hans, 1989, *Symbolism: Cultural Icons and Their Meanings,* Toronto, Meridian Books.

Cayce H.L., 1962, *Dreams: The Language of the Unconscious,* Virginia, A.R.E. Press.

Dunne, John William, 1927, *An Experiment with Time,* New York, MacMillan Publishing.

Freud, Sigmund, 1899, *The Interpretation of Dreams,* Oxford Press.

Gurney, Myers and Podmore, 1886, *Phantasms of the Living,* Volume II, London, Trubner and Sons.

Hobson, J. Allan, 1988, *The Dreaming Brain,* New York, Basic Books.

Jung, C.G., 1909, *The Analysis of Dreams,* Paris.

Jung, C.G., 1909, *General Aspects of Dream Psychology,* Zurich.

Jung, C.G., 1909, *On the Nature of Dreams,* Zurich.

Keller, Helen, 1947, *The World I Live In,* New York, Random House.

Knappert, Jan, 1995, *Pacific Mythology,* Great Britain, Diamond Books.

LaBerge, Stephen, 1985, *Lucid Dreaming,* New York, Ballantine.

Lewis, James, 1995, *The Dream Encyclopedia,* Detroit, Visible Ink Press.

Petersen, William, 1961, *Dreams: Our Judge and Jury,* Edgar Cayce Publishing Company.

Redfield, James, 1997, *The Celestine Vision,* New York, Warner Books.

Saint-Exupery, Antoine de, 1943, *Le Petite Prince,* New York, Harcourt, Brace and World.

Sechrist, Elsie, 1968, *Dreams—Your Magic Mirror,* New York, Dell Publishing.

Stevensen, Ian, 1960, *Analysis of Paranormal Experiences Connected with the Sinking of the Titanic.* New York, ASPR Journal, October, Volume 54.

Stevensen, Ian, 1960, *Seven More Paranormal Experiences Connected with the Sinking of the Titanic.* New York, ASPR Journal, October, Volume 59.

Ullman, M., Krippner, S., and Vaughn, A., 1973, *Dream Telepathy,* New York, MacMillan.

# About the Author

While many writers find their callings in life's events, Suz Andreasen has been putting pen to paper since her childhood. Andreasen resides in New York City and her literary work is often centered in human mythology. She is well known for her writings on dream interpretation and spiritual potential, authoring three weekly columns for American Online. Every week Suz receives thousands of letters on every subject you can name—love, relationships, spirituality, compatibility, and more. If you would like to write to Suz Andreasen and share your dreams, be sure to visit her online home at www.dearsuz.com.

When it comes to Suz's knowledge of the esoteric, you will find her exploring many things. She has written over twenty-two volumes of dream journals and personal logs, which she began at the age of fourteen. She is an avid study on many topics, including astrology, numerology, clairvoyance, dream interpretation, mythology, and also karma and reincarnation. She has studied the works of Carl Jung, Lao Tsu, and Edgar Cayce and firmly believes that all studies are of value and wholly interdependent on one another. To quote her, "Each thing we do relates to each result. Each result relates to change, each change to life."

Note: Many of the dreams published in this book were submitted via www.theMindSite.com and are published with written permission of the authors.

## DISCOVER HOW THE EDGAR CAYCE MATERIAL CAN HELP YOU!

The Association for Research and Enlightenment, Inc. (A.R.E.®), was founded in 1931 by Edgar Cayce. Its international headquarters are in Virginia Beach, Virginia, where thousands of visitors come year round. Many more are helped and inspired by A.R.E.'s local activities in their own hometowns or by contact via mail (and now the Internet!) with A.R.E. headquarters.

People from all walks of life, all around the world, have discovered meaningful and life-transforming insights in the A.R.E. programs and materials, which focus on such areas as personal spirituality, holistic health, dreams, family life, finding your best vocation, reincarnation, ESP, meditation, and soul growth in small-group settings. Call us today on our toll-free number:

**1-800-333-4499**

or

Explore our electronic visitors center on the Internet: **http://www.edgarcayce.org.**

We'll be happy to tell you more about how the work of the A.R.E. can help you!

A.R.E.
215 67th Street
Virginia Beach, VA 23451-2061